2nd Workshop on Data Science with Human-in-the-loop: Language Advances (DaSH-LA 2021)

Online
11 June 2021

ISBN: 978-1-7138-3021-4

Printed from e-media with permission by:

Curran Associates, Inc.
57 Morehouse Lane
Red Hook, NY 12571

Association for Computational Linguistics
209 N. Eighth Street
Stroudsburg, Pennsylvania 18360

Phone: 1-570-476-8006
Fax: 1-570-476-0860

acl@aclweb.org

Additional copies of this publication are available from:

Curran Associates, Inc.
57 Morehouse Lane
Red Hook, NY 12571 USA
Phone: 845-758-0400
Fax: 845-758-2633
Email: curran@proceedings.com
Web: www.proceedings.com

DaSH-LA

The 2nd Workshop on Data Science with Human-in-the-loop: Language Advances

Proceedings of the Workshop

June 11, 2021

Message from the Workshop Co-chairs

The 2nd Workshop on Data Science with Human-in-the-loop (DaSH) builds on the success of the inaugural workshop that took place at KDD in 2020. The current workshop (DaSH-LA) is co-located with NAACL-HLT 2021, and its focus is on human-in-the-loop aspects in computational linguistics and natural language processing (NLP).

The aim of the DaSH-LA workshop is to stimulate research on human-computer interaction challenges in data science within the broad areas related to language, including but not limited to information extraction, text classification, machine translation, dialog systems, question answering, language generation, information retrieval, digital humanity, and more. We expect the overall series of the DaSH workshops to help develop and grow a strong community of researchers who are interested in this topic and to yield future collaborations and scientific exchanges across the relevant areas of computational linguistics, data mining, machine learning, data and knowledge management, human-machine interaction, and user interfaces.

The participants of the DaSH-LA workshop include researchers and practitioners interested in understanding how to optimize human-computer cooperation and how to minimize human effort along various NLP pipelines in a wide range of tasks and real-life applications. The full-day program includes two keynote talks (by Dan Weld and Joyce Chai), three regular sessions with 14 accepted papers, a special session with highlights from two recent papers with human-in-the-loop focus, as well as a panel of experts (including Danqi Chen, Joel Tetreault and the two keynote speakers).

We would like to thank all people who in one way or another helped with the workshop. We are thankful to the members of the program committee who did an excellent job in reviewing the submitted papers under strict time constraints, and also to the steering committee for their helpful suggestions. Last but not least we would like to thank all authors, speakers and participants at the workshop.

Eduard Dragut, Yunyao Li, Lucian Popa, and Slobodan Vucetic
June 2021

Workshop Co-chairs

Eduard Dragut, Temple University
Lucian Popa, IBM Research
Slobodan Vucetic, Temple University
Yunyao Li, IBM Research

Program Committee

Mohit Bansal, University of North Carolina (UNC) Chapel Hill
Cornelia Caragea, University of Illinois at Chicago
Marina Danilevsky, IBM Research
Aritra Dasgupta, New Jersey Institute of Technology
Nemanja Djuric, Aurora Innovation
Kenneth Forbus, Northwestern University
Anna Lisa Gentile, IBM Research
Iryna Gurevych, Technical University of Darmstadt
Lifu Huang, Virginia Tech
Dongyeop Kang, Carnegie Mellon University
Jonathan K. Kummerfeld, University of Michigan
Bing Liu, University of Illinois at Chicago
Jeff Pan, University of Edinburgh
Soujanya Poria, Singapore University of Technology and Design
Daniel Preotiuc-Pietro, Bloomberg
Kun Qian, Amazon
Xiang Ren, University of Southern California
Shashank Srivastava, University of North Carolina (UNC) Chapel Hill
Gabriel Stanovsky, Hebrew University of Jerusalem
Benjamin Van Durme, Johns Hopkins University
Dakuo Wang, IBM Research
Rui Zhang, Penn State University

Steering Committee

AnHai Doan, University of Wisconsin
ChengXiang Zhai, University of Illinois at Urbana-Champaign
Dan Weld, University of Washington
Marti A. Hearst, University of California, Berkeley
Sunita Sarawagi, IIT Bombay

Table of Contents

Conference Program

Keynote Talk 1: Daniel Weld

Regular Session 1: Support for Text Analytics with Human in the Loop

Leveraging Wikipedia Navigational Templates for Curating Domain-Specific Fuzzy Conceptual Bases
Krati Saxena, Tushita Singh, Ashwini Patil, Sagar Sunkle and Vinay Kulkarni

It is better to Verify: Semi-Supervised Learning with a human in the loop for large-scale NLU models
Verena Weber, Enrico Piovano and Melanie Bradford

ViziTex: Interactive Visual Sense-Making of Text Corpora
Natraj Raman, Sameena Shah, Tucker Balch and Manuela Veloso

A Visualization Approach for Rapid Labeling of Clinical Notes for Smoking Status Extraction
Saman Enayati, Ziyu Yang, Benjamin Lu and Slobodan Vucetic

Semi-supervised Interactive Intent Labeling
Saurav Sahay, Eda Okur, Nagib Hakim and Lama Nachman

Highlights: Human in the Loop Papers from Recent Conferences

Human-In-The-LoopEntity Linking for Low Resource Domains
Jan-Christoph Klie, Richard Eckart de Castilho and Iryna Gurevych

Bridging Multi-disciplinary Collaboration Challenges in ML Development via Domain Knowledge Elicitation
Soya Park

Regular Session 2: Human in the Loop for NLP Tasks

Keynote Talk 2: Joyce Chai

Regular Session 3: Human in the Loop Tools

Panel

Leveraging Wikipedia Navigational Templates for Curating Domain-Specific Fuzzy Conceptual Bases

Krati Saxena, Tushita Singh, Ashwini Patil, Sagar Sunkle, Vinay Kulkarni
Tata Consultancy Services Research
Pune, India

Abstract

Domain-specific conceptual bases use key concepts to capture domain scope and relevant information. Conceptual bases serve as a foundation for various downstream tasks, including ontology construction, information mapping, and analysis. However, building conceptual bases necessitates domain awareness and takes time. Wikipedia navigational templates offer multiple articles on the same/similar domain. It is possible to use the templates to recognize fundamental concepts that shape the domain. Earlier work in this domain used Wikipedia's structured and unstructured data to construct open-domain ontologies, domain terminologies, and knowledge bases. We present a novel method for leveraging navigational templates to create domain-specific fuzzy conceptual bases in this work. Our system generates knowledge graphs from the articles mentioned in the template, which we then process using Wikidata and machine learning algorithms. We filter important concepts using fuzzy logic on network metrics to create a crude conceptual base. Finally, the expert helps by refining the conceptual base. We demonstrate our system using an example of RNA virus antiviral drugs.

1 Introduction

Domain-specific conceptual bases are a method for grasping the domain at a high level by capturing the notions that generally make up a domain. While ontology focus on formal representations and system of categories encompassing the domain information and conceptual models focus on linking the general ontological categories (Fonseca and Martin, 2007), the conceptual bases are abstract models addressing the most crucial concepts that are invariably found in a domain. Aside from defining the scope and outlining the concepts, the conceptual bases may be used for a variety of downstream activities, such as developing less abstract conceptual constructs, such as ontology, or applications such as entity mapping in knowledge graphs, creating instances for named entity recognition, and summarizing or analyzing the domain.

Creating a conceptual base is a difficult task that necessitates a thorough understanding of the domain and a considerable amount of time to establish the importance of concepts. Online sources such as Wikipedia contain a vast amount of information on many domains (Wikipedia, 2021a). In this research, we propose a novel approach to create domain-specific conceptual bases using Wikipedia navigational templates (Wikipedia, 2021b). The navigational templates make it simple to connect similar topics invariably. Similar topics are present as navigational boxes at the bottom of the article or sidebars on the right side of the article.

Our system uses knowledge from the articles in the navigational templates and identifies relevant notions consistently present in various articles of the same field. For this, we parse the articles' information and create a basic knowledge graph. We map the information to their Wikidata instances and cluster similar concepts. We apply fuzzy rules based on network metrics to decide the importance of concepts. In the end, the expert cleans and refines the resultant conceptual base to create the final version.

Our specific contributions are:

- Our framework allows users to build domain-specific conceptual bases from knowledge graphs in various domains using Wikipedia navigational templates.
- The novelty lies in the application of fuzzy rules on network metrics. We also provide modifiable fuzzy rules to expand or contract the conceptual bases as required.

We organize the paper as follows. We discuss the method in Section 2. We illustrate the outcomes of the approach using an example of RNA virus antivirals in Section 3. We also review the outcomes and limitations in that section, followed by

Proceedings of the 2nd Workshop on Data Science with Human in the Loop: Language Advances, pages 1–7
June 11, 2021. ©2021 Association for Computational Linguistics

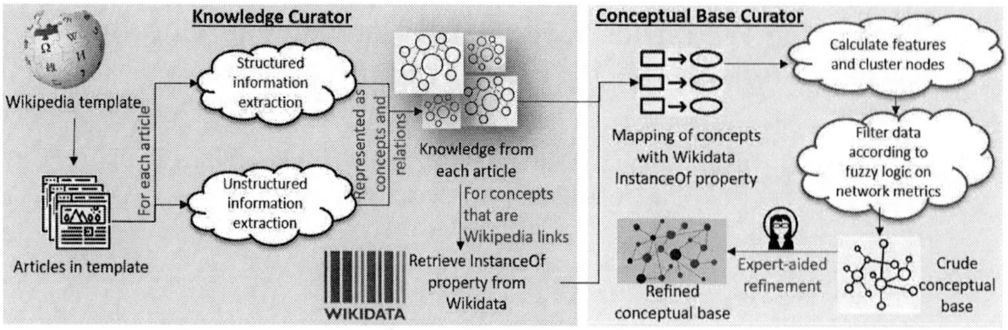

Figure 1: Method overview

related works in Section 4. We conclude the paper in Section 5.

2 Proposed Method

We show the overview of the method in Figure 1. Our system consists of two parts: Knowledge Curator and Conceptual Base Curator. The Knowledge Curator extracts information from articles and Wikidata to construct a basic knowledge graph, and the Conceptual Base Curator employs machine learning techniques for processing and fuzzy rules to filter the relevant concepts.

2.1 Knowledge Curator

Collecting articles Our framework uses the template name as an input to gather information from a particular domain. The pattern "Template:Template name>" defines the Wikipedia templates. We use Wikipedia's special export webpage[1] to export the template's data into XML for faster processing. To remove unnecessary text from the XML, we use pattern-based cleaning and rule-based parsing. To retrieve the article names in the template, we use rule-based parsing. We export the information as XML for each article and use pattern-based cleaning to clean it.

Information extraction from articles Structured material, such as content information and infoboxes, can be found in Wikipedia articles. In the same way, they contain unstructured information in the context of the article's text. We extract this information by rule-based text processing on the cleaned article's XMLs.

Graph representation We represent the extracted information as a graph for further processing. For each article, we create a separate knowledge graph where the article node is the central node. We add section-subsection information using the relations: has_section and has_subsection. We add infobox information by adding has_ in front of the first column labels of the infobox and the first column label as the node. For example, Earth[2] info box contains information on mass. We add the has_mass relation to the *Earth* node with *mass* node. We process the text in the article by text normalization and sentence segmentation[3]. We tokenize[4] the sentences and extract noun chunks[5] from the sentences and consider the noun chunks as the nodes. We join the first noun chunk of the sentences with the section node using the relation has_info_about. The trailing noun chunks are added to the previous noun chunk nodes using in-between tokens as the relation. We also create a list of nodes that are links to other articles.

Retrieving Wikidata instance For all the nodes that are links to other Wikipedia articles, we parse the instanceOf[6] property using web crawling and save them to a file.

2.2 Conceptual Base Curator

Mapping We map the nodes to their Wikidata instances. If an instance is present, we replace the node with the instance name. If there are multiple instances, we create multiple nodes and add all the connecting nodes to the instance nodes. For example, a node A is connected to node B and C and A has Wikidata instanceOf as A_{i1} and A_{i2}. Then we

[1] https://en.wikipedia.org/wiki/Special:Export

[2] https://en.wikipedia.org/wiki/Earth

[3] https://spacy.io/usage/linguistic-features#sbd

[4] https://spacy.io/usage/linguistic-features#tokenization

[5] https://spacy.io/usage/linguistic-features#dependency-parse

[6] https://www.wikidata.org/wiki/Property:P31

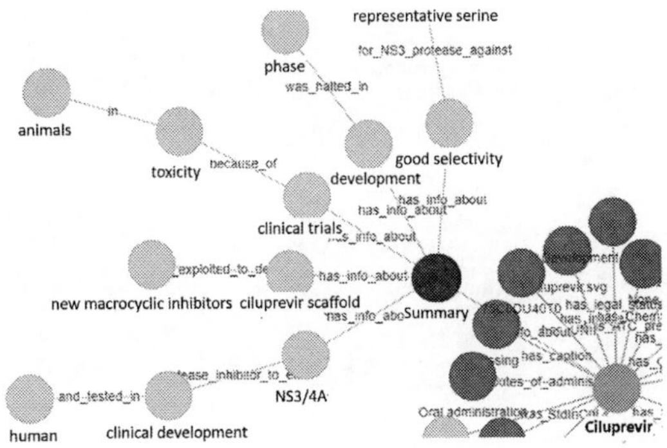

Figure 2: Screenshot of a small part of graph for *Ciluprevir* drug: the dark green node is the article node. Red, navy blue and light green nodes are information from infoboxes, section and text, respectively. Light green nodes constitutes noun chunk information connected via in-between tokens or has_info_about relations.

replace A-B and A-C with A_{i1}-B, A_{i1}-C, A_{i2}-B, A_{i2}-C in the graph.

Clustering nodes There are several similar nodes in the graphs of all the articles. We calculate the Levenshtein distance (Levenshtein, 1966) based feature matrix for all the nodes. We perform affinity propagation clustering (Frey and Dueck, 2007) which outputs cluster and cluster exemplars. We replace the nodes in the clusters with their exemplars for further use.

Node filtering and knowledge graphs collation The uncertainty factor of the concepts is the impetus for using fuzzy logic to construct a conceptual base. If we fill the conceptual base with all possible notions, the structure assumes that all concepts and relations are equally representative of the domain. However, this is not the case. Some notions are more applicable than others. Consider the following three medications: Remdesivir[7], Ledipasvir[8] and Dasabuvir[9]. Medical uses, side effects, and trade names are all common concepts. As a result, these can be said to be true in the drug domain with some certainty. The Remdesivir article contains information about medical usage controversy, which is absent in other drugs. As a consequence, this concept can be categorized as less significant.

We use fuzzy logic to find relevant concepts in a particular domain. For this, we filter out the nodes whose relation does not contain a word with VERB pos-tag. We collate the graphs for all the articles and remove "a, an, the" from the nodes.

Fuzzy logic on network metrics We calculate two network metrics: degree centrality and betweenness centrality (Freeman, 1977). The centrality metric identifies the network's most influential nodes. The number of connections a node has determines its degree centrality. The degree centrality of a vertex v, for a given graph $G := (V, E)$ with $|V|$ vertices and $|E|$ edges, is defined as:

$$C_{Deg}(v) = deg(v) \tag{1}$$

Where, $deg(v)$ is the degree of vertex v. The number of times a node appears in the shortest path of other nodes is known as betweenness centrality. It is a metric that reflects a node's power over other network nodes. It is defined by the equation:

$$C_{Btw}(v) = \sum_{i \neq v \neq j} \frac{\sigma_{ij}(v)}{\sigma_{ij}} \tag{2}$$

where σ_{ij} is the total number of shortest paths from node i to node j and $\sigma_{ij}(v)$ is the number of those paths that pass through v.

The fuzzy logic uses the above-defined network metrics to decide the relevancy of the concepts. The fuzzy logic consists of four main components: fuzzifier, rule base, inference engine, and defuzzifier. Fuzzifier converts inputs to fuzzy sets characterized by membership functions (MF). Rule base consists of IF-THEN rules used to drive the inference engine. The inference engine makes fuzzy inference on the fuzzy input based on the defined rules. Defuzzifier converts fuzzy set to the required output.

In our system, the input is degree centrality and betweenness centrality measures for all the nodes. We have experimented with the Gaussian membership function. The Gaussian MF is defined as:

$$GaussMF(x; \mu, \sigma) = e^{-\frac{1}{2}(\frac{x-\mu}{\sigma})^2} \tag{3}$$

where, x is the input, μ is the mean and σ is the standard deviation of x. We generate gaussian MF for both the centrality measures.

We use categorical inference on the concept relevance (HIGH, MEDIUM, LOW) and Mamdani Implication for getting the output. Assuming a rule $R_i = (D_i \text{ OR } B_i) \rightarrow N_i$, is defined by $\mu_{R_i} = \mu_{D_i ORB_i \rightarrow N_j}(d, b; n)$, where μ is membership function, D_i and B_i are fuzzy sets for degree and betweenness centrality and $N_j wherej \in$

[7] https://en.wikipedia.org/wiki/Remdesivir

[8] https://en.wikipedia.org/wiki/Ledipasvir/sofosbuvir

[9] https://en.wikipedia.org/wiki/Dasabuvir

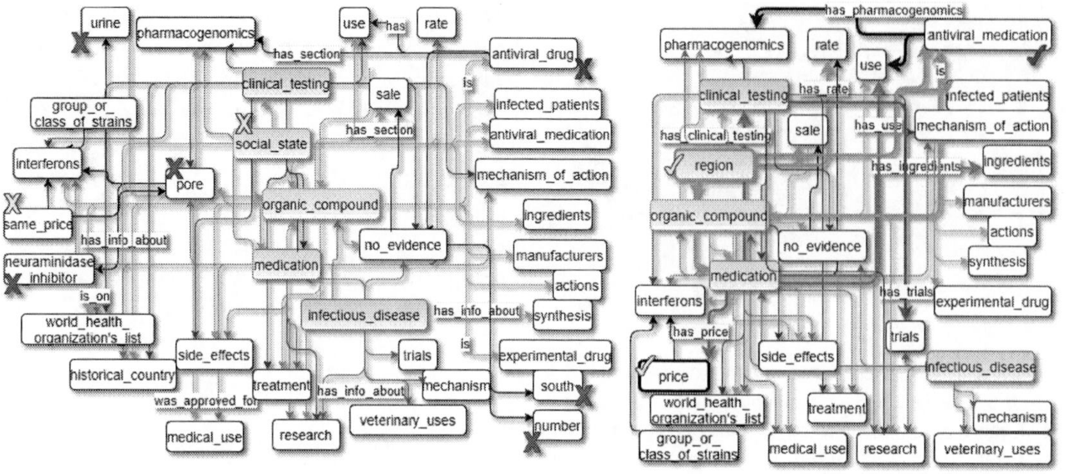

Figure 3: (a) Left: automatically generated crude conceptual base, (b) Right: refined conceptual base, consisting of concepts from section and text. (a) Left: red crosses depict nodes removed, yellow crosses depict the modified nodes, and blue crosses depict the node merged to another node. (b) Right: refined nodes and edges are shown in bold. Yellow ticked nodes are modified, and blue ticked are merged. For clarity, we show the five most central nodes and nodes connecting to them with different colors.

$[1, 2, 3] \equiv [HIGH, MEDIUM, LOW]$ denotes relevance set for nodes. Then, the Mamdani Implication uses minimum operator ($\wedge$) for fuzzy implication.

$$\begin{aligned} \mu_{N_j}(n) &= \alpha_i \wedge \mu_{N_j}(n) \\ where, \alpha_i &= (\mu_{D_i} \wedge \mu_{B_i}) \end{aligned} \tag{4}$$

We define three rules for inference:

- IF $\mu_{d_n} \wedge \mu_{b_n}$ <= 0.6 THEN $\mu_{N_j}(n) = HIGH$
- IF 0.6 < $\mu_{d_n} \wedge \mu_{b_n}$ <= 0.8 THEN $\mu_{N_j}(n) = MEDIUM$
- IF $\mu_{d_n} \wedge \mu_{b_n}$ > 0.8 THEN $\mu_{N_j}(n) = LOW$

The values in the rules are modifiable to increase or decrease the span of concepts covered in various relevance levels.

We filter out node-edge-node pairs using nodes of varying significance. We consider a node-edge-node pair highly relevant if any node in the pair is highly relevant and the node-edge-node pair has appeared in more than two articles. Similarly, we translate the medium and low importance at node level to node-edge-node pair level. We only use highly relevant node-edge-node pairs in this paper, but medium and low relevance pairs may be added to extend the conceptual base if required. We measure the resultant network's largest connected component and present it to the domain expert for further refinement.

Refining the concept base The domain expert refines the crude conceptual base. Removal or modification of semantically related concepts and removal or modification of notions that reflect the same object are both parts of the refinement process. The expert makes node connections to the modified nodes by naming "has_<node>" to new relations. There is no modification of the relations where the node is not modified.

3 Results and Discussion

3.1 Case Study on RNA Virus Antiviral Drugs

We present the results of our approach using an example of RNA virus antiviral drugs[10]. The system is implemented in Python. All the steps automatically retrieve or process the data until stated otherwise.

The system first curates the knowledge graph from all the articles using the section, infobox, and text information. We show a screenshot of a small part of the knowledge graph for the *Ciluprevir* drug in Figure 2. The system also retrieves and maps the Wikidata instanceOf property to all the link-based nodes.

Next, we apply affinity propagation to cluster similar information together. We experimented by clustering section, infoboxes and text together and independently. Infoboxes present a structured summary of the article's information. We note that the

[10] https://en.wikipedia.org/wiki/Template:RNA_antivirals

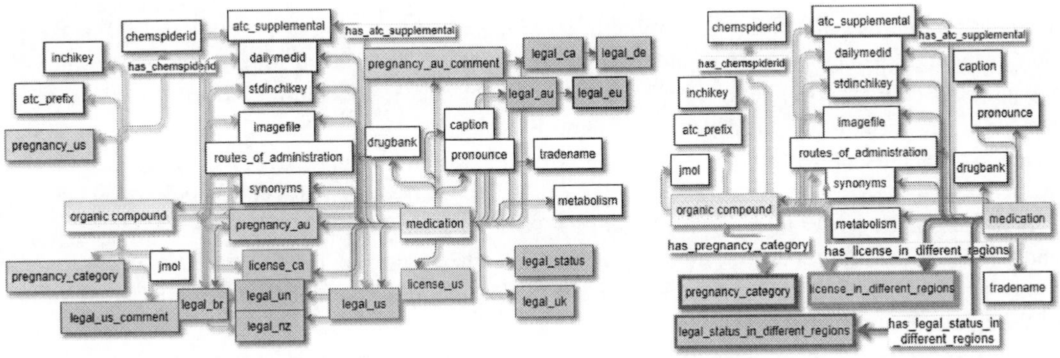

Figure 4: (a) Left: Crude and (b) Right: refined conceptual base from infoboxes. Same color nodes represent instances of the same concept.

clustering of infoboxes tends to lose information because different information identifiers may come under a single cluster, although they represent independent information. As a result, the final conceptual base contains minimal information from infoboxes. In our experiment, the automatically created conceptual base that uses clusters of all information together contains 49.4%, 4%, and 46.6% concepts coming from section, infoboxes, and text, respectively. Hence, we cluster only section and text information (independently) and use infoboxes information as it is.

After this, the application of fuzzy logic results in a crude conceptual base. Due to space restrictions, we show snippets of the model with only a few mentions of the edge names: consisting of section and text information in Figure 3(a) and infobox information in Figure 4(a). The respective refined models are shown in Figure 3(b) and 4(b). Edges or relations mostly consists of names such as has_info_about, has_section, has_subsection, has_type and verbs such as is, approved_by, is_not_recommended_during, etc. We call our output conceptual base and not conceptual model because the relations such as has_info_about, has_section, has_subsection does not provide any meaningful link between the concepts. Meaningful modification of such relations can be considered as a downstream task.

The templates contain few articles of different domains as well. For instance, RNA antiviral template contains disease and virus names as well. But, the proposed approach ensures that we consider only statistically significant concepts for the conceptual base. We manually validate that the crude conceptual base contains 14%, 16%, and 70% of concepts from section, text, and infoboxes, respectively.

3.2 Discussion

Our observations suggest that the crude conceptual base can capture most of the relevant information from both the section and text information and infobox information. There are few ambiguous names in the nodes like *pore*, *south*, *rate* (marked using crosses) in Figure 3(a) and *legal_us*, *legal_uk*, etc. (colored nodes) in Figure 4(a), which the domain expert removes or corrects. The expert also modifies edges, where nodes are modified.

The crude base contains two types of nodes: 1) nodes representing the same object in the current context but can have different meanings, and 2) nodes that are instances of another concept. For example, in Figure 3(a), the nodes *medication*, *antiviral drug* and *antiviral medication* represents antiviral drugs in the current context. These nodes appear because an article node is the most central in their knowledge graph, and they can have multiple Wikipedia instanceOf properties. Similarly, there are many instances of legal status and pregnancy category in Figure 4(a). Instances appear in the infobox conceptual base because we do not cluster those nodes. As a result, original data is retained for calculation of relevance.

Since the refinement process is manual, the expert can decide how to modify the crude conceptual base as per the need. In Figure 3(b) and 4(b), we have shown basic refinement. In Figure 3(a), we show red crosses on the nodes that are removed because of ambiguity or no meaningful information, yellow crosses on the nodes that are modified because of inappropriate names but are meaningful, and blue cross on the node that is merged with another similar node. Here, *antiviral drug* is merged to *antiviral medication*. The refined version in Figure 3(b) depicts bold boundary nodes and edges that the expert modifies. In Figure 4(a), same-colored nodes represent instances of same concepts, which the expert merge into one in Figure 4(b).

In the presented case study, the expert modifies about 30% of the total nodes (section+ text+ infoboxes). However, this is subject to the structure of Wikipedia articles in the navigational template. For example, most of the articles in the Distillation[11] template do not contain infoboxes, which reduces the percentage of nodes that needs to be modified.

Following are the limitations of our approach:

- Parsing information from web pages is a time-consuming task, so we use XML and text processing for information gathering. Sometimes, rule-based text processing incorrectly extracts the information, and seldom, the XML does not contain full information. We manually check the infobox content after cleaning the XMLs. We find that approximately 47.5% of infobox entries are incorrect or empty in our case study. In the future, we plan to check the performance and scalability of other tools.
- Sections constitute a small part of the article's information, but we lose a considerable amount of textual information because of the filtering process. We are currently exploring techniques to create enhanced knowledge graphs using language models where filtration of nodes results in minimum or no information loss.
- Currently, we do not provide any aid for refining the conceptual base. We plan to create a GUI for this purpose that will include controllers for fuzzy logic and an interface for effortless refinement, further reducing the time and effort needed to create the conceptual base.

4 Related Works

Many researchers have worked on fuzzy ontology creation and their downstream applications, such as generating taxonomies, ontologies, and conceptual models from various data sources.

The use of fuzzy logic for creating concept lattices and ontologies has been studied previously by various researchers. There have been studies regarding fuzzy ontology creation (De Maio et al., 2009), (Tho et al., 2006), using fuzzy ontology and concept models in various domain-specific tasks and dataset (Parry, 2006), (Abulaish, 2009), (Quach and Hoang, 2018). As opposed to the previous work, we employ fuzzy logic using network metrics attributes.

There are a few significant open-domain, community-driven projects for structured knowledge creation. DBpedia (Lehmann et al., 2015) extracts structured information in multiple languages from Wikipedia infoboxes. Yago (Suchanek et al., 2007) has released various versions, and this also uses Wikipedia infoboxes. It also employs Wikipedia categories to determine the type of information, which is then mapped to WordNet taxonomy. Wikidata (Vrandečić and Krötzsch, 2014) a collaborative database, also links Wikipedia data with unique identifiers. Apart from the community-driven projects, researchers also used Wikipedia in other open-domain tasks such as document topic classification (Hassan et al., 2012), collaborative ontology creation (Hepp et al., 2006), semantic conceptual modeling and semantic relatedness interpretation (Saif et al., 2018), explaining facts in AI (Sarker et al., 2020), learning named entities (Nothman et al., 2013), large-scale taxonomy generation (Ponzetto and Strube, 2007). Researchers also used Wikipedia in domain-specific tasks like exploiting Wikipedia knowledge for classification tasks (Warren, 2012) and extracting domain-terms and terminologies from Wikipedia (Vivaldi and Rodríguez, 2010), (Vivaldi and Rodríguez, 2011), (Vivaldi et al., 2012). In this research, we provide domain-specific conceptual base construction from a small set of articles extracted on-the-fly from Wikipedia navigational templates instead of full Wiki dumps or other domain-specific corpora/texts. We also exploit unstructured text in addition to the structured information like Wikipedia info-boxes and article content structure.

5 Conclusion

We use Wikipedia navigational templates to build domain-specific conceptual bases in this study. To compute the relevance of the concepts, our system generates a graph representation of the article's knowledge and uses fuzzy logic on top of its network metrics. With a bit of human intervention, the system outputs a refined conceptual base that can be used further for various downstream purposes.

[11] https://en.wikipedia.org/wiki/Template:Distillation

References

Muhammad Abulaish. 2009. An ontology enhancement framework to accommodate imprecise concepts and relations. *Journal of Emerging technologies in web intelligence*, 1(1).

Carmen De Maio, Giuseppe Fenza, Vincenzo Loia, and Sabrina Senatore. 2009. Towards an automatic fuzzy ontology generation. In *2009 IEEE International Conference on Fuzzy Systems*, pages 1044–1049. IEEE.

Frederico Fonseca and James Martin. 2007. Learning the differences between ontologies and conceptual schemas through ontology-driven information systems. *Journal of the Association for Information Systems*, 8(2):4.

Linton C Freeman. 1977. A set of measures of centrality based on betweenness. *Sociometry*, pages 35–41.

Brendan J Frey and Delbert Dueck. 2007. Clustering by passing messages between data points. *science*, 315(5814):972–976.

Mostafa M Hassan, Fakhri Karray, and Mohamed S Kamel. 2012. Automatic document topic identification using wikipedia hierarchical ontology. In *2012 11th International Conference on Information Science, Signal Processing and their Applications (ISSPA)*, pages 237–242. IEEE.

Martin Hepp, Daniel Bachlechner, and Katharina Siorpaes. 2006. Harvesting wiki consensus-using wikipedia entries as ontology elements. In *SemWiki*. Citeseer.

Jens Lehmann, Robert Isele, Max Jakob, Anja Jentzsch, Dimitris Kontokostas, Pablo N Mendes, Sebastian Hellmann, Mohamed Morsey, Patrick Van Kleef, Sören Auer, et al. 2015. Dbpedia–a large-scale, multilingual knowledge base extracted from wikipedia. *Semantic web*, 6(2):167–195.

Vladimir I Levenshtein. 1966. Binary codes capable of correcting deletions, insertions, and reversals. In *Soviet physics doklady*, volume 10, pages 707–710. Soviet Union.

Joel Nothman, Nicky Ringland, Will Radford, Tara Murphy, and James R Curran. 2013. Learning multilingual named entity recognition from wikipedia. *Artificial Intelligence*, 194:151–175.

David Parry. 2006. Fuzzy ontologies for information retrieval on the www. In *Capturing Intelligence*, volume 1, pages 21–48. Elsevier.

Simone Paolo Ponzetto and Michael Strube. 2007. Deriving a large scale taxonomy from wikipedia. In *AAAI*, volume 7, pages 1440–1445.

Xuan Hung Quach and Thi Lan Giao Hoang. 2018. Fuzzy ontology modeling by utilizing fuzzy set and fuzzy description logic. In *Modern Approaches for Intelligent Information and Database Systems*, pages 15–26. Springer.

Abdulgabbar Saif, Nazlia Omar, Mohd Juzaiddin Ab Aziz, Ummi Zakiah Zainodin, and Naomie Salim. 2018. Semantic concept model using wikipedia semantic features. *Journal of Information Science*, 44(4):526–551.

Md Kamruzzaman Sarker, Joshua Schwartz, Pascal Hitzler, Lu Zhou, Srikanth Nadella, Brandon Minnery, Ion Juvina, Michael L Raymer, and William R Aue. 2020. Wikipedia knowledge graph for explainable ai. In *Iberoamerican Knowledge Graphs and Semantic Web Conference*, pages 72–87. Springer.

Fabian M Suchanek, Gjergji Kasneci, and Gerhard Weikum. 2007. Yago: a core of semantic knowledge. In *Proceedings of the 16th international conference on World Wide Web*, pages 697–706.

Quan Thanh Tho, Siu Cheung Hui, Alvis Cheuk M Fong, and Tru Hoang Cao. 2006. Automatic fuzzy ontology generation for semantic web. *IEEE transactions on knowledge and data engineering*, 18(6):842–856.

Jorge Vivaldi, Luis Adrián Cabrera-Diego, Gerardo Sierra, and María Pozzi. 2012. Using wikipedia to validate the terminology found in a corpus of basic textbooks. In *LREC*, pages 3820–3827.

Jorge Vivaldi and Horacio Rodríguez. 2010. Finding domain terms using wikipedia. In *LREC*.

Jorge Vivaldi and Horacio Rodríguez. 2011. Extracting terminology from wikipedia. *Procesamiento del lenguaje natural*, 47:65–73.

Denny Vrandečić and Markus Krötzsch. 2014. Wikidata: a free collaborative knowledgebase. *Communications of the ACM*, 57(10):78–85.

Robert Warren. 2012. Creating specialized ontologies using wikipedia: The muninn experience. *Berlin, DE: Proceedings of Wikipedia Academy: Research and Free Knowledge (WPAC2012). URL: http://hangingtogether. org.*

Wikipedia. 2021a. Wikipedia category contents. `https://en.wikipedia.org/wiki/Wikipedia:Contents/Categories`.

Wikipedia. 2021b. Wikipedia navigation template. `https://en.wikipedia.org/wiki/Wikipedia:Navigation_template`.

It is better to Verify: Semi-Supervised Learning with a human in the loop for large-scale NLU models

Verena Weber, Enrico Piovano and **Melanie Bradford**
Amazon Alexa AI, Berlin, Germany
{wverena,piovano,neunerm}@amazon.com

Abstract

When a NLU model is updated, new utterances must be annotated to be included for training. However, manual annotation is very costly. We evaluate a semi-supervised learning workflow with a human in the loop in a production environment. The previous NLU model predicts the annotation of the new utterances, a human then reviews the predicted annotation. Only when the NLU prediction is assessed as incorrect the utterance is sent for human annotation. Experimental results show that the proposed workflow boosts the performance of the NLU model while significantly reducing the annotation volume. Specifically, in our setup, we see improvements of up to 14.16% for a recall-based metric and up to 9.57% for a F1-score based metric, while reducing the annotation volume by 97% and overall cost by 60% for each iteration.

1 Introduction

Natural Language Understanding (NLU) models are a key component of task-oriented dialog systems such as as Amazon Alexa or Google Assistant which have gained more popularity in recent years. To improve their performance and extend their functionalities, new versions of the NLU model are released to customers on a regular basis. In the classical supervised learning approach, new training data between model updates is acquired by sampling utterances from live traffic and have them annotated by humans. The main drawback is the high cost of manual annotation. We refer to this conventional workflow as *human annotation* workflow. In this paper, we propose a new workflow with the aim to reduce the annotation cost while still maintaining high quality NLU models. We refer to it as the *human verification* workflow. The proposed workflow uses the previous (current) version of the NLU model to annotate the new training data before each model update. The predicted annotation produced by the NLU model, which we refer to as NLU hypothesis or interpretation, is then reviewed by humans. If the NLU hypothesis is assessed as correct, the NLU hypothesis is used as the ground-truth annotation of the utterance during training. If the NLU hypothesis is assessed as incorrect, the utterance is sent for human annotation before being ingested for training. With the proposed workflow, only utterances for which the hypothesis of the NLU model was assessed as incorrect are annotated by humans, thereby reducing the annotation volume drastically. Since verifying is faster and cheaper than annotating, a cost reduction is achieved. We investigate the adoption of this workflow once the system has reached a certain maturity, not from the start. While these two workflows would provide the same annotation for any utterance in an ideal world, the results may differ in the real world depending on the presence of annotation or verification errors. In this paper, we would like to answer the following fundamental question: in terms of human annotation errors, human verification errors and model performance, is it better to manually verify or annotate in order to iteratively update NLU systems?

To answer this question, we investigate the impact of human annotation vs. verification in a large scale NLU system. To this end, we consider two model architectures utilized for NLU models in the current production systems, a Conditional Random Field (CRF) (Lafferty et al., 2001; Okazaki, 2007) for slot filling and a Maximum Entropy (MaxEnt) classifier (Berger et al., 1996) for intent classification as well as a transformer based BERT architecture (Devlin et al., 2018). We evaluate the proposed workflow both explicitly by measuring annotation quality as well as implicitly by comparing the resulting model performance. Our experimental results show that the *human verification* workflow boosts the model performance while reducing human annotation volumes. In addition, we show that human annotation resources are better spent on utterances selected through Active Learning (Cohn et al., 1996; Settles, 2009; Konyushkova et al., 2017).

Proceedings of the 2nd Workshop on Data Science with Human in the Loop: Language Advances, pages 8–15
June 11, 2021.

2 Related Work

Using a model to label data instead of humans is an approach that has been studied extensively since human labelling is costly while unlabelled data can be acquired easily. Under the term Semi-supervised learning (SSL) (Zhou and Belkin, 2014; Zhu, 2005) many different approaches to leverage unlabelled data emerged in the literature. SSL aims at exploiting unlabelled data based on a small set of labelled data. One approach is self-training, also referred to as self-teaching or bootstrapping (Zhu, 2005; Triguero et al., 2015). In self-training labels are generated by feeding the unlabelled data in a model trained on the the available labelled data. Typically, the predicted labels for instances with high confidence are then used to retrain the model and the procedure is repeated. For neural networks, Lee (2013) suggested pseudo-labelling which optimizes a combination of supervised and unsupervised loss instead of retraining the model on pseudo-labels. Self-training has been applied to several natural language processing tasks. To name only a few examples, Yarowsky (1995) uses self-training for word sense disambiguation, Riloff et al. (2003) to identify subjective nouns. In McClosky et al. (2006) self learning is used for parsing.

The two main drawbacks of self-training are that instances with low confidence scores cannot be labelled and that prediction errors with high confidence can reinforce itself. To mitigate the latter issue strategies to identify mis-labeled instances have been discussed. An exhaustive review is beyond the scope of this paper, we just name a few examples. Li and Zhou (2005) use local information in a neighborhood graph to identify unreliable labels, Shi et al. (2018) add a distance based uncertainty weight for each sample and propose Min-Max features for better between-class separability and within-class compactness.

In this paper we suggest to use human verification to ensure the ingested predicted labels are reliable. In addition, we rely on human annotation for those utterances that the model cannot interpret correctly. The goal is to mitigate the two afore-mentioned problems of self-training.

A so called human-in-the-loop approach has been investigated for different applications. Zhang et al. (2020) investigate a human-in-the-loop approach for image segmentation and annotation. Schulz et al. (2019) examine the use of suggestion models to support human experts with segmentation and classification of epistemic activities in diagnostic reasoning texts. Zhang and Chaudhuri (2015) suggest active learning from weak and strong labelers where these labelers can be humans with different levels of expertise in the labelling task. Shivaswamy and Joachims (2015) show that a human expert is not always needed but that user behavior is valuable feedback that can be collected more easily.

The contribution of this paper is two-fold: First, we propose a SSL approach with a human in the loop for large-scale NLU models. Second, we show this workflow boosts the performance in a production system while reducing human annotation significantly.

Active Learning (AL) (Cohn et al., 1996; Settles, 2009; Konyushkova et al., 2017) proposes to label those instances that promise the highest learning effect for the model instead of blindly labelling data. Since the proposed workflow reduces the human annotation volume, we spend some of these freed up resources on annotation of AL data.

3 Setup and Approach

In this section, we briefly discuss the NLU model, the used metrics, the concept of iterative model updates and evaluation.

3.1 NLU task

A common approach to NLU is dividing the recognition task into two subtasks. Predicting the intent and the slots of a user's utterance constitutes a way to map the utterance on a semantic space. Accordingly, our NLU model consists of two models, each performing one of these subtasks. Intent classification (IC) predicts the user's specific intent, e.g. play music or turn on a light. Slot filling (SF), finally extracts the semantic constituents from the utterance. Taking the example "Where is MCO?" from the ATIS data (Tur et al., 2010) (Do and Gaspers, 2019), should be labelled as $where-[O]\ is-[O]\ MCO-[B-airport\_code]$ by slot filling. The intent should be recognized as city. When an utterance is humanly annotated for training, the annotator performs the same operation of the NLU model by mapping the utterance to a specific intent and slots in order to be ingested for training.

3.2 Metrics

We report results considering two metrics utilized to evaluate the performance of NLU models in production systems, Semantic Error Rate (SemER) and Intent Classification Error rate (ICER). SemER takes into consideration both intent and slot classification errors, while ICER only takes intent errors into consideration. SemER is computed as follows:

$$SemER = \frac{\#(slot\ +\ intent\ errors)}{\#(slots\ +\ intents\ in\ reference)} \tag{1}$$

ICER simply is the percentage of utterances with mis-classified intent, only intent classification counts while slot errors are ignored.

$$ICER = \frac{\#(intent\ errors)}{\#(total\ utterances)} \tag{2}$$

Note that both SemER and ICER are error metrics, i.e. a metric reduction reflects an improvement. Both are one-sided metrics that do not take precision into account. Therefore, we also report F-metrics for SemER and ICER, which are referred to as F-SemER and F-ICER, respectively. They are defined as the harmonic mean of the recall-based metric and the precision. We report macro-averages over intents for all metrics.

3.3 Iterative Model Updates

NLU models need to be regularly updated to improve their capability to understand new customer requests and extend the functionalities of the virtual assistant. Therefore new models trained on recent customer data are released on a regular basis. New data is sampled from live traffic between two NLU model releases and annotated. A part of the legacy training data is then discarded and replaced by the new annotated data for two reasons: 1) practical constraints to the building time of the new release model, 2) using too old and therefore unrepresentative data could degrade model performance. As a consequence, each NLU model is trained on an almost constant number of training utterances. For example, assuming that the overall training size is constrained to 400.000 utterances, then, if in a new release 10.000 new utterances are added, the oldest 10.000 will be removed.

3.4 Maturity and workflow evaluation

When NLU models are released for the first time, only human annotated data are used for training as previous versions of the NLU model are not available. This means in theory, the two workflows can be implemented from the second release onward. This implies that during the first few releases the majority of the training data is human annotated data. However, due to the data elimination procedure described in Section 3.3, after a certain number of releases with the verification workflow the manually annotated data from the first release will be fully removed from the training set. Here we assume to be in that maturity stage, where the full training dataset is derived from either the verification or annotation workflow, and hence no mixed training set between the two workflows is considered. For evaluation of the proposed workflows, we simulate the described updates and consider a specific model update for evaluation. A schematic timeline is shown in Figure 1. As we are considering a mature NLU model, this evaluation is representative of other model updates.

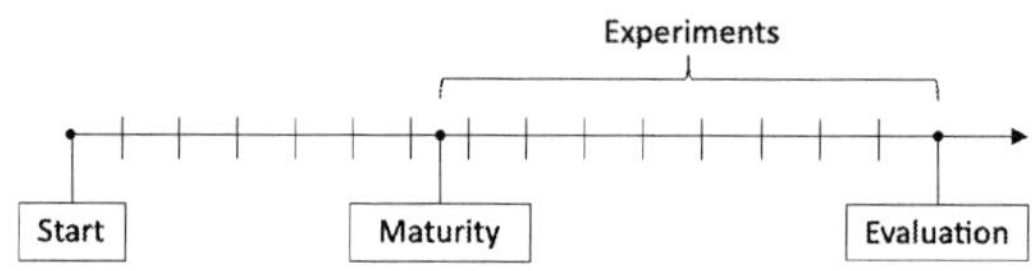

Figure 1: Schematic depiction of the NLU model updates timeline. Each dash represents a release. Results are reported for Evaluation point.

4 Proposed workflow

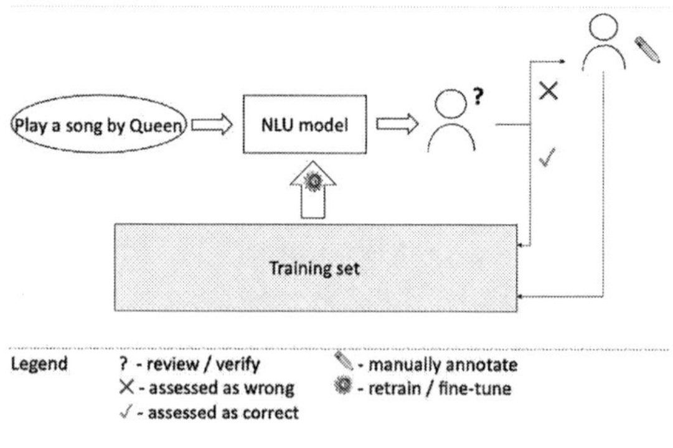

Figure 2: Schematic depiction of the proposed verification workflow. Note that the NLU model is updated periodically.

4.1 Detailed Workflow Description

This section describes the two workflows in detail. Throughout this paper we denote the *human annotation* workflow as the benchmark.

1. **Human annotation workflow** - *benchmark*: In each model update, the new training utterances are sent for manual annotation. Hence, the whole training dataset on which the NLU model is retrained (or-fine-tuned) periodically is human annotated, including the recently added utterances. The annotator only has access to the annotation guideline, but cannot see any kind of hypothesized annotation of the utterance.

2. **Human verification workflow** - *proposed*: Before each model update, the new training instances are first fed into the previous NLU model. The NLU hypothesis is then sent for human verification to assess if the NLU hypothesis is correct or not. If the annotation is evaluated as correct, the NLU hypothesis is ingested as ground-truth in the new NLU model training dataset. If the annotation is evaluated as incorrect, the utterance is sent for human annotation before being ingested. In this workflow, the evaluator has access to both the annotation guideline as well as the NLU annotation hypothesis of the utterance. Figure 2 depicts the proposed workflow. The training dataset on which the NLU model is retrained (or fine-tuned) only partially consists of human-annotated data.

With the proposed workflow, the cost is dramatically reduced as verifying is faster and cheaper than annotating. However, the question is if the verification workflow is also favorable in terms of data quality and model performance. In our experiments we therefore evaluate which of the two workflows is able to generate higher quality training data and enhance the NLU model performance. Results are discussed in Section 7.

5 Datasets

For training, we start with a dataset of unlabelled utterances representative of the user engagement with a dialog system. The dataset spans over a large number of intent and slots representative of multiple functionalities. High level statistics are listed in Table 5.

In order to have the same annotation and verification quality as in the production system, we requested the support from professional annotators. Trained and experienced annotators mimicked both workflows. For each utterance, one annotator of the team followed the *human annotation* workflow, while another followed the *human verification* workflow. For each training utterance, we also have the corresponding NLU hypothesis from the production model when the utterance was sampled. As a result two labelled training datasets were generated from one unlabelled dataset following each workflow. The overall training dataset has been built over multiple NLU releases as explained in Section 3.3.

The two training sets are then used to re-train or fine-tune each of the considered architecture. As a test set, we also consider a dataset of utterances representative of the engagement of the users with a voice assistant (see Table 5), also sampled as explained in Section 3.3. In order to have a correct and unbiased test set, test data are annotated following a different pipeline than the ones for training. For each test utterances three annotators need to produce the same annotation (100% agreement). This allows us to assume that the annotation of the test data is almost surely correct. The updated models are then evaluated on the test set to compare performance.

6 Experiments

This section describes the conducted experiments to evaluate both workflows and provides more details about how we selected utterances for annotation through AL.

6.1 Considered Model Architectures

To evaluate the proposed verification workflow, we consider two NLU architectures:

- CRF+MaxEnt classifier architecture:
  We use a Conditional Random Field (CRF) (Lafferty et al., 2001; Okazaki, 2007) for slot filling and a Maximum Entropy (MaxEnt) classifier (Berger et al., 1996) for intent classification. The new NLU model is obtained by re-training from scratch on the updated training dataset.

- BERT architecture:
  We use a transformer based BERT model (Devlin et al., 2018) that jointly solves the task of intent classification and NER. Hidden states are fed into a softmax layer to solve the two tasks. We use pre-trained mono-lingual BERT for German trained on unsupervised data from

	# utterances	# distinct intents	# distinct slots
training set	400 000	316	282
test set	100 000	316	282

Table 1: High level statistics for training and test set.

Wikipedia pages. We tokenize the input sentence, feed it to BERT, get the last layer's activations, and pass them through a final layer to make intent and NER predictions. In this case the updated NLU model is obtained by fine-tuning the initial NLU model on the new training dataset.

For both approaches we keep the set of features, hyperparameters and configuration constant for our experiments. All experiments are conducted for German. For each architecture, the models are trained by using the annotated data from the annotation vs verification workflows, respectively. For the BERT models, this step is preceeded by pre-training both models on unsupervised Wikipedia data. We then compare the performance of the resulting models.

6.2 Active Learning

We perform AL in two steps considering a corpus of millions of unlabelled utterances initially:

1. For each domain, select through a binary classifier which utterances from the unsupervised corpus are relevant to the domain.

2. Out of the candidate pool, select those with the lowest confidence score product of MaxEnt classifier (IC) and CRF (NER) and send them for annotation.

Note that a low product of IC and NER score indicates that the utterance is difficult to label for the model. We selected a total of 30.000 utterances through AL for human annotation.

7 Results

This section discusses all obtained results. We first evaluate the annotation quality for both workflows and quantify the possible cost reduction for the proposed workflow, see Sections 7.1 and 7.2. Second, we compare the performance of the NLU models when trained on data labeled through the respective workflow. Results are shown in Section 7.3.

7.1 Annotation reduction with the proposed workflow

To investigate by how much human annotation could be reduced through the proposed workflow, we calculate the percentage of utterances for which the NLU hypothesis of the previous model was assessed as correct between each update. We find that 97% of the annotation from the NLU model are assessed as correct. This means that only 3% of the utterances would be manually annotated constituting a significant reduction in annotation volume. Annotating an utterance takes about 2.5 the time of verification. Note that time is proportional to cost as we assume that human annotation specialists are paid a certain wage per hour and are able to process a certain amount of utterances depending on the task, annotation vs. verification. Let N denote the number of sampled utterances, t_A the annotation time per utterance and t_V the verification time per utterance in minutes. Then $t_A = 2.5 \cdot t_V$ or $t_V = 0.4 \cdot t_A$. The total cost for the verification workflow can then be written as:

$$total_V = N \cdot t_V + 0.03 \cdot N \cdot t_A \qquad (3)$$

Substituting $t_V = 0.4 \cdot t_A$ into 3 gives $total_V = 0.43 \cdot N \cdot t_A$. Note that $N \cdot t_A$ denotes the total cost of the annotation workflow $total_A$, so

$$total_V = 0.43 \cdot total_A. \qquad (4)$$

Thus the verification workflow leads to an overall cost reduction of almost 60 %.

7.2 Quality of evaluation vs annotation

To compare the frequency of human errors in *annotation* and *verification workflow*, we requested an assessment by specialized annotators for the annotations from each workflow for one sample of utterances. For each utterance, three specialists had to agree in their assessment. Note that we took a sample of utterances assessed as correct in the *human verification workflow* as we wanted to estimate the percentage of incorrect training data that might be ingested through the verification workflow.

Table 3 shows the human errors in the *verification workflow* relative to the *annotation workflow*.

		ICER	SemER	F-ICER	F-SemER	Annotation Reduction
1	MaxEnt+CRF	-3.85%	-2.62%	-6.81%	-3.45%	-97%
2	MaxEnt+CRF+AL	-24.58%	-20.44%	-26.04%	-17.26%	-90%
3	BERT	-14.16%	-8.77%	-9.47%	-1.80%	-97%

Table 2: Rel. difference in error metrics for *verification* vs *annotation* (baseline) workflow for all experiments.

An annotation or verification is treated as incorrect if the intent or at least one of the slots is incorrect. We can see the *verification workflow* reduces overall human errors by 66% compared to the *annotation workflow*. Note that this large human error reduction is mostly driven by fewer intent errors, which are reduced by 80% for the *verification workflow* relative to the *annotation workflow*. Overall, the frequency of verification human errors is significantly lower than the frequency of annotation human errors. This means that looking at an already annotated utterance helps to reduce the number of low-quality training data compared to annotating an utterance from scratch, where the person has no indication.

To evaluate the annotation consistency in each training dataset generated through the respective workflow, we calculate the average entropy across each dataset on token level in Table 4. Entropy will be lower the fewer interpretations we see for the same token and the more consistent the annotation is. The entropy of the training set from the verification workflow is 5% lower than for the annotation workflow.

	Rel. human error
Intent Errors	-80%
Slot Errors	-50%
Overall Errors	-66%

Table 3: Human error frequencies for *verfication* vs *annotation* on a sample of utterances.

	Avg. entropy
annotation workflow	0.5677
verification workflow	0.5378
relative	-5.3%

Table 4: Average entropy on token level for each training dataset generated through the respective workflow.

7.3 Experiment Results

Table 2 displays all the experimental results to measure the impact of the *verification workflow* vs *annotation workflow* on model performance. Specifically, we show the relative percentage change of the metric values considering the verification workflow relative to the metric values considering the annotation workflow as a baseline. As SemER and ICER are error based metrics, a "-" means an improvement of the performance for verification compared to annotation, while "+" means a degradation.

It is evident that the *verification workflow* outperforms the *annotation workflow*, often even by a substantial margin, for all experiments and metrics while drastically reducing manual annotation volume for each iteration. This is in line with the previous observation of a lower error rate and higher consistency in the training data from the verification annotation workflow, see Section 7.2. Moreover, the gain in terms of ICER is higher than SemER for all experiments, which is driven by the greater reduction of intent errors in the verification workflow. We assume the display of the NLU hypothesis influences verifiers and results in a more consistent annotation when it comes to ambiguous utterances that have multiple valid interpretations. This again leads to more consistency in the training data by reducing the number of utterances for which the model sees two different annotations.

The gains for BERT are larger than for MaxEnt+CRF, except for F-SemER. This suggests that BERT is more sensitive to contradictory training data which is why the proposed workflow yields even higher performance gains compared to the MaxEnt+CRF architecture.

Given the high reduction in annotation volume through the proposed workflow, we used some of the freed up capacities instead to have AL data annotated. We added an additional 30.000 AL utterances for the most confused intents and slots to the training dataset of each workflow. As shown in Table 2, adding comparatively few AL data boosts model performance of the verification vs annotation models by more than 20% for almost all metrics while increasing the annotation volume by less than 10%. The great relative difference in performance for verification vs annotation suggests that AL is even more beneficial for the verification workflow.

8 Conclusion

With the aim of reducing annotation costs, we test a methodology where mature NLU models are iteratively updated by ingesting labelled data via a *human verification* instead of a *human annotation* workflow. Our findings show that the proposed verification workflow not only cuts annotation costs by almost 60 %, but it also boosts the performance of the NLU system for both considered architectures. This is in line with the annotation quality evaluation we performed, where we found that the human error rate for verification is lower than the human error rate for annotation yielding more consistent training data in the former. Our findings have an important practical implication: verifying is better than annotating for mature systems. Moreover, a fraction of the annotation savings should be utilized to annotate more impactful data, for instance AL data, which generated a large performance gain in the proposed workflow with a minimal increase in annotation volume.

Acknowledgements

The authors would like to thank the Alexa DeepNLU team for providing the pre-trained BERT model for German language.

The authors would also like to thank Tobias Falke for his valuable comments on an earlier draft of this paper.

References

Adam L. Berger, Vincent J. Della Pietra, and Stephen A. Della Pietra. 1996. A maximum entropy approach to natural language processing. *Comput. Linguist.*, 22(1):39–71.

David A Cohn, Zoubin Ghahramani, and Michael I Jordan. 1996. Active learning with statistical models. *Journal of artificial intelligence research*, 4:129–145.

Jacob Devlin, Ming-Wei Chang, Kenton Lee, and Kristina Toutanova. 2018. BERT: pre-training of deep bidirectional transformers for language understanding. *CoRR*, abs/1810.04805.

Quynh Ngoc Thi Do and Judith Gaspers. 2019. Cross-lingual transfer learning for spoken language understanding. *Proceedings of the 2019 IEEE International Conference on Acoustics, Speech and Signal Processing, ICASSP*.

Ksenia Konyushkova, Raphael Sznitman, and Pascal Fua. 2017. Learning active learning from data. In *Advances in Neural Information Processing Systems*, pages 4225–4235.

John D. Lafferty, Andrew McCallum, and Fernando C. N. Pereira. 2001. Conditional random fields: Probabilistic models for segmenting and labeling sequence data. In *Proceedings of the Eighteenth International Conference on Machine Learning*, ICML '01, pages 282–289, San Francisco, CA, USA. Morgan Kaufmann Publishers Inc.

Dong-Hyun Lee. 2013. Pseudo-label: The simple and efficient semi-supervised learning method for deep neural networks. In *Workshop on challenges in representation learning, ICML*, volume 3.

Ming Li and Zhi-Hua Zhou. 2005. Setred: Self-training with editing. In *Pacific-Asia Conference on Knowledge Discovery and Data Mining*, pages 611–621. Springer.

David McClosky, Eugene Charniak, and Mark Johnson. 2006. Effective self-training for parsing. In *Proceedings of the Human Language Technology Conference of the NAACL, Main Conference*, pages 152–159.

Naoaki Okazaki. 2007. Crfsuite: a fast implementation of conditional random fields (crfs). *URL http://www. chokkan. org/software/crfsuite*.

Ellen Riloff, Janyce Wiebe, and Theresa Wilson. 2003. Learning subjective nouns using extraction pattern bootstrapping. In *Proceedings of the seventh conference on Natural language learning at HLT-NAACL 2003*, pages 25–32.

Claudia Schulz, Christian M Meyer, Jan Kiesewetter, Michael Sailer, Elisabeth Bauer, Martin R Fischer, Frank Fischer, and Iryna Gurevych. 2019. Analysis of automatic annotation suggestions for hard discourse-level tasks in expert domains. *arXiv preprint arXiv:1906.02564*.

Burr Settles. 2009. Active learning literature survey. Technical report, University of Wisconsin-Madison Department of Computer Sciences.

Weiwei Shi, Yihong Gong, Chris Ding, Zhiheng MaXiaoyu Tao, and Nanning Zheng. 2018. Transductive semi-supervised deep learning using min-max features. In *Proceedings of the European Conference on Computer Vision (ECCV)*.

Pannaga Shivaswamy and Thorsten Joachims. 2015. Coactive learning. *Journal of Artificial Intelligence Research*, 53:1–40.

Isaac Triguero, Salvador García, and Francisco Herrera. 2015. Self-labeled techniques for semi-supervised learning: taxonomy, software and empirical study. *Knowledge and Information systems*, 42(2):245–284.

Gokhan Tur, Dilek Hakkani-Tür, and Larry Heck. 2010. What is left to be understood in atis? In *2010 IEEE Spoken Language Technology Workshop*, pages 19–24. IEEE.

David Yarowsky. 1995. Unsupervised word sense disambiguation rivaling supervised methods. In *33rd annual meeting of the association for computational linguistics*, pages 189–196.

Chicheng Zhang and Kamalika Chaudhuri. 2015. Active learning from weak and strong labelers. *arXiv preprint arXiv:1510.02847*.

Xiaoya Zhang, Lianjie Wang, Jin Xie, and Pengfei Zhu. 2020. Human-in-the-loop image segmentation and annotation. *Science China Information Sciences*, 63(11):1–3.

Xueyuan Zhou and Mikhail Belkin. 2014. Chapter 22 - semi-supervised learning. In Paulo S.R. Diniz, Johan A.K. Suykens, Rama Chellappa, and Sergios Theodoridis, editors, *Academic Press Library in Signal Processing: Volume 1*, volume 1 of *Academic Press Library in Signal Processing*, pages 1239 – 1269. Elsevier.

Xiaojin Jerry Zhu. 2005. Semi-supervised learning literature survey. Technical report, University of Wisconsin-Madison Department of Computer Sciences.

ViziTex: Interactive Visual Sense-Making of Text Corpora

Natraj Raman[1], Sameena Shah[2], Tucker Balch[2], Manuela Veloso[2]
J.P.Morgan AI Research
[1]London, UK.
[2]New York, USA.
first.last@jpmorgan.com

Abstract

Information visualization is critical to analytical reasoning and knowledge discovery. We present an interactive studio that integrates perceptive visualization techniques with powerful text analytics algorithms to assist humans in sense-making of large complex text corpora. The novel visual representations introduced here encode the features delivered by modern text mining models using advanced metaphors such as hypergraphs, nested topologies and tessellated planes. They enhance human-computer interaction experience for various tasks such as summarization, exploration, organization and labeling of documents. We demonstrate the ability of the visuals to surface the structure, relations and concepts from documents across different domains.

1 Introduction

Despite admirable progress in machine learning, human participation in data analysis and decision making is a reality. Human efforts are often required for bootstrapping labels, interpreting decisions and verifying outcomes. It is important to design intuitive visualizations that can exploit the pattern recognition and spatial reasoning capabilities of humans in order to transform the human-computer interaction experience. While traditional bar charts and heat map displays hold value, complex interactive graphical representations (Yuan et al., 2020) are often required to effectively slice and dice high-dimensional data. Furthermore, it is essential for these visuals to encode all the features delivered by machine learning models.

Interactive information processing in large complex text corpora pose a significant challenge due to the sheer volume, lack of structure and multi-faceted nature of text material. Existing efforts around visual interfaces for sense-making of text documents do not characterize the true potential of the text analytics algorithms (Liu et al., 2012), are often tied to a particular model (Vig, 2019) or remain fragmented with task specific solutions (Wang et al., 2016).

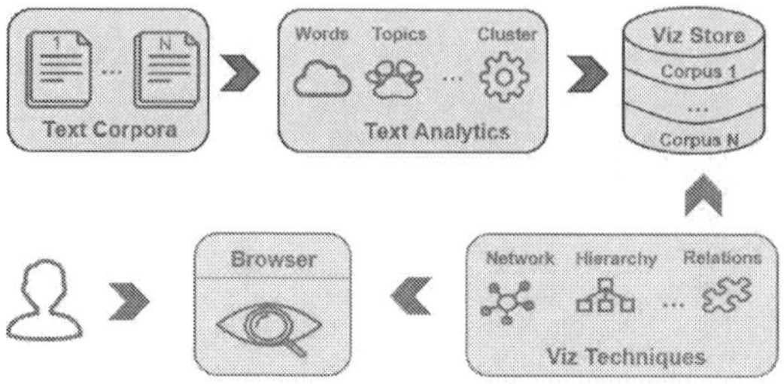

Figure 1: Architecture Overview.

There is a compelling opportunity for perceptive visualization techniques that fully leverage the capabilities of text mining models and cater to analysis at various levels of task granularity and human expertise. Towards this effort, we propose an interactive studio that delivers novel visual representations for common text oriented tasks such as theme discovery, document organization and label exploration. Visualizations presented here include a hypergraph that encodes distributional similarity between words, a multi-level radial layout to capture distinguishing terms, a clutter-free parallel coordinate plot of topic relations, a nested topology for document hierarchies and a tessellated plane to capture boundary points. These visualizations highlight interesting linguistic patterns in the corpus, surface complex relations between documents and reduce the burden of annotations for labeling exercises.

The structure of the framework, which follows a loosely coupled architecture pattern, is outlined in Fig. 1. There are three main components that drive the system: a text corpora, a suite of text analytics algorithms and a set of visualization techniques. We particularly focus on metadata rich corpus with multiple facets or data dimensions along which a corpus can be subdivided. The visualizations are

Proceedings of the 2nd Workshop on Data Science with Human in the Loop: Language Advances, pages 16–23
June 11, 2021.

independent of the analytical models and newer algorithms can be flexibly plugged-in. All the generated graphical elements are interactive, with the end user being able to zoom, pan, hover and click for receiving contextual information. The users merely require a web-browser to access the visuals.

We demonstrate the domain agnostic nature of the visuals by providing illustrations from publicly available datasets that span across informal, legal and scientific language formats. In the following sections, we review related efforts and present eight different visualizations.

2 Related Work

Research in visual text analytics has gained prominence and surveys such as (Liu et al., 2018) provide an overview of recent progress. Differently, Kucher and Kerren (2015) present a visual survey by collating the images generated by the various visualization methods and offer an interactive filter for exploration.

There has been several efforts towards the development of software tools for analyzing text data. For example, the Leximancer (Angus et al., 2013) application plots word frequency statistics to help an analyst examine concepts in text. Tiara (Liu et al., 2012) is a visual text analysis tool that uses topic models to summarize documents. The popular pyLDAViz package (Sievert and Shirley, 2014) offers interactive visualization for topic models. Our work differs from these by introducing new metaphors and integrating a variety of text mining tasks.

Designing interactive graphics for the creation of interesting visualization techniques is popular. StoryPrint (Watson et al., 2019) is a visualization method for script-based media that presents prominence and emotion of characters in a scene. The visual analytic system in Verifi (Karduni et al., 2019) enables investigation of misinformation on social media. Vig (2019) introduced a multi-scale visualization tool to illustrate the inner workings of attention patterns generated by neural Transformers. Unlike these application and model specific efforts, our work is intended to be agnostic both to the data domain and underlying algorithm.

3 Visualizations

We present several techniques for visually analyzing a corpus at word, topic and document levels below. Samples from three different datasets namely

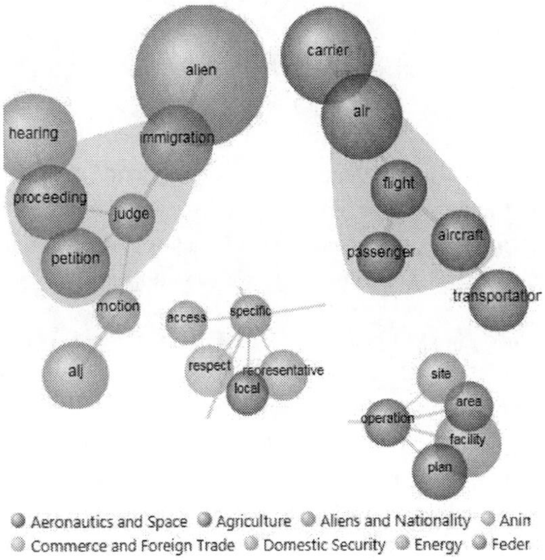

Figure 2: Hypergraph depicting word co-occurrences.

Amazon Reviews (McAuley and Leskovec, 2013), Arxiv Abstracts[1] and Code of Federal Regulations (CFR)[2] are used to illustrate the visualizations.

3.1 Word Hypergraph

A usual first step in text analytics is to plot the frequency of words in the corpus with a word cloud. However, the absence of context limits the ability of a word cloud visual to provide any insights beyond a basic overview. Following the principle of "characterizing a word by the company it keeps", we depict the co-occurrences of words (Weeds and Weir, 2005) to indicate semantic proximity. Rather than the structure-less cloud visual, a graph format with word nodes inter-connected by weighted edges is used. The words are scaled by a measure of how often they appear and colored by their dominant facet. The co-occurrence strength between words is encoded in the edge thickness. Furthermore, hyper-edges are used to connect the linked nodes that share similar attributes.

Formally, we are given a corpus with D documents comprising of N terms and a discrete attribute associated with each document. Let $G = (V, E, H)$ be a hypergraph with term nodes $\{v_n\}_{n=1}^{N}$, a set of edges $E \subset V \times V$ and hyperedges $H \subset \mathcal{P}(V)$. We set the dyadic connections between terms i and j based on weighted mutual

[1] https://doi.org/10.6078/D1708G

[2] https://www.ecfr.gov/

information as

$$e_{ij} = \frac{|t_i \cap t_j|}{D} \log \frac{N^2 |t_i \cap t_j|}{D|t_i||t_j|}, \quad (1)$$

where $|t|$ is an occurrence measure and $e_{ij} \in E$. Let $c_i \in \{C_1 ... C_P\}$ be the dominant attribute of term i. An hyper-edge $h \in H$ connecting potentially arbitrary number of nodes is defined as

$$h_i = \{v_i\} \cup \{v_k : c_i = c_k \wedge e_{ik} > \tau, \forall k \in V_{\setminus i}\} \quad (2)$$

where τ is a threshold to control visual clutter.

This hypergraph visualization allows the user to identify words that are central to characterizing a particular subset of the corpus. For example, by paying attention to the hyper-edges connecting nodes *air, flight, passenger* and *aircraft* in Fig. 2, the user can conclude that *flight* is a key-word in the *Aeronautics* subset of the CFR corpus while words such as *operation* or *access* is more ambiguous in describing the corpus.

3.2 Word Relations

Domain experts are often interested in understanding how subsets of a text collection differ. The identification of terms that are distinct to particular subsets will aid in this effort. To achieve this, we construct a radial layout of the top relevant terms that are shared across the various subsets. Each subset occupies a non-uniform slice based on its bandwidth in an inner concentric circle while its corresponding terms appear along the outer circle. The prominence of a term to a particular subset is reflected in its font-size. The relations between the terms are modeled as a B-Spline curve (Holten, 2006) in order to reduce visual clutter. The curve is drawn with a linear interpolation of the term colors and its width depends on the relationship strength.

In detail, let $\eta_p = \{w_i\}_{i=1}^{N_p}, \exists p' : w_i \in \eta_{p'}$ be the set of relevant terms in subset p of the corpus. The arc length for p is set to $N_p / \sum_{p'} N_{p'}$ and the curve width between p and p' for term i is computed as

$$\gamma_{pp'}^{i} = [1/Z] f(w_i^p) + f(w_i^{p'}), \quad (3)$$

where f is a measure of term occurrence and Z is a normalization constant. Fig. 3 shows the relation between words across different facets of the Amazon corpus. When inspecting the word *music*, the user can visually infer that this word is common to *CDs, Android Apps, Movies/TV* and *Video Games* subsets unlike a word such as *great* that is prevalent across all subsets, thereby unearthing distinguishing terms.

3.3 Topic Graph

Summarizing a corpus using a small set of underlying topics is a popular text mining technique to discover semantic structures. We improve over existing topic model visualizations by introducing three new features: the ability to capture correlations between topics, rank a topic by the significance of its semantic content, and associate meaningful labels with a topic. Consequently, the topics are now represented as a graph with the links between topic nodes denoting the extent of their correlation (Blei and Lafferty, 2006). While a node is colored by the dominant facet of its topic, its opacity is controlled by the topic's significance (Röder et al., 2015). Thus topics that are less coherent are deemphasized, blending into the background. Both the automatically extracted topic label (Mei et al., 2007) and the top ranked terms of a topic are displayed, with the latter decorated in an elliptical arc around a node.

In order to extract the topic label, we first construct a set of candidate phrases $1...L$ and score the semantic relevance of a phrase l to topic k as

$$score(l, k) = \sum_m \log \frac{p(w_{mk})}{p(w_m)}, \quad (4)$$

where $p(w_{mk})$ denotes the probability of the mth term in the phrase for topic k and $p(w_m)$ is the probability of the term across all topics. The topic label is then selected from the top ranked scores.

The utility of this visualization is evident in Fig. 4. The presence of labels such as *convex optimization problem* and *multivariate asset return* makes the topic theme of Arxiv corpus more interpretable than merely viewing a generic term such as *problem* or *model*.

3.4 Topic Relations

It is useful to discover differentiating topics across corpus subsets, similar to the identification of distinguishing words. However, it is difficult to accommodate the additional topic level grouping in the radial layout discussed above without disrupting legibility. Hence we employ a parallel co-ordinate (Siirtola et al., 2009; Collins et al., 2009) representation to portray this high-dimensional data. Specifically, the subsets are visualized along parallel columns and the top ranked topics for a subset

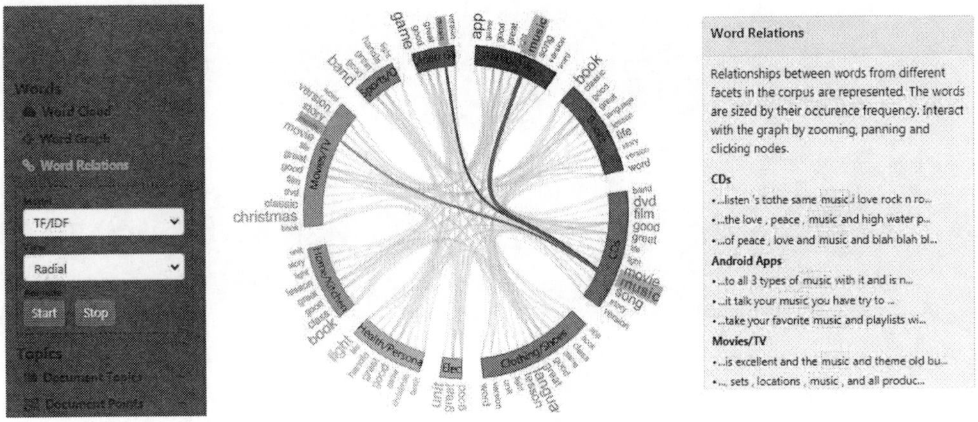

Figure 3: Relations between words across different subsets are displayed in a radial layout.

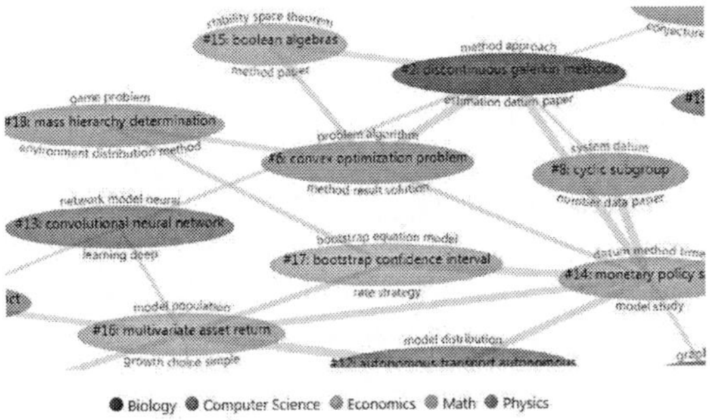

Figure 4: Topic Graph encoded with correlations, coherence and labels.

are scaled by their corresponding topic distribution. The topic terms themselves are relatively sized.

Naively showing all the links between related topics will clutter the visual. Hence the edges appear clipped by default, and are expanded only when the user hovers over a topic of interest. Fig. 5 demonstrates this concept, with the full-links shown only for *Topic 3* and rest of the elements are de-emphasized. The user can judge whether a topic is distinctive or not from the presence or absence of the clipped edges. For example, unlike *Topic 1*, *Topic 2* does not contain any edge implying that it captures *Aliens* subset specific terms.

3.5 Document Clusters

Visualizing the documents in the corpus in a manner that reflects the similarity and differences between them is essential for efficient organization and navigation. The spatial relations between the documents can be determined by comparing their embedding representations, which may range from a simple bag-of-words model to a modern pre-trained contextual text encoder (Devlin et al., 2018). Instead of simply plotting a 2D projection of these document embeddings, we cluster the documents using their original high-dimensional representation and visualize their relative positions in the clustered space.

Formally, we convert a document d to a fixed length continuous vector of size m through a function $\phi : d \to \mathbb{R}^m$. The pdf of the document is modeled based on this vector as a mixture of K multi-variate Gaussian densities as follows:

$$p(d) = \sum_{k=1}^{K} \pi_k \mathcal{N}(\mu_k, \Sigma_k). \tag{5}$$

Here $\mu_k \in \mathbb{R}^m$, $\Sigma_k \in \mathbb{R}^{m \times m}$ and $\pi_k \in \mathbb{R}$ denotes a mixture proportion. The above model partitions the corpus into K different clusters and the cluster index of a document sampled from this density function is used to determine its position in the cluster network.

Fig. 6 illustrates such a cluster network of documents for the CFR corpus. The documents are centered around their corresponding cluster and colored by their facet. Nearby clusters are linked together denoting their similarity and a cluster can be collapsed interactively to simplify the view. The visual enables the user to reason say "Why is an *Aeuronatics* document grouped in a cluster with predominantly *Federal Elections* documents?" and provide feedback, thereby improving the tagging process in an active learning setting.

3.6 Document Hierarchy

Examining the relationship between documents within a same cluster is critical to gaining granular insights about the corpus structure. Instead

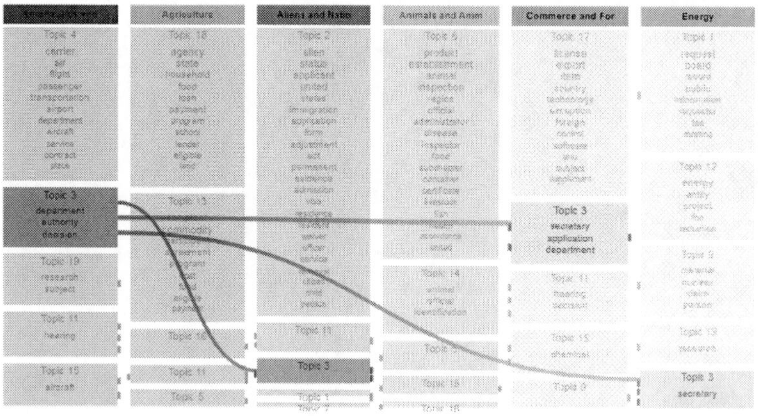

Figure 5: Topic Relations rendered using a parallel coordinate plot and clipped edges. Topic boxes and links are highlighted on hover to reduce clutter.

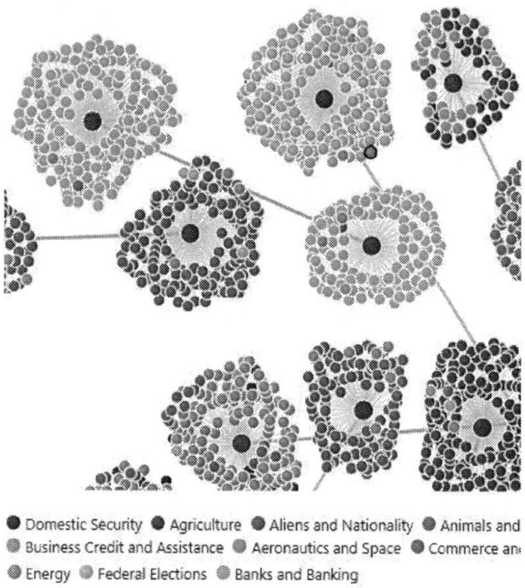

Figure 6: Network representation of document clusters.

of partitioning the documents exclusively, a better alternative is to organize them in a hierarchical fashion, from generic to specific (Ibrahim et al., 2019). This would empower the users to decide the level of detail, as dictated by their target task. We recursively partition the corpus to create hierarchical clusters and visualize them using a nested structure enclosure diagram.

Each circle in Fig.7 denotes an hierarchical level, with the circles contained inside the same parent being more similar. Leaf level circles denote the documents and are colored by their facet. The user can zoom-in to each circle and access the document content to explore anomalous patterns. For example, we investigated the reasons for the placement of an orange point (*Clothing/Shoes*) in the midst of violet points (*Android Apps*) and observed that it was a data quality issue.

3.7 Document Boundaries

Selecting the right data to label is important for annotation exercises and in active learning tasks. An effective strategy when sampling the data points is to identify points that are near decision boundaries (Monarch, 2021). The idea being that such uncertain points may have subjective interpretation and hence are worthy of human attention. We focus on presenting such boundary documents to the user in conjunction with documents that the machine is confident about.

In detail, the documents are first partitioned using a flat clustering algorithm based on their embedding representations using (5). Let $\mathcal{D}_k \subset \mathbb{R}^m$ denote the set of documents in cluster k. A convex hull encompassing the points in this cluster is defined from their convex combinations of $\mathcal{D}_k$ as

$$\Big\{ \sum_j \lambda_j \mathcal{D}_{kj} : \sum_j \lambda_j = 1 \wedge \lambda_j \geq 0 \wedge \mathcal{D}_{kj} \subset \mathcal{D}_k \Big\}. \quad (6)$$

The vertices of the hull are treated as the boundary points of a cluster. For visualization, a Voronoi diagram (Phillips, 2021) is constructed by using the cluster centroids as seed points. Thus each cluster is now visualized as a Voronoi cell bounded by a polygon with the polygon segments overlapping for nearby cells. The boundary points of a cluster are placed adjacent to the polygon sides while the interior points are arranged in a radial fashion at the center. Fig. 8 depicts this structure. The user

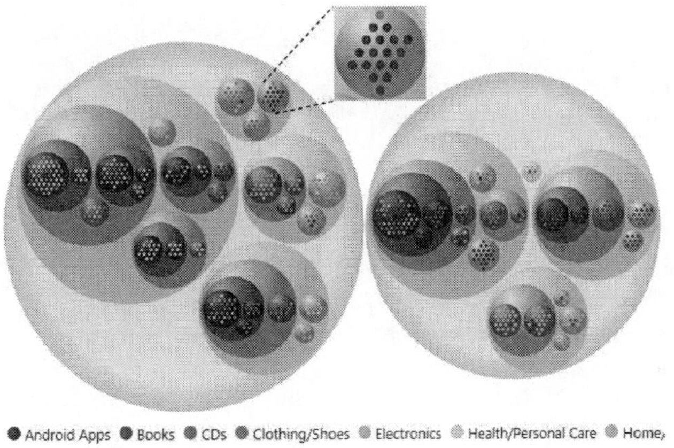

Figure 7: Hierarchical relations between the documents portrayed using a nested topology. Documents inside the same circle are more similar than the documents in sibling and parent circles.

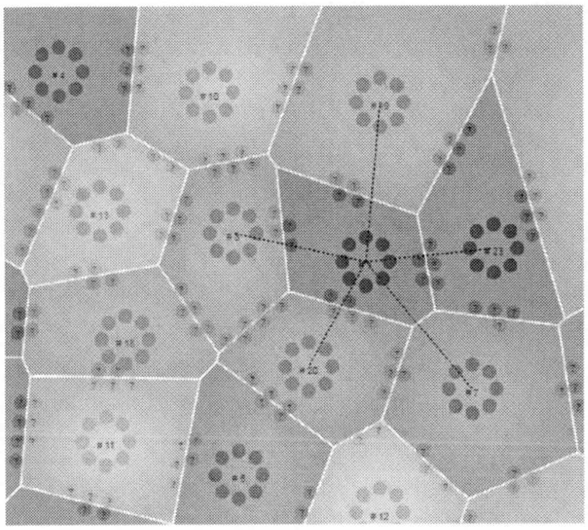

Figure 8: Voronoi tessellation of the cluster space showing both boundary and interior points.

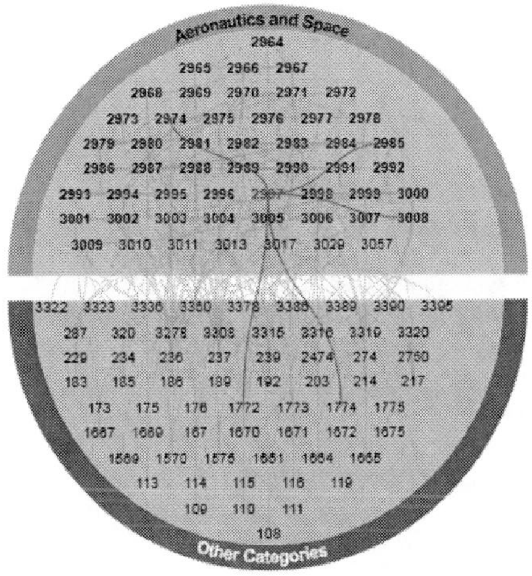

Figure 9: Relations (intra vs inter) between documents.

can drill down to see details about the boundary points and the sampled interior points. The Voronoi cells adjacent to *Cluster 1* is highlighted, signifying that the boundary points for this cluster may be assigned to its neighbors such as *Cluster 20* or *23*.

3.8 Document Relations

All the document specific visualizations outlined above consider the corpus holistically. Sometimes it is required to anchor the analysis to a particular subset of the corpus and compare with the rest of the subsets in a one-vs-all setting. Such intra and inter subset relations is explored in Fig. 9. The top hemisphere contains the ids of documents only from *Aeuronatics and Space* subset of CFR corpus. The documents from other subsets that are close to these documents in the embedding space are listed in the bottom hemisphere, with related documents being linked. The documents with strong intra-segment links are highlighted in bold font. The user can analyze the similarity and differences between a select set of documents based on the link cues.

4 Conclusion

Large and complexly related text collections require perceptive information visualization techniques to assist human understanding and reasoning. The interactive visualizations proposed here facilitates discovering concepts, themes, clusters, outliers and structure in a corpus by integrating text analytics models with novel visual representations. In future, we wish to extend the suite of statistical models for selection and incorporate new visuals for temporal analysis that exploits animations.

Acknowledgments

This paper was prepared for information purposes by the Artificial Intelligence Research group of JPMorgan Chase & Co and its affiliates ("JP Morgan"), and is not a product of the Research Department of JP Morgan. J.P. Morgan makes no representation and warranty whatsoever and disclaims all liability for the completeness, accuracy or reliability of the information contained herein. This document is not intended as investment research or investment advice, or a recommendation, offer or solicitation for the purchase or sale of any security, financial instrument, financial product or service, or to be used in any way for evaluating the merits of participating in any transaction, and shall not constitute a solicitation under any jurisdiction or to any person, if such solicitation under such jurisdiction or to such person would be unlawful.

References

Daniel Angus, Sean Rintel, and Janet Wiles. 2013. Making sense of big text: a visual-first approach for analysing text data using leximancer and discursis. *International Journal of Social Research Methodology*, 16(3):261–267.

David Blei and John Lafferty. 2006. Correlated topic models. *Advances in neural information processing systems*, 18:147.

Christopher Collins, Fernanda B Viegas, and Martin Wattenberg. 2009. Parallel tag clouds to explore and analyze faceted text corpora. In *2009 IEEE Symposium on Visual Analytics Science and Technology*, pages 91–98. IEEE.

Jacob Devlin, Ming-Wei Chang, Kenton Lee, and Kristina Toutanova. 2018. Bert: Pre-training of deep bidirectional transformers for language understanding. *arXiv preprint arXiv:1810.04805*.

Danny Holten. 2006. Hierarchical edge bundles: Visualization of adjacency relations in hierarchical data. *IEEE Transactions on visualization and computer graphics*, 12(5):741–748.

R Ibrahim, S Zeebaree, and K Jacksi. 2019. Survey on semantic similarity based on document clustering. *Adv. Sci. Technol. Eng. Syst. J*, 4(5):115–122.

Alireza Karduni, Isaac Cho, Ryan Wesslen, Sashank Santhanam, Svitlana Volkova, Dustin L Arendt, Samira Shaikh, and Wenwen Dou. 2019. Vulnerable to misinformation? verifi! In *Proceedings of the 24th International Conference on Intelligent User Interfaces*, pages 312–323.

Kostiantyn Kucher and Andreas Kerren. 2015. Text visualization techniques: Taxonomy, visual survey, and community insights. In *2015 IEEE Pacific Visualization Symposium (PacificVis)*, pages 117–121. IEEE.

Shixia Liu, Xiting Wang, Christopher Collins, Wenwen Dou, Fangxin Ouyang, Mennatallah El-Assady, Liu Jiang, and Daniel A Keim. 2018. Bridging text visualization and mining: A task-driven survey. *IEEE transactions on visualization and computer graphics*, 25(7):2482–2504.

Shixia Liu, Michelle X Zhou, Shimei Pan, Yangqiu Song, Weihong Qian, Weijia Cai, and Xiaoxiao Lian. 2012. Tiara: Interactive, topic-based visual text summarization and analysis. *ACM Transactions on Intelligent Systems and Technology (TIST)*, 3(2):1–28.

Julian McAuley and Jure Leskovec. 2013. Hidden factors and hidden topics: understanding rating dimensions with review text. In *Proceedings of the 7th ACM conference on Recommender systems*, pages 165–172.

Qiaozhu Mei, Xuehua Shen, and ChengXiang Zhai. 2007. Automatic labeling of multinomial topic models. In *Proceedings of the 13th ACM SIGKDD international conference on Knowledge discovery and data mining*, pages 490–499.

Robert Monarch. 2021. *Human-in-the-Loop Machine Learning: Active learning and annotation for human-centered AI*, volume 1. Manning, Shelter Island, NY.

M Jeff Phillips. 2021. *Mathematical Foundations for Data Analysis*, volume 1. Springer.

Michael Röder, Andreas Both, and Alexander Hinneburg. 2015. Exploring the space of topic coherence measures. In *Proceedings of the eighth ACM international conference on Web search and data mining*, pages 399–408.

Carson Sievert and Kenneth Shirley. 2014. Ldavis: A method for visualizing and interpreting topics. In *Proceedings of the workshop on interactive language learning, visualization, and interfaces*, pages 63–70.

Harri Siirtola, Tuuli Laivo, Tomi Heimonen, and Kari-Jouko Räihä. 2009. Visual perception of parallel coordinate visualizations. In *2009 13th International Conference Information Visualisation*, pages 3–9. IEEE.

Jesse Vig. 2019. A multiscale visualization of attention in the transformer model. In *Proceedings of the 57th Annual Meeting of the Association for Computational Linguistics: System Demonstrations*, pages 37–42, Florence, Italy. Association for Computational Linguistics.

Xiting Wang, Shixia Liu, Junlin Liu, Jianfei Chen, Jun Zhu, and Baining Guo. 2016. Topicpanorama: A full picture of relevant topics. *IEEE transactions on visualization and computer graphics*, 22(12):2508–2521.

Katie Watson, Samuel S Sohn, Sasha Schriber, Markus Gross, Carlos Manuel Muniz, and Mubbasir Kapadia. 2019. Storyprint: an interactive visualization of stories. In *Proceedings of the 24th International Conference on Intelligent User Interfaces*, pages 303–311.

Julie Weeds and David Weir. 2005. Co-occurrence retrieval: A flexible framework for lexical distributional similarity. *Computational Linguistics*, 31(4):439–475.

Jun Yuan, Changjian Chen, Weikai Yang, Mengchen Liu, Jiazhi Xia, and Shixia Liu. 2020. A survey of visual analytics techniques for machine learning. *Computational Visual Media*, pages 1–34.

A Visualization Approach for Rapid Labeling of Clinical Notes for Smoking Status Extraction

Saman Enayati
saman.enayati@temple.edu

Ziyu Yang
tug27634@temple.edu

Benjamin Lu
lu.ben@pennmutual.com

Slobodan Vucetic
vucetic@temple.edu

Abstract

Labeling is typically the most human-intensive step during the development of supervised learning models. In this paper, we propose a simple and easy-to-implement visualization approach that reduces cognitive load and increases the speed of text labeling. The approach is fine-tuned for task of extraction of patient smoking status from clinical notes. The proposed approach consists of the ordering of sentences that mention smoking, centering them at smoking tokens, and annotating to enhance informative parts of the text. Our experiments on clinical notes from the MIMIC-III clinical database demonstrate that our visualization approach enables human annotators to label sentences up to 3 times faster than with a baseline approach.

1 Introduction

Deep learning algorithms achieve state-of-the-art accuracy on a range of natural language processing tasks. However, to achieve high accuracy, deep learning algorithms typically require a lot of labeled data. In extremely error-sensitive applications, such as those in the medical domain, the trade-off between labeling effort and prediction accuracy is strongly skewed towards maximizing the accuracy. In such applications, data labeling arises as the most costly and human-intensive step during the development of deep learning models. In this paper, we focus on a scenario where the requirement is to label all available data because the goal is to maximize the accuracy using the available corpus of documents. In such a scenario, none of the labeling shortcuts developed in the machine learning community such as active learning are of much help on their own.

Our focus is on presenting textual information to human annotators in a way that minimizes their cognitive load, thus improving their focus, and maximizes their labeling speed, thus reducing the cost of labeling. Our proposed visualization approach is fine-tuned to enable text labeling in the specific application where the objective is to extract information about smoking status of patients from their medical notes. Smoking status of patients is critical information in many practical applications, ranging from recruiting participants in clinical trials to determining medical and life insurance premiums for prospective customers.

Smoking status extraction is a specific instance of information extraction problems. Our visualization approach relies on several key observations about this particular type of problem. We first observed that smoking status could typically be extracted from sentences that contain one of the smoking keywords such as *smoke, smoking, tobacco, nicotine*. Thus, our first step was to extract from the corpus only sentences containing one of those keywords. Our second observation was that smoking status can typically be deduced from several words surrounding the keyword. Thus, it might be possible to prune very long sentences to sub-sentences surrounding the keyword without loss of information. This observation allows reserving only a single line to display each relevant sentence.

Our third observation is that the space of possible smoking-related sentences occurring in clinical notes is relatively limited and that for any smoking-related sentence there are likely very similar sentences in the corpus. We hypothesized that displaying similar sentences next to each other would allow human annotators to process the text much faster than if sentences are shown in random order. Our fourth observation is that some common discriminative keywords reveal the smoking status, such as *denies, quit, former, packs*. We hypothesized that highlighting those keywords in the text could allow a human annotator to work faster.

Our final observation was that by training a predictive model on the currently available labels, even when the number of available labels is relatively

Proceedings of the 2nd Workshop on Data Science with Human in the Loop: Language Advances, pages 24–30
June 11, 2021.

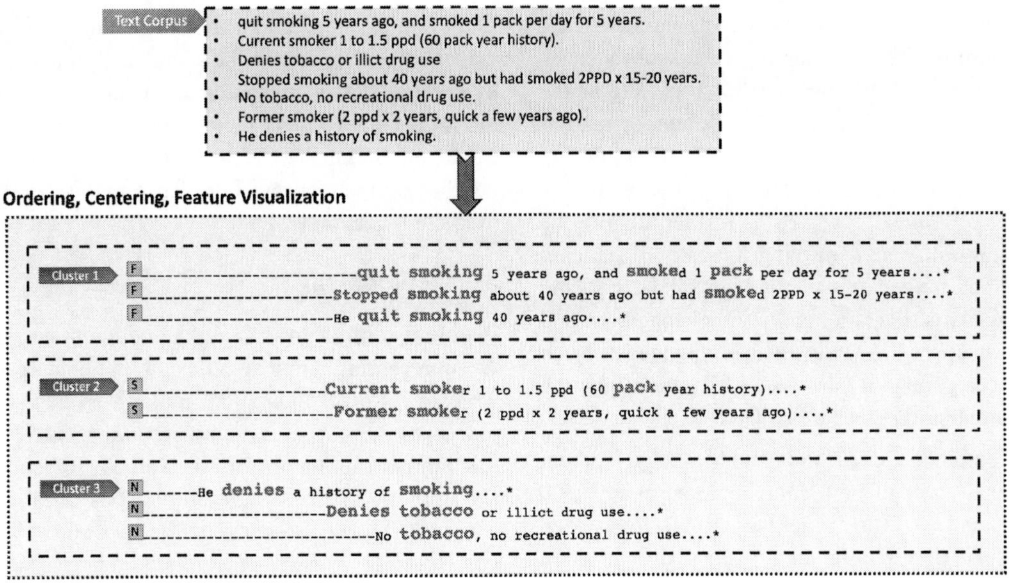

Figure 1: An illustration of the proposed sequence visualization approach for rapid labeling. The predicted labels for each sentence are shown inside the yellow boxes. where N refers to Non-Smoker, F to Former Smoker, and S to Smoker. Only the 5th sentence in the bottom panel is misclassified by the current prediction model and has to be overwritten by a human annotator.

small, would likely result in prediction accuracy that is significantly higher than a baseline that assigns labels randomly or based on the majority class labels. Thus, providing labels obtained by the current prediction model would allow a human annotator to skip the correctly labeled sentences and only enter the labels for the incorrectly labeled ones. As the number of labels grows, the accuracy of the prediction model is expected to increase, and the effort to correct the labels would decrease, thus increasing the speed of labeling.

The resulting visualization approach developed by exploiting the stated observations is illustrated in Figure 1. A panel at the top shows 7 randomly selected smoking-related sentences from our corpus. A panel at the bottom shows the same sentences displayed using our approach. The main features of our visualization approach are (1) sentence ordering, (2) sentence centering around the smoking keyword, (3) text annotation to emphasize discriminative keywords, and (4) displaying of the predicted labels. We are claiming, and our user study (described in Section 4) confirms it, that the bottom panel makes it much easier and faster for a human annotator to label a large corpus of smoking related sentences for the smoking status of a patient.

To produce the bottom panel in Figure 1, we had to decide (1) what are the smoking keywords, (2) what keywords are discriminative of the smoking status, (3) how to order the sentences, (4) how to provide predicted labels, (5) what to do during the cold start when no or very few sentences are labeled, and (6) how to implement the visualization approach. Details about the proposed approach are provided in Section 3. In Section 2 we provide a brief overview of the related work. In Section 4 we describe the experimental design, explain our user study, and provide experimental results that convincingly indicate the usefulness of the proposed approach.

2 Related Work

Extracting smoking status of patients from Electronic Health Records [EHR] has been crucial in clinical settings, and especially useful to health care providers to select the best care plan for patients at risk of smoking-related diseases. (Rajendran and Topaloglu, 2020) investigates the application of three Deep Learning models on EHR data to extract the smoking status of patients. Authors compare their approach with traditional machine learning models on both binary (Smoker vs Non-Smoker) and multi-class classification (Current Smoker vs. Former Smoker vs. Non-smoker) tasks. (Wang et al., 2016) extracts smoking status from three different sources such as narrative texts, patient-provided-information, and diagnosis codes. They conclude that narrative text proves to be the most useful source for smoking status extraction. (Palmer et al., 2019; Hegde et al., 2018) develop rule-based algorithms to determine tobacco use by patients. (Palmer et al., 2019) further identify the cessation date and smoking intensity of patients. Common for the aforementioned work on smoking status extraction is a need to label sentences and train an appropriate machine learning model. None of those papers discuss issues related to labeling nor attempt to reduce labeling costs.

A common approach to annotate a large amount of data is through crowdsourcing (Fang et al., 2014; Good and Su, 2013; Lim et al., 2020). It has been used in variety of tasks such as Image Classification (Fang et al., 2014), Bioinformatics (Good and Su, 2013), and Text mining (Li et al., 2020). Although crowdsourcing is a cost-effective way to collect labeled data, it can still be costly when the required labeling effort is significant. Moreover, when using imperfect annotators with varying levels of expertise, it is important to develop appropriate label integration approaches (Settles, 2011). Beyond the crowdsourcing issues, one popular approach to reduce labeling costs is to apply Active Learning and label only the most informative examples (Fang et al., 2014).

More recently, Human-In-the-Loop [HIL] approaches were proposed to improve the efficiency of annotation (Klie et al., 2020; Kim and Pardo, 2018). (Kim and Pardo, 2018) present a HIL system for sound event detection, which directs the annotator's attention to the most promising regions of an audio clip for labeling. (Klie et al., 2020) apply a similar technique on Entity Linking [EL] task, in which the machine learning component makes recommendations about the most relevant entries in a knowledge base, and the annotator selects the correct candidate. The recommender improves itself based on the obtained feedback. In addition, (Qian et al., 2020) present an interface for entity normalization annotation in which they measure the number of clicks in a tool to quantify the human effort.

While many papers attempt to minimize labeling effort, a vast majority of them are measuring the effort by counting the number of labeled examples. There are very few papers (Zhang et al., 2019) that measure labeling effort in terms of elapsed time. The uniqueness of our work is in demonstrating that annotation speed can be significantly impacted by the way data is presented to an annotator. Furthermore, our work is specific in its focus on an extreme labeling scenario where the task is to label the complete corpus in order to maximize the prediction accuracy.

3 Methodology

Problem Definition: Given a document corpus D representing clinical notes of patients from which a set of N unlabeled smoking-related sentences $S_1, S_2, ..., S_N$ is extracted, the goal is to ask human annotators to label all N sentences for smoking status. There are 4 types of labels: *Smoker (S), Non-Smoker (N), Former Smoker (F), and Other (O)*, where *Others* refer to sentences that do not reveal the smoking status.

In this section, we describe a visualization approach that improves human annotation speed. The main components of the approach are sequence ordering, label prediction, and text visualization. The details are explained in the following subsections.

3.1 Ordering

Our goal is to order sentences in a computationally-efficient manner by combining clustering and alignment algorithms. We use clustering to find groups of similar sequences that will subsequently be ordered with help of an alignment algorithm.

In order to cluster sentences, we rely on their vector embeddings. In particular, we use sequence embeddings of the pre-trained BERT model (Devlin et al., 2019). K-Means Clustering, whose computational cost is $O(N)$ as implemented by (Pedregosa et al., 2011), is used to find k clusters, where k is selected such that the average cluster size is limited to a specified size.

Sentences in each cluster are then ordered, such that neighboring sentences are perceived by a human annotator to be as similar as possible. Rather than ordering sentences based on BERT embeddings, we instead resort to sequence alignment distance, which we hypothesize are closer to human perception of similarity. In particular, we apply Needleman–Wunsch algorithm [NWA] [1] (Needleman and Wunsch, 1970), which is a dynamic programming algorithm that finds a similarity score between a pair of sentences in $O(L^2)$ time, where L

[1] `http://emboss.sourceforge.net/docs/emboss_tutorial/node3.html`

is the length of a sentence, For each cluster, we create a pairwise score matrix, $Score$, of size $N_c \times N_c$, where N_c is the number of sequences within the cluster c.

To find the order of the sentences in each cluster, we apply the following greedy algorithm. It starts by selecting the first sentence at random. The next sentence is its nearest neighbor, according to $Score$ matrix. The process continues by adding the nearest neighbors of previous sentences.

3.2 Sentence Visualization

Once the sentences are sorted, our next objective is to display them in a way that reduces the cognitive load of a human annotator. Our first idea is to center the sequences around smoking-related keywords such as *Smoke, Smoking, Tobacco, Nicotine.* We find those keywords by applying word2vec (Mikolov et al., 2013) to our document corpus D and by finding neighbors of word *Smoke* in the resulting embedding. Then, we manually select neighbors that are indicative of smoking-related sentences.

According to the maximum screen width, we align the sentences such that the smoking keyword appears in the middle of the screen. In addition, we fill the empty spaces before the sentence starts with dashes (-) to improve readability.

Our labeling approach proceeds in batches. After selecting the first batch of M unlabeled sentences at random (in our experiments we use $M = 200$), we do not display any predicted labels and orders. After we obtain labels for the first batch, we train a baseline machine learning model such as logistic regression using the bag of words representation (in our experiments we used the most frequent 500 non-stop words). Then, we analyze the statistical significance of the logistic regression weights and select K words associated with the most significant weights as discriminative words. Examples of discriminative keywords are *cigarette, denies, quit, former, packs.*

We select the second batch of unlabeled sentences at random, order them, and display them centered with the discriminative words in bold red font to improve readability. In addition, we display the predicted labels by the logistic regression next to the ordered sentences.

Rather than building a specialized sentence visualization and annotation tool, we use MS Excel[2]. Each sentence occupies one row in the Excel spreadsheet, where the first column is reserved for prediction labels, and the second column is reserved for the centered annotated sentences. An advantage of Excel is that it enables the use of the built-in cell drag feature to quickly change annotations of neighboring sentences. In addition, we use *Courier* as the font format, since it is a monospaced font type. The monospaced font displays each character or letter in the same amount of horizontal space. As a result, it makes the alignment and centering precise.

We continue selecting batches, labeling them, and retraining the prediction models. Once the number of labels becomes sufficiently large ($1,000$ in our experiments) we replace logistic regression with deep learning. We also allow for the batches to become larger over time.

4 Experimental Design

We performed our experiments using 52,726 discharge notes from the MIMIC-III dataset (Johnson et al., 2016), which contains de-identified records of the Beth Israel Deaconess Medical Center's Intensive Unit emergency department patients from 2001 to 2012.

We defined smoking-related keywords by selecting keyword *smoke* and its selected word2vec nearest neighbors. We collected 26 unique keywords. Using those keywords, we found 34,149 unique matching sentences.

4.1 Results

We evaluate the effectiveness of our proposed approach in three different rounds of labeling. We performed a user study with 2 human annotators (the first two co-authors of this paper) to measure labeling time in each of the 3 rounds of labeling. The total number of sentences annotated by each user in our experiments was 3,000 sentences each. In addition, in Section 4.2, we performed an ablation study to analyze the impact of different components of the proposed visualization approach.

In addition to labeling time, we also report the labeling rate, which is the number of sentences labeled per minute:

$$Rate = \frac{\#\ of\ annotated\ sequences}{elapsed\ time}$$

[2] `https://www.microsoft.com/en-us/microsoft-365/excel`

Groups & Settings	User 1 (mins)	User 2 (mins)	Rate User 1 (Sent/min)	Rate User 2 (Sent/min)	Total rate (Sent/min)
Round 1					
Batch1 (Unordered)	27	19	7	10	17
Round 2					
Batch1 (Unordered)	19	17	10	11	21
Batch2 (Ordered)	12	11	16	17	33
Batch3 (Ordered)	**11**	**9**	**17**	**21**	**38**
Batch4 (Unordered)	16	16	12	12	24

Table 1: The annotation results in Round 1 and 2. The experiments are conducted in the same order as the numbers indicate. Each group contains 200 sentences. Unordered refers to the baseline, and Ordered is our visualization approach.

Groups and Settings	User 1 (mins)	User 2 (mins)	Rate User 1 (Sent/min)	Rate User 2 (Sent/min)	Total rate (Sent/min)
Batch1 (Unordered)	40	35	12	14	26
Batch2 (Ordered)	23	23	21	21	42
Batch3 (Ordered)	**19**	**20**	**26**	**24**	**50**
Batch4 (Unordered)	34	34	14	14	28

Table 2: The results for Round 3. The experiments are conducted in the same order as the numbers indicate. Each Group contains 500 samples. The labels for these experiments are provided by fine-tuned Clinical BERT model. Unordered refers to the baseline, and Ordered is our visualization approach.

In the following subsections, we explain the basics of each baseline method as well as the experimental design for each round of labeling.

4.1.1 Round 1

In this round of the experiment, we select 200 random sentences. We display them in the same way as it is shown in the upper panel in Figure 1. Once we obtain the labels from the first batch, we train a logistic regression model. The first row of Table 1 shows the annotation details.

4.2 Round 2

We asked users to annotate 800 sentences in 4 batches. We chose the Latin square design to proceed as unordered, ordered, ordered, and unordered batches. We have also use logistic regression model to predict the labels for all the batches. Table 1 demonstrates the result of this round.

On average, the annotation rate using our method is 1.9× compared to round 1. Additionally, it is 1.5× faster compared to the unordered set in Round 2. By repeating the annotation task in batches 3 and 4, we can speed up the rate in our method by 15% (from 33 to 38) and in the unordered set by 14% (from 21 to 24).

4.2.1 Round 3

We annotated 2,000 sentences in 4 batches, each batch containing 500 sentences. Similar to Round 2, we set up the experiments with the Latin Triangle mixture design (unordered, ordered, ordered, unordered).

Given the annotated data from Round 1 and 2, we replaced the classifier with a deep learning algorithm. We use the Clinical BERT, which is pretrained on all the discharge summary notes in the MIMIC dataset. We split the data into 800 training and 200 for testing. The hyperparameters are selected according to (Devlin et al., 2019). We set the batch size to 16, learning rate to $2e{-}5$, maximum sentence length to 200, and fine-tuned it for 4 epochs. We have also performed experiments with SVM, logistic regression. Table 3 demonstrates the performance of all the classifiers.

According to Table 2, the annotation rate increased from Round 2 to Round 3 by 29% (from 35.5 to 46) with our approach. However, it increased by 16% (from 22.5 in Round 2 to 27 in Round 3) using the baseline approach.

Comparing the annotation speed in Round 3, our approach is 1.7× faster than the baseline (46 compared to 27). Since the size of the batches increased in Round 3, there was more redundancy in the sentences and our approach was more helpful to the annotators than in Round 2. In particular, ordering resulted in smoother transitions between sentences, which contributed to faster human annotation.

Last but not the least, by repeating the labeling task, we expect users to get used to the data, and therefore, we expected the annotation rate to increase regardless of the visualization approach. Confirming this assumption, users on average got 19% faster with our method during Round 3 (rate increased from 42 to 50), while they got only 7% faster with the baseline approach (rate increased from 26 to 28).

Model	Accuracy Round 1	Accuracy Round 2
Baseline	0.35	0.36
Logistic Regression	0.76	0.79
SVM	0.78	0.80
Fine-tuned Clinical BERT	0.78	0.89

Table 3: All the classifiers are trained to predict 4 classes: Smoker, NonSmoker, Former, and Other. Baseline accuracy is the fraction of the majority class in the test set. In Round 1, there are 800 training and 200 test sentences. In Round 2, there are 3,400 training and 600 test sentences.

4.3 Ablation Study

In this section, we analyze the impact of two components of our system on the final annotation rate. We asked one of the users to annotate an additional 1,000 sentences. We split the set into two groups, each group with 500 samples. First, we studied the impact of centering. Therefore, we aligned all the data to the left and kept the ordering and feature visualization. Second, we removed the feature visualization component, and kept the ordering and centering. Table 4 shows the results of these two experiments.

Components	User 2 (mins)	Rate User 2 (Sent/min)
No centering	22	22
No coloring	21	23

Table 4: Ablation study on the impact of centering and feature visualization. In the first row, we do not center the sentences around the smoke keywords. In the second row, we do not highlight the important features.

According to the results for Round 2 in Table 2, the highest rate for User 2 was 24 sentences per minute. However, when we removed the centering component, the rate decreased by 8%, to 22 per minute. In addition, by removing the coloring component, the rate decreased by 4%, to 23 per minute. The centering component had a stronger impact on the labeling rate than the coloring component. However, both of the removals reduced the rate of labeling.

Given the annotated data from the ablation study, and adding all the labeled data from the first and second rounds, we re-trained all the classifiers on 3,400 training sentences and used 600 sentences for testing. We observed 15% improvement in the BERT model accuracy and 3% improvement in the Logistic Regression model accuracy compared to the models trained on Round data.

5 Conclusion

We presented a visualization approach that enables rapid annotation of sentences for smoking status of patients. Our framework contains three main components: sentence ordering, sentence presentation, and sentence labeling by the prediction model. Our approach does not depend on high-quality ML predictors to provide initial labels. The display has a significant impact on speeding up the annotation process. We evaluated our visualization approach with a user study on sentences from MIMIC-III discharge summaries. We achieved close to 3$\times$ faster annotation rate compared to the baseline method that displayed sentences randomly in their original shape. As the annotation progressed, as the batches of unlabeled sentences became larger, and as the prediction models improved, the annotation speed kept increasing in our user experiments. The proposed visualization approach is applicable to similar text classification tasks. It is a topic of further research to study how to modify the presented approach to make it applicable to a large number of text annotation tasks in natural language processing.

References

Jacob Devlin, Ming-Wei Chang, Kenton Lee, and Kristina Toutanova. 2019. BERT: Pre-training of deep bidirectional transformers for language understanding. In *Proceedings of the 2019 Conference of the North American Chapter of the Association for Computational Linguistics: Human Language Technologies, Volume 1 (Long and Short Papers)*, pages 4171–4186, Minneapolis, Minnesota. Association for Computational Linguistics.

Meng Fang, Jie Yin, and Dacheng Tao. 2014. Active learning for crowdsourcing using knowledge transfer. *Proceedings of the AAAI Conference on Artificial Intelligence*, 28(1).

Benjamin M. Good and Andrew I. Su. 2013. Crowdsourcing for bioinformatics. *Bioinformatics*, 29(16):1925–1933.

Harshad Hegde, Neel Shimpi, Ingrid Glurich, and Amit Acharya. 2018. Tobacco use status from clinical notes using natural language processing and rule based algorithm. *Technology and Health Care*, 26(3):445–456.

Alistair EW Johnson, Tom J Pollard, Lu Shen, H Lehman Li-wei, Mengling Feng, Mohammad Ghassemi, Benjamin Moody, Peter Szolovits, Leo Anthony Celi, and Roger G Mark. 2016. Mimic-iii, a freely accessible critical care database. *Scientific data*, 3:160035.

Bongjun Kim and Bryan Pardo. 2018. A human-in-the-loop system for sound event detection and annotation. *ACM Transactions on Interactive Intelligent Systems (TiiS)*, 8(2):1–23.

Jan-Christoph Klie, Richard Eckart de Castilho, and Iryna Gurevych. 2020. From Zero to Hero: Human-In-The-Loop Entity Linking in Low Resource Domains. In *Proceedings of the 58th Annual Meeting of the Association for Computational Linguistics*, pages 6982–6993, Online. Association for Computational Linguistics.

Maolin Li, Hiroya Takamura, and Sophia Ananiadou. 2020. A neural model for aggregating coreference annotation in crowdsourcing. In *Proceedings of the 28th International Conference on Computational Linguistics*, pages 5760–5773, Barcelona, Spain (Online). International Committee on Computational Linguistics.

Sora Lim, Adam Jatowt, Michael Färber, and Masatoshi Yoshikawa. 2020. Annotating and analyzing biased sentences in news articles using crowdsourcing. In *Proceedings of the 12th Language Resources and Evaluation Conference*, pages 1478–1484, Marseille, France. European Language Resources Association.

Tomas Mikolov, Kai Chen, Greg Corrado, and Jeffrey Dean. 2013. Efficient estimation of word representations in vector space. *arXiv preprint arXiv:1301.3781*.

Saul B Needleman and Christian D Wunsch. 1970. A general method applicable to the search for similarities in the amino acid sequence of two proteins. *Journal of molecular biology*, 48(3):443–453.

Ellen L Palmer, Saeed Hassanpour, John Higgins, Jennifer A Doherty, and Tracy Onega. 2019. Building a tobacco user registry by extracting multiple smoking behaviors from clinical notes. *BMC medical informatics and decision making*, 19(1):1–10.

F. Pedregosa, G. Varoquaux, A. Gramfort, V. Michel, B. Thirion, O. Grisel, M. Blondel, P. Prettenhofer, R. Weiss, V. Dubourg, J. Vanderplas, A. Passos, D. Cournapeau, M. Brucher, M. Perrot, and E. Duchesnay. 2011. Scikit-learn: Machine learning in Python. *Journal of Machine Learning Research*, 12:2825–2830.

Kun Qian, Lucian Popa, and Yunyao Li. 2020. An intuitive user interface for human-in-the-loop entity name parsing and entity variant generation. In *Proceedings of (DaSH@KDD)*. Association for Computing Machinery.

Suraj Rajendran and Umit Topaloglu. 2020. Extracting smoking status from electronic health records using nlp and deep learning. *AMIA Summits on Translational Science Proceedings*, 2020:507.

Burr Settles. 2011. Closing the loop: Fast, interactive semi-supervised annotation with queries on features and instances. In *Proceedings of the 2011 Conference on Empirical Methods in Natural Language Processing*, pages 1467–1478, Edinburgh, Scotland, UK. Association for Computational Linguistics.

Liwei Wang, Xiaoyang Ruan, Ping Yang, and Hongfang Liu. 2016. Comparison of three information sources for smoking information in electronic health records. *Cancer informatics*, 15:CIN–S40604.

Shanshan Zhang, Lihong He, Eduard Dragut, and Slobodan Vucetic. 2019. How to invest my time: Lessons from human-in-the-loop entity extraction. In *Proceedings of the 25th ACM SIGKDD International Conference on Knowledge Discovery amp; Data Mining*, KDD '19, page 2305–2313, New York, NY, USA. Association for Computing Machinery.

Semi-supervised Interactive Intent Labeling

Saurav Sahay **Eda Okur** **Nagib Hakim** **Lama Nachman**
Intel Labs, USA
{saurav.sahay,eda.okur,nagib.hakim,lama.nachman}@intel.com

Abstract

Building the Natural Language Understanding (NLU) modules of task-oriented Spoken Dialogue Systems (SDS) involves a definition of intents and entities, collection of task-relevant data, annotating the data with intents and entities, and then repeating the same process over and over again for adding any functionality/enhancement to the SDS. In this work, we showcase an Intent Bulk Labeling system where SDS developers can interactively label and augment training data from unlabeled utterance corpora using advanced clustering and visual labeling methods. We extend the Deep Aligned Clustering (Zhang et al., 2021) work with a better backbone BERT model, explore techniques to select the seed data for labeling, and develop a data balancing method using an oversampling technique that utilizes paraphrasing models. We also look at the effect of data augmentation on the clustering process. Our results show that we can achieve over 10% gain in clustering accuracy on some datasets using the combination of the above techniques. Finally, we extract utterance embeddings from the clustering model and plot the data to interactively bulk label the samples, reducing the time and effort for data labeling of the whole dataset significantly.

1 Introduction

Acquiring an accurately labeled corpus is necessary for training machine learning (ML) models in various classification applications. Labeling is an expensive and labor-intensive activity requiring annotators to understand the domain well and to label the instances one at a time. In this work, we explore the task of labeling multiple intents visually with the help of a semi-supervised clustering algorithm. The clustering algorithm helps learn an embedding representation of the training data that is well-suited for downstream labeling. In order to label, we further reduce the high dimensional representation using the UMAP (McInnes et al., 2018). Since utterances are short, uncovering their semantic meaning to group them together is very challenging. SBERT (Reimers and Gurevych, 2019) showed that out-of-the-box BERT (Devlin et al., 2018) maps sentences to a vector space that is not very suitable to be used with common measures like cosine-similarity and euclidean distances. This happens because in the BERT network, there is no independent sentence embedding computation, which makes it difficult to derive sentence embeddings. Researchers utilize the mean pooling of word embeddings as an approximate measure of the sentence embedding. However, results show that this practice yields inappropriate sentence embeddings that are often worse than averaging GloVe embeddings (Pennington et al., 2014; Reimers and Gurevych, 2019). Many researchers have developed sentence embedding methods: Skip-Thought (Kiros et al., 2015), InferSent (Conneau et al., 2017), USE (Cer et al., 2018), SBERT (Reimers and Gurevych, 2019). State-of-the-art SBERT adds a pooling operation to the output of BERT to derive a fixed-sized sentence embedding and fine-tunes a Siamese network on the sentence-pairs from the NLI (Bowman et al., 2015; Williams et al., 2017) and STSb (Cer et al., 2017) datasets.

The Deep Aligned Clustering (DAC) (Zhang et al., 2021) introduced an effective method for clustering and discovering new intents. DAC transfers the prior knowledge of a limited number of known intents and incorporates a technique to align cluster centroids in successive training epochs. The limited known intents are used to pre-train the model. The authors use the pre-trained BERT model (Devlin et al., 2018) to extract deep intent features, then pre-train the model with a randomly selected subset of labeled data. The pre-trained parameters are used to obtain well-initialized intent representations. K-Means clustering is performed on the extracted intent features along with

Proceedings of the 2nd Workshop on Data Science with Human in the Loop: Language Advances, pages 31–40
June 11, 2021.

a method to estimate the number of clusters and the alignment strategy to obtain the final cluster assignments. The K-Means algorithm selects cluster centroids that minimize the Euclidean distance within the cluster. Due to this Euclidean distance optimization, clustering using the SBERT model to extract feature embeddings naturally outperforms other embedding methods. In our work, we have extended the DAC algorithm with the SBERT as an embedding backbone for clustering of utterances.

In semi-supervised learning, the seed set is selected using a sampling strategy: "A simple random sample of size n consists of n individuals from the population chosen such that every set of n individuals has an equal chance to be the sample actually selected." (Moore and McCabe, 1989). However, these sample subsets may not represent the original data adequately because randomization methods do not exploit the correlations in the original population. In a stratified random sample, the population is classified first into groups (called strata) with similar characteristics. Then a simple random sample is chosen from each strata separately. These simple random samples are combined to form the overall sample. Stratified sampling can help ensure that there are enough observations within each strata to make meaningful inferences. DAC uses the Random Sampling method for seed selection. In this work, we have explored a couple of stratified sampling approaches for seed selection in hope to mitigate the limitations of random sampling and improve the clustering outcome.

Another issue we address in this work is class sample imbalance. Seed selection generally yields an imbalanced dataset, which in turn impairs the predictive capability of the classification algorithms (Douzas et al., 2018). Some methods manipulate the training data, aiming to change the class distribution towards a more balanced one by undersampling or oversampling (Kotsiantis et al., 2006; Galar et al., 2011). SMOTE (Chawla et al., 2002) is a popular oversampling technique proposed to improve random oversampling. In one variant of SMOTE, borderline minority instances are heuristically selected and linearly interpolated to create synthetic samples. In this work, we take inspiration from the SMOTE method and choose borderline minority instances and paraphrase them using a Sequence to Sequence Paraphrasing model. The paraphrases provide natural and meaningful augmentations of the dataset that are not synthetic.

Previous work has shown that data augmentation can boost performance on text classification tasks (Barzilay and McKeown, 2001; Dolan and Brockett, 2005; Lan et al., 2017; Hu et al., 2019). Wieting et al. (2017) used Neural Machine Translation (NMT) (Sutskever et al., 2014) to translate the non-English side of the parallel text to get English-English paraphrase pairs. This method has been scaled to generate large paraphrase corpora (Wieting and Gimpel, 2018). Prior work in learning paraphrases has used autoencoders (Socher et al., 2011), encoder-decoder architectures as in BART (Lewis et al., 2019), and other learning frameworks such as NMT (Sokolov and Filimonov, 2020). Data augmentation using paraphrasing is a simple yet effective strategy that we explored in this work to improve the clustering.

For interactive visual labeling of utterances, we build up from the learnt embedding representation of the data and fine-tune it using the clustering. DAC learns to cluster with a weak self-supervised signal to update its representation and to optimize both local (via K-Means) and global information (via cluster alignment). This results in an optimized intent-level feature representation. This high dimensional latent representation can be reduced to 2-3 dimensions using the Uniform Manifold Approximation and Projection (UMAP) (McInnes et al., 2018). We use Rasa WhatLies[1] library (Warmerdam et al., 2020) to extract the UMAP embeddings. For interactive labeling, we utilize an interactive visualization library called Human Learn[2] (Warmerdam et al., 2021) that allows us to draw decision boundaries on a plot. By building on top of the work of Rasa Bulk Labelling[3] UI (Warmerdam, 2020; Bokeh Development Team, 2018), we augment the interface with our learnt representation for interactive labeling. Although we focus on NLU, other studies like 'Conversation Learner' (Shukla et al., 2020) focus on interactive dialogue managers (DM) with human-in-the-loop annotations of dialogue data via machine teaching. Note also that although the majority of task-oriented SDS still involves defining intents/entities, there are recent examples that argue for a richer target representation than the classical intent/entity model, such as SMCalFlow (Andreas et al., 2020).

[1] `rasahq.github.io/whatlies/`

[2] `koaning.github.io/human-learn/`

[3] `github.com/RasaHQ/rasalit/blob/main/notebooks/bulk-labelling/bulk-labelling-ui.ipynb`

Figure 1: Interactive Labeling System Architecture

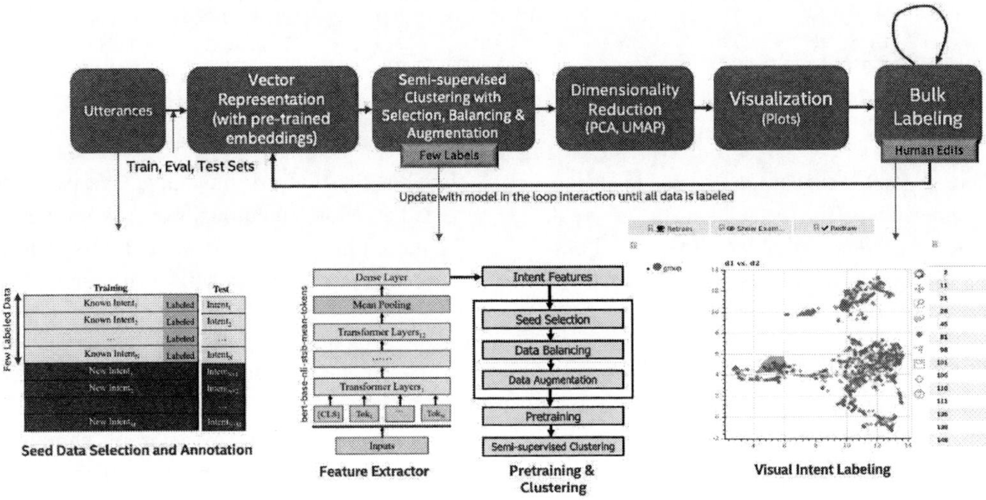

2 Methodology

Figure 1 describes the semi-supervised labeling process. We start with the unlabeled utterance corpus and apply seed sampling methods to select a small subset of the corpus. Once the selected subset is manually labeled, we address the data imbalance with our paraphrase-based minority oversampling method. We can also augment the labeled corpus with paraphrasing to provide more data for the clustering process. The DAC algorithm is applied with improved embeddings to extract the utterance representation for interactive labeling.

2.1 Sentence Representation

For sentence representation, we use the HuggingFace Transformers model BERT-base-nli-stsb-mean-tokens[4]. This model was first fine-tuned on a combination of Stanford Natural Language Inference (SNLI) (Bowman et al., 2015) (570K sentence-pairs with labels contradiction, entailment, and neutral) and Multi-Genre Natural Language Inference (Williams et al., 2017) (430K diverse sentence-pairs with same labels as SNLI) datasets, then on Semantic Textual Similarity benchmark (STSb) (Cer et al., 2017) (provide labels between 0 and 5 on the semantic relatedness of sentence pairs) training set. This model achieves a performance of 85.14 (Spearman's rank correlation between the cosine-similarity of the sentence embeddings and the gold labels) on STSb regression evaluation. For context, the average BERT embeddings achieve a performance of 46.35 on this evaluation (Reimers and Gurevych, 2019).

[4]https://huggingface.co/sentence-transformers/bert-base-nli-stsb-mean-tokens/tree/main

2.2 Seed Selection

We explore two selection and sampling strategies for seed selection as follows:

- **Cluster-based Selection (CB)**: In this method, we apply K-Means clustering on the N utterances to partition the data into n seed number of subsets. For example, if 10% of the data has 100 utterances, this method creates 100 clusters from the dataset. We then pick the centroid's nearest neighbor as part of the seed set for all the clusters. The naive intuition for this strategy is that it would create a large number of clusters spread all over the data distribution (N/n instances per cluster on average for uniformly distributed instances).

- **Predicted Cluster Sampling (PCS)**: This is a stratified sampling method where we first predict the number of clusters and then sample instances from each cluster. We use the cluster size estimation method from the DAC work as follows: K-Means is performed with a large K' (initialized with twice the ground truth number of classes). The assumption is that real clusters tend to be dense and the cluster mean size threshold is assumed to be N/K'.

$$K = \sum_{i=1}^{K'} \delta(|S_i| >= t)$$

Dataset	#Classes	#Train	#Valid	#Test	Vocab	Length (max / mean)
CLINC	150	18,000	2,250	2,250	7,283	28 / 8.31
BANKING	77	9,003	1,000	3,080	5,028	79 / 11.91
KidSpace	19	1,289	445	419	2,581	74 / 5.10

Table 1: Dataset Statistics

where $|S_i|$ is the size of the ith produced cluster, and $\delta(condition)$ is an indicator function. It outputs 1 if condition is satisfied, and outputs 0 if not. The method seems to perform well as reported in DAC work.

2.3 Data Balancing and Augmentation

For handling data imbalance, we propose a paraphrasing-based method to over-sample the minority classes. The method is described as follows:

1. For every instance p_i $(i = 1, 2, ..., p_{num})$ in the minority class P, we calculate its m nearest neighbors from the whole training set T. The number of majority examples among the m nearest neighbors is denoted by m' $(0 \leq m' \leq m)$.

2. If $m' = m$, i.e., all the m nearest neighbors of p_i are majority examples, p_i is considered to be noise and is not operated in the following steps. If $\frac{m}{2} \leq m' < m$, namely the number of p_i's majority nearest neighbors is larger than the number of its minority ones, p_i is considered to be easily misclassified and put into a set DANGER. If $0 \leq m' < \frac{m}{2}$, p_i is safe and does not need to participate in the following steps.

3. The examples in DANGER are the borderline data of the minority class P, and we can see that DANGER $\subseteq P$. We set DANGER $= \{p'_1, p'_2, ..., p'_{d_{num}}\}$, $0 \leq d_{num} \leq p_{num}$

4. For each borderline data (that can be easily misclassified), we paraphrase the instance. For paraphrasing, we fine-tuned the BART Sequence to Sequence model (Lewis et al., 2019) on a combination of 3 datasets: ParaNMT (Wieting and Gimpel, 2018), PAWS (Zhang et al., 2019; Yang et al., 2019), and the MSRP corpus (Dolan and Brockett, 2005).

5. We classify the paraphrased sample with a RoBERTa (Liu et al., 2019) based classifier fine-tuned on the labeled data and only add the instance if the classifier predicts the same label as the minority instance. We call this the 'ParaMote' method in our experiments. Without this last step (5), we call this overall approach our 'Paraphrasing' method.

We use the Paraphrasing model and the classifier as a data augmentation method to augment the labeled training data (refer to as 'Aug' in our experiments).

Note that we augment the paraphrased sample if it belongs to the same minority class ('ParaMote') as we do not want to inject noise while solving the data imbalance problem. The opposite is also possible for other purposes such as generating semantically similar adversaries (Ribeiro et al., 2018).

3 Experimental Results

To conduct our experiments, we use the BANKING (Casanueva et al., 2020) and CLINC (Larson et al., 2019) datasets similar to the DAC work (Zhang et al., 2021). We also use another dataset called KidSpace that includes utterances from a Multimodal Learning Application for 5-to-8 years-old children (Sahay et al., 2019; Anderson et al., 2018). We hope to utilize this system to label future utterances into relevant intents. Table 1 shows the statistics of the 3 datasets where 25% random classes are kept unseen at pre-training.

3.1 Sentence Representation

The choice of pre-trained embeddings has the largest impact on the clustering results. We observe huge performance gains for the single domain KidSpace and BANKING datasets. For the multi-domain and diverse CLINC dataset with the largest number of intents, we saw a slight degradation in performance. While this needs further investigation, we believe the dataset is diverse enough and already has very high clustering scores and that the improved sentence representations may not be helping further.

3.2 Seed Selection

Seed selection is an important problem for limited data tasks. Law of large numbers does not hold and

Dataset	BERT	Data Bal/Aug	Seed Selection	NMI	ARI	ACC
BANKING	Standard	None	RandomSampling	79.22	52.96	63.84±1.91
			ClusterBased	78.51	51.53	63.73±1.73
			PredictedClusterSampling	78.62	51.72	62.72±0.97
	Sentence	None	RandomSampling	82.96	60.72	71.27±2.28
			ClusterBased	80.65	55.03	65.44±1.24
			PredictedClusterSampling	82.11	58.43	69.78±2.08
	Sentence	Paraphrasing	RandomSampling	83.00	60.95	71.95
			PredictedClusterSampling	82.20	58.86	69.62
	Sentence	ParaMote	RandomSampling	82.58	59.54	69.92
			PredictedClusterSampling	81.88	58.13	69.74
	Sentence	Aug (3x)	RandomSampling	82.94	60.78	71.66
			PredictedClusterSampling	81.69	58.18	69.99
CLINC	Standard	None	RandomSampling	93.90	79.70	86.34±1.47
			ClusterBased	90.60	69.60	77.87±1.70
			PredictedClusterSampling	93.76	79.42	86.41±0.65
	Sentence	None	RandomSampling	93.80	79.06	85.76±1.17
			ClusterBased	90.25	67.23	74.25±1.83
			PredictedClusterSampling	93.60	78.57	85.43±0.96
	Sentence	Paraphrasing	RandomSampling	93.78	79.14	85.86
			PredictedClusterSampling	93.40	77.68	84.89
	Sentence	ParaMote	RandomSampling	93.79	79.10	85.81
			PredictedClusterSampling	93.48	77.97	84.86
	Sentence	Aug (3x)	RandomSampling	93.69	78.67	85.52
			PredictedClusterSampling	92.96	76.50	83.96
KidSpace	Standard	None	RandomSampling	71.40	48.26	58.55±4.22
			ClusterBased	68.13	39.26	53.48±4.47
			PredictedClusterSampling	70.53	45.33	56.80±4.56
	Sentence	None	RandomSampling	75.62	63.41	68.66±4.96
			ClusterBased	71.27	53.16	62.10±9.59
			PredictedClusterSampling	75.74	61.99	67.04±7.66
	Sentence	Paraphrasing	RandomSampling	76.41	63.02	68.83
			PredictedClusterSampling	75.52	61.53	68.21
	Sentence	ParaMote	RandomSampling	76.28	61.20	68.09
			PredictedClusterSampling	76.33	62.05	68.21
	Sentence	Aug (3x)	RandomSampling	76.48	61.33	68.07
			PredictedClusterSampling	76.37	58.97	68.78

Table 2: Semi-supervised DeepAlign Clustering Results with BERT Model, Data Balance/Augmentation and Seed Selection on BANKING, CLINC, and KidSpace datasets (averaged results over 10 runs with different seed values; labeled ratio is 0.1 for BANKING and CLINC, 0.2 for KidSpace; known class ratio is 0.75 in all cases)

random sampling strategy may lead to larger variance in outcomes. We explored Cluster-based Selection (CB) and Predicted Cluster Sampling (PCS) besides other techniques (see detailed results in Appendix A.1). Our results trend towards smaller standard deviations and similar performance for the BANKING and CLINC datasets with the PCS method. Surprisingly, this does not hold for the KidSpace dataset that needs further investigation. Figure 2 shows the KidSpace data visualised with various colored clusters and centroids. While we non-randomly choose seed data, we still hide 25% of the classes at random (to enable unknown intent discovery). Our recommendation is to use PCS if one cannot run the training multiple times for certain situations to have less variance in results.

3.3 Data Balancing for Imbalanced Data

Figure 3 shows the histogram for the seed data, which is highly imbalanced and may adversely impact the clustering performance. We apply Paraphrasing and ParaMote methods to balance the data. Paraphrasing almost always improves the performance while the additional classifier to check for class-label consistency (ParaMote) does not help.

Figure 2: Cluster Visualization

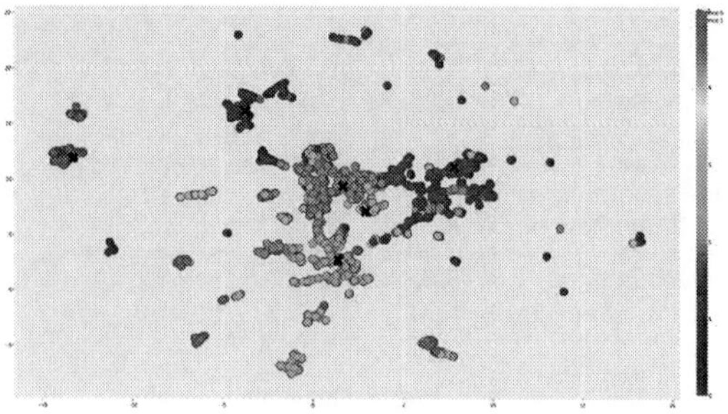

Figure 3: Label Distribution

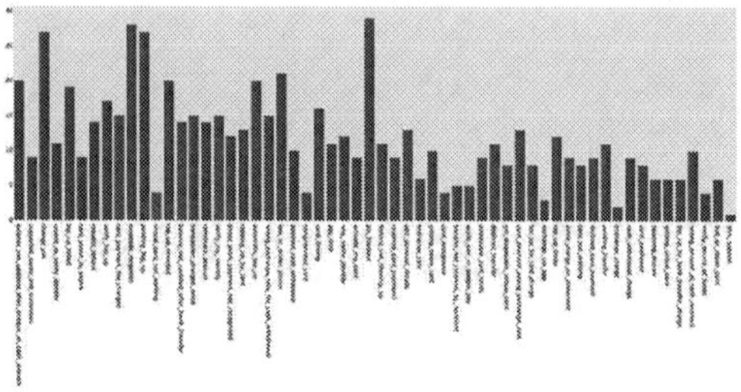

3.4 Data Augmentation

We augmented the entire labeled data including the majority class using Paraphrasing (with class-label consistency) by 3x in our experiments. We aimed to understand if this could help get a better pre-trained model that could eventually improve the clustering outcome. We do not observe any performance gains with the augmentation process.

3.5 Interactive Data Labeling

Our goal in this work is to develop a well-segmented learnt representation of the data with deep clustering and then to use the learnt representation to enable fast visual labeling. Figure 4 shows the two clustered representations, one without pre-training and BERT-base embedding while the other with a fine-tuned sentence BERT representation and pre-training. We can obtain well separated visual clusters using the latter approach. We use the drawing library human-learn to visually label the data. Figure 5 shows selected region of the data with various labels and class confusion. We notice that this representation not only helps with the labeling but also helps with correcting the labels and identify utterances that belong to multiple classes which cannot be easily segmented. For example,

Figure 4: Cluster Visualization on KidSpace with BERT-base/SBERT w/wo pre-training

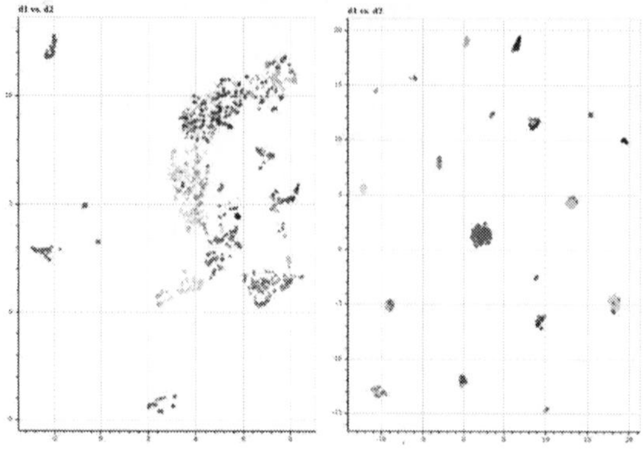

Figure 5: Cluster Mixup on KidSpace due to Game Semantics

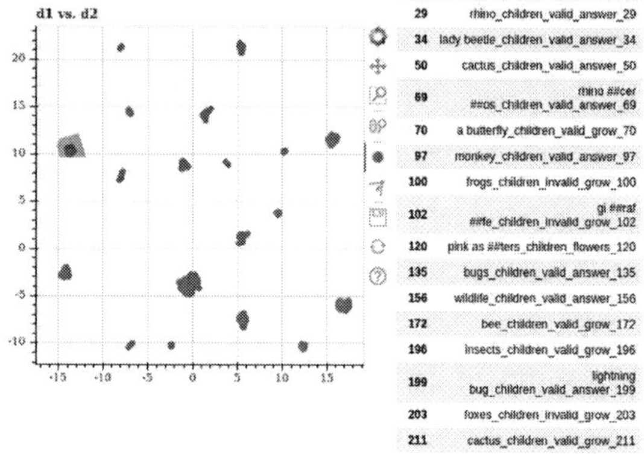

'children-valid-answer' and 'children-invalid-grow' (invalid answers) contain semantically similar content depending on the game logic of the interaction. We perhaps need to group these together and use an alternative logic for implementing game semantics.

3.6 Conclusion

In this exploration, we have used fine-tuned sentence BERT model to significantly improve the clustering performance. Predicted Cluster Sampling strategy for seed data selection seems to be a promising approach with possibly lower variance in clustering performance for smaller data labeling tasks. Paraphrasing-based data imbalance handling slightly improves the clustering performance as well. Finally, we have utilized the learnt representation to develop a visual intent labeling system.

References

Glen J. Anderson, Selvakumar Panneer, Meng Shi, Carl S. Marshall, Ankur Agrawal, Rebecca Chierichetti, Giuseppe Raffa, John Sherry, Daria Loi, and Lenitra Megail Durham. 2018. Kid space: Interactive learning in a smart environment. In *Proceedings of the Group Interaction Frontiers in Technology*, GIFT'18, New York, NY, USA. Association for Computing Machinery.

Jacob Andreas, John Bufe, David Burkett, Charles Chen, Josh Clausman, Jean Crawford, Kate Crim, Jordan DeLoach, Leah Dorner, Jason Eisner, Hao Fang, Alan Guo, David Hall, Kristin Hayes, Kellie Hill, Diana Ho, Wendy Iwaszuk, Smriti Jha, Dan Klein, Jayant Krishnamurthy, Theo Lanman, Percy Liang, Christopher H. Lin, Ilya Lintsbakh, Andy McGovern, Aleksandr Nisnevich, Adam Pauls, Dmitrij Petters, Brent Read, Dan Roth, Subhro Roy, Jesse Rusak, Beth Short, Div Slomin, Ben Snyder, Stephon Striplin, Yu Su, Zachary Tellman, Sam Thomson, Andrei Vorobev, Izabela Witoszko, Jason Wolfe, Abby Wray, Yuchen Zhang, and Alexander Zotov. 2020. Task-Oriented Dialogue as Dataflow Synthesis. *Transactions of the Association for Computational Linguistics*, 8:556–571.

Regina Barzilay and Kathleen R. McKeown. 2001. Extracting paraphrases from a parallel corpus. In *Proceedings of the 39th Annual Meeting of the Association for Computational Linguistics*, pages 50–57, Toulouse, France. Association for Computational Linguistics.

Bokeh Development Team. 2018. *Bokeh: Python library for interactive visualization.*

Samuel R. Bowman, Gabor Angeli, Christopher Potts, and Christopher D. Manning. 2015. A large annotated corpus for learning natural language inference. In *Proceedings of the 2015 Conference on Empirical Methods in Natural Language Processing*, pages 632–642, Lisbon, Portugal. Association for Computational Linguistics.

Iñigo Casanueva, Tadas Temčinas, Daniela Gerz, Matthew Henderson, and Ivan Vulić. 2020. Efficient intent detection with dual sentence encoders. In *Proceedings of the 2nd Workshop on Natural Language Processing for Conversational AI*, pages 38–45, Online. Association for Computational Linguistics.

Daniel Cer, Yinfei Yang, Sheng-yi Kong, Nan Hua, Nicole Limtiaco, Rhomni St. John, Noah Constant, Mario Guajardo-Cespedes, Steve Yuan, Chris Tar, Yun-Hsuan Sung, Brian Strope, and Ray Kurzweil. 2018. Universal sentence encoder. *CoRR*, abs/1803.11175.

Daniel M. Cer, Mona T. Diab, Eneko Agirre, Iñigo Lopez-Gazpio, and Lucia Specia. 2017. Semeval-2017 task 1: Semantic textual similarity - multilingual and cross-lingual focused evaluation. *CoRR*, abs/1708.00055.

Nitesh V Chawla, Kevin W Bowyer, Lawrence O Hall, and W Philip Kegelmeyer. 2002. Smote: synthetic minority over-sampling technique. *Journal of artificial intelligence research*, 16:321–357.

Alexis Conneau, Douwe Kiela, Holger Schwenk, Loïc Barrault, and Antoine Bordes. 2017. Supervised learning of universal sentence representations from natural language inference data. In *Proceedings of the 2017 Conference on Empirical Methods in Natural Language Processing*, pages 670–680, Copenhagen, Denmark. Association for Computational Linguistics.

Jacob Devlin, Ming-Wei Chang, Kenton Lee, and Kristina Toutanova. 2018. BERT: pre-training of deep bidirectional transformers for language understanding. *CoRR*, abs/1810.04805.

William B. Dolan and Chris Brockett. 2005. Automatically constructing a corpus of sentential paraphrases. In *Proceedings of the Third International Workshop on Paraphrasing (IWP2005)*.

Georgios Douzas, Fernando Bacao, and Felix Last. 2018. Improving imbalanced learning through a heuristic oversampling method based on k-means and smote. *Information Sciences*, 465:1–20.

Mikel Galar, Alberto Fernandez, Edurne Barrenechea, Humberto Bustince, and Francisco Herrera. 2011. A review on ensembles for the class imbalance problem: bagging-, boosting-, and hybrid-based approaches. *IEEE Transactions on Systems, Man, and Cybernetics, Part C (Applications and Reviews)*, 42(4):463–484.

J. Edward Hu, Abhinav Singh, Nils Holzenberger, Matt Post, and Benjamin Van Durme. 2019. Large-scale, diverse, paraphrastic bitexts via sampling and clustering. In *Proceedings of the 23rd Conference on Computational Natural Language Learning (CoNLL)*, pages 44–54, Hong Kong, China. Association for Computational Linguistics.

Ryan Kiros, Yukun Zhu, Russ R Salakhutdinov, Richard Zemel, Raquel Urtasun, Antonio Torralba, and Sanja Fidler. 2015. Skip-thought vectors. In *Advances in Neural Information Processing Systems*, volume 28. Curran Associates, Inc.

Sotiris Kotsiantis, Dimitris Kanellopoulos, Panayiotis Pintelas, et al. 2006. Handling imbalanced datasets: A review. *GESTS International Transactions on Computer Science and Engineering*, 30(1):25–36.

Wuwei Lan, Siyu Qiu, Hua He, and Wei Xu. 2017. A continuously growing dataset of sentential paraphrases. *CoRR*, abs/1708.00391.

Stefan Larson, Anish Mahendran, Joseph J. Peper, Christopher Clarke, Andrew Lee, Parker Hill, Jonathan K. Kummerfeld, Kevin Leach, Michael A. Laurenzano, Lingjia Tang, and Jason Mars. 2019. An evaluation dataset for intent classification and out-of-scope prediction. In *Proceedings of the*

2019 Conference on Empirical Methods in Natural Language Processing and the 9th International Joint Conference on Natural Language Processing (EMNLP-IJCNLP), pages 1311–1316, Hong Kong, China. Association for Computational Linguistics.

Mike Lewis, Yinhan Liu, Naman Goyal, Marjan Ghazvininejad, Abdelrahman Mohamed, Omer Levy, Veselin Stoyanov, and Luke Zettlemoyer. 2019. BART: denoising sequence-to-sequence pretraining for natural language generation, translation, and comprehension. *CoRR*, abs/1910.13461.

Yinhan Liu, Myle Ott, Naman Goyal, Jingfei Du, Mandar Joshi, Danqi Chen, Omer Levy, Mike Lewis, Luke Zettlemoyer, and Veselin Stoyanov. 2019. Roberta: A robustly optimized BERT pretraining approach. *CoRR*, abs/1907.11692.

L. McInnes, J. Healy, and J. Melville. 2018. UMAP: Uniform Manifold Approximation and Projection for Dimension Reduction. *ArXiv e-prints*.

David S. Moore and George P. McCabe. 1989. *Introduction to the practice of statistics*.

Jeffrey Pennington, Richard Socher, and Christopher Manning. 2014. GloVe: Global vectors for word representation. In *Proceedings of the 2014 Conference on Empirical Methods in Natural Language Processing (EMNLP)*, pages 1532–1543, Doha, Qatar. Association for Computational Linguistics.

Nils Reimers and Iryna Gurevych. 2019. Sentence-bert: Sentence embeddings using siamese bert-networks. In *Proceedings of the 2019 Conference on Empirical Methods in Natural Language Processing*. Association for Computational Linguistics.

Marco Tulio Ribeiro, Sameer Singh, and Carlos Guestrin. 2018. Semantically equivalent adversarial rules for debugging NLP models. In *Proceedings of the 56th Annual Meeting of the Association for Computational Linguistics (Volume 1: Long Papers)*, pages 856–865, Melbourne, Australia. Association for Computational Linguistics.

Saurav Sahay, Shachi H. Kumar, Eda Okur, Haroon Syed, and Lama Nachman. 2019. Modeling intent, dialog policies and response adaptation for goal-oriented interactions. In *Proceedings of the 23rd Workshop on the Semantics and Pragmatics of Dialogue*, London, United Kingdom. SEMDIAL.

Swadheen Shukla, Lars Liden, Shahin Shayandeh, Eslam Kamal, Jinchao Li, Matt Mazzola, Thomas Park, Baolin Peng, and Jianfeng Gao. 2020. Conversation Learner - a machine teaching tool for building dialog managers for task-oriented dialog systems. In *Proceedings of the 58th Annual Meeting of the Association for Computational Linguistics: System Demonstrations*, pages 343–349, Online. Association for Computational Linguistics.

Richard Socher, Eric H. Huang, Jeffrey Pennington, Andrew Y. Ng, and Christopher D. Manning. 2011. Dynamic pooling and unfolding recursive autoencoders for paraphrase detection. In *Proceedings of the 24th International Conference on Neural Information Processing Systems*, NIPS'11, page 801–809, Red Hook, NY, USA. Curran Assoc. Inc.

Alex Sokolov and Denis Filimonov. 2020. Neural machine translation for paraphrase generation. *arXiv preprint arXiv:2006.14223*.

Ilya Sutskever, Oriol Vinyals, and Quoc V. Le. 2014. Sequence to sequence learning with neural networks. *CoRR*, abs/1409.3215.

Vincent Warmerdam, Thomas Kober, and Rachael Tatman. 2020. Going beyond T-SNE: Exposing whatlies in text embeddings. In *Proceedings of Second Workshop for NLP Open Source Software (NLP-OSS)*, pages 52–60, Online. Association for Computational Linguistics.

Vincent D. Warmerdam. 2020. Rasa algorithm whiteboard - bulk labelling ui. The relevant notebook can be found on GitHub: `https://github.com/RasaHQ/rasalit/blob/main/notebooks/bulk-labelling/bulk-labelling-ui.ipynb`.

Vincent D. Warmerdam, Gabriel Luiz Freitas Almeida, Joshua Adelman, and Kay Hoogland. 2021. koaning/human-learn: 0.2.5.

John Wieting and Kevin Gimpel. 2018. ParaNMT-50M: Pushing the limits of paraphrastic sentence embeddings with millions of machine translations. In *Proceedings of the 56th Annual Meeting of the Association for Computational Linguistics (Volume 1: Long Papers)*, pages 451–462, Melbourne, Australia. Association for Computational Linguistics.

John Wieting, Jonathan Mallinson, and Kevin Gimpel. 2017. Learning paraphrastic sentence embeddings from back-translated bitext. In *Proceedings of the 2017 Conference on Empirical Methods in Natural Language Processing*, pages 274–285, Denmark. Association for Computational Linguistics.

Adina Williams, Nikita Nangia, and Samuel R. Bowman. 2017. A broad-coverage challenge corpus for sentence understanding through inference. *CoRR*, abs/1704.05426.

Yinfei Yang, Yuan Zhang, Chris Tar, and Jason Baldridge. 2019. PAWS-X: A Cross-lingual Adversarial Dataset for Paraphrase Identification. In *Proc. of EMNLP*.

Hanlei Zhang, Hua Xu, Ting-En Lin, and Rui Lyu. 2021. Discovering new intents with deep aligned clustering. In *Proceedings of the AAAI Conference on Artificial Intelligence*.

Yuan Zhang, Jason Baldridge, and Luheng He. 2019. PAWS: Paraphrase Adversaries from Word Scrambling. In *Proc. of NAACL*.

Dataset	BERT	Seed Selection	labeled_ratio	NMI	ARI	ACC
BANKING	Standard	RandomSampling	0.1	79.22	52.96	63.84±1.91
		ClusterBased	0.1	78.51	51.53	63.73±1.73
		KnownClusterBased	0.1	68.86	34.87	47.76±1.81
		ClusterBasedSentenceEmb	0.1	79.35	53.89	65.83±1.22
		PredictedClusterSampling	0.1	78.62	51.72	62.72±0.97
	Sentence	RandomSampling	0.1	82.96	60.72	71.27±2.28
		ClusterBased	0.1	80.65	55.03	65.44±1.24
		KnownClusterBased	0.1	74.21	42.37	53.89±2.53
		ClusterBasedSentenceEmb	0.1	80.87	56.07	66.72±1.42
		PredictedClusterSampling	0.1	82.11	58.43	69.78±2.08
CLINC	Standard	RandomSampling	0.1	93.90	79.70	86.34±1.47
		ClusterBased	0.1	90.60	69.60	77.87±1.70
		KnownClusterBased	0.1	85.33	55.35	66.65±3.14
		ClusterBasedSentenceEmb	0.1	90.70	69.92	78.17±2.03
		PredictedClusterSampling	0.1	93.76	79.42	86.41±0.65
	Sentence	RandomSampling	0.1	93.80	79.06	85.76±1.17
		ClusterBased	0.1	90.25	67.23	74.25±1.83
		KnownClusterBased	0.1	84.95	53.34	63.89±1.55
		ClusterBasedSentenceEmb	0.1	90.03	66.23	73.60±1.73
		PredictedClusterSampling	0.1	93.60	78.57	85.43±0.96
KidSpace	Standard	RandomSampling	0.2	71.40	48.26	58.55±4.22
		ClusterBased	0.2	68.13	39.26	53.48±4.47
		KnownClusterBased	0.2	-	-	-
		KnownClusterBased	0.4	69.76	55.52	61.10±6.15
		ClusterBasedSentenceEmb	0.2	66.92	38.46	53.87±6.58
		PredictedClusterSampling	0.2	70.53	45.33	56.80±4.52
	Sentence	RandomSampling	0.2	75.62	63.41	68.66±4.96
		ClusterBased	0.2	71.27	53.16	62.10±9.59
		KnownClusterBased	0.2	62.42	36.02	48.83±3.75
		KnownClusterBased	0.4	63.31	37.83	49.91±4.62
		ClusterBasedSentenceEmb	0.2	69.51	47.19	60.05±8.03
		PredictedClusterSampling	0.2	75.74	61.99	67.04±7.66
	Sentence	RandomSampling	0.1	65.21	38.04	48.85±2.47
		ClusterBased	0.1	62.60	35.41	49.62±5.40
		KnownClusterBased	0.1	63.32	38.00	50.95±4.65
		ClusterBasedSentenceEmb	0.1	61.96	34.98	47.76±2.85
		PredictedClusterSampling	0.1	66.98	40.55	51.20±4.15

Table 3: Semi-supervised DeepAlign Clustering Results with BERT Model, Data Balance/Augmentation and Seed Selection on BANKING, CLINC, and KidSpace datasets (averaged results over 10 runs with different seed values; known class ratio is 0.75 in all cases)

A Appendix

A.1 Additional Experimental Results

In addition to the Cluster-based Selection (CB) and Predicted Cluster Sampling (PCS) methods, we have explored other seed selection techniques compared with the Random Sampling. These are the Known Cluster-based Selection (KCB) and Cluster-based Sentence Embedding (CSE) methods. KCB is a variation of CB where we cluster into a number of known labels' subsets (based on known class ratio) and pick up certain % of data (based on labeled ratio) from each cluster's data points. CSE, on the other hand, is another variation of CB where, instead of BERT word embeddings as the pre-trained representations, we use the sentence embeddings model before running K-Means (the rest is the same as the CB method).

Table 3 presents detailed clustering performance results on three datasets using all five seed selection methods we explored, with varying labeled ratio and BERT embeddings (standard/BERT-base vs. sentence/SBERT models). In Table 4, we expand our analysis on the KidSpace dataset with data balancing/augmentation approaches on top of these five seed selection methods, once again with standard/sentence BERT embeddings. Table 5 presents additional results on the BANKING dataset to compare data balancing/augmentation methods on top of standard vs. the sentence BERT representations.

Dataset	BERT	Data Bal/Aug	Seed Selection	labeled_ratio	NMI	ARI	ACC
KidSpace	Standard	None	RandomSampling	0.2	71.40	48.26	58.55
			ClusterBased	0.2	68.13	39.26	53.48
			KnownClusterBased	0.2	-	-	-
			ClusterBasedSentenceEmb	0.2	66.92	38.46	53.87
			PredictedClusterSampling	0.2	70.53	45.33	56.80
	Standard	Paraphrasing	RandomSampling	0.2	71.99	50.35	59.21
			ClusterBased	0.2	68.04	39.80	55.06
			KnownClusterBased	0.2	66.31	39.40	51.10
			ClusterBasedSentenceEmb	0.2	67.44	39.49	54.42
			PredictedClusterSampling	0.2	72.15	51.78	61.12
	Standard	ParaMote	RandomSampling	0.2	71.46	47.77	58.64
			ClusterBased	0.2	67.82	39.59	54.56
			KnownClusterBased	0.2	67.67	46.99	55.88
			ClusterBasedSentenceEmb	0.2	66.64	39.61	53.82
			PredictedClusterSampling	0.2	72.38	49.98	59.98
	Sentence	None	RandomSampling	0.2	75.62	63.41	68.66
			ClusterBased	0.2	71.27	53.16	62.10
			KnownClusterBased	0.2	62.42	36.02	48.83
			ClusterBasedSentenceEmb	0.2	69.51	47.19	60.05
			PredictedClusterSampling	0.2	75.74	61.99	67.04
	Sentence	Paraphrasing	RandomSampling	0.2	76.41	63.02	68.83
			ClusterBased	0.2	70.71	48.19	60.88
			KnownClusterBased	0.2	67.58	54.05	58.62
			ClusterBasedSentenceEmb	0.2	70.93	52.60	62.67
			PredictedClusterSampling	0.2	75.52	61.53	68.21
	Sentence	ParaMote	RandomSampling	0.2	76.28	61.20	68.09
			ClusterBased	0.2	70.98	51.03	62.82
			KnownClusterBased	0.2	67.13	49.47	56.64
			ClusterBasedSentenceEmb	0.2	71.02	51.03	62.39
			PredictedClusterSampling	0.2	76.33	62.05	68.21
	Sentence	Aug (3x)	RandomSampling	0.2	76.48	61.33	68.07
			PredictedClusterSampling	0.2	76.37	58.97	68.78

Table 4: Semi-supervised DeepAlign Clustering Results with BERT Model, Data Balance/Augmentation and Seed Selection on KidSpace dataset (averaged results over 10 runs with different seed values; known class ratio is 0.75 in all cases)

Dataset	BERT	Data Bal/Aug	Seed Selection	labeled_ratio	NMI	ARI	ACC
BANKING	Standard	None	RandomSampling	0.1	79.22	52.96	63.84
			PredictedClusterSampling	0.1	78.62	51.72	62.72
	Standard	Paraphrasing	RandomSampling	0.1	79.31	53.31	64.83
			PredictedClusterSampling	0.1	78.79	52.41	64.62
	Standard	ParaMote	RandomSampling	0.1	79.62	54.08	65.37
			PredictedClusterSampling	0.1	79.30	53.08	65.08
	Sentence	None	RandomSampling	0.1	82.96	60.72	71.27
			PredictedClusterSampling	0.1	82.11	58.43	69.78
	Sentence	Paraphrasing	RandomSampling	0.1	83.00	60.95	71.95
			PredictedClusterSampling	0.1	82.20	58.86	69.62
	Sentence	ParaMote	RandomSampling	0.1	82.58	59.54	69.92
			PredictedClusterSampling	0.1	81.88	58.13	69.74
	Sentence	Aug (3x)	RandomSampling	0.1	82.94	60.78	71.66
			PredictedClusterSampling	0.1	81.69	58.18	69.99

Table 5: Semi-supervised DeepAlign Clustering Results with BERT Model, Data Balance/Augmentation and Seed Selection on BANKING dataset (averaged results over 10 runs with different seed values; known class ratio is 0.75 in all cases)

Human-In-The-Loop
Entity Linking for Low Resource Domains

Jan-Christoph Klie **Richard Eckart de Castilho** **Iryna Gurevych**
Ubiquitous Knowledge Processing Lab (UKP-TUDA)
Department of Computer Science
Technical University of Darmstadt, Germany
`www.ukp.tu-darmstadt.de`

Abstract

Entity linking (EL) is concerned with disambiguating entity mentions in a text against a knowledge base (KB). To quickly annotate texts with EL in low-resource domains and noisy text, we present a novel Human-In-The-Loop EL approach. We show that it greatly outperforms a strong baseline in simulation. In a user study, annotation time is reduced by 35 % compared to annotating without interactive support; users report that they strongly prefer our new approach. An open-source and ready-to-use implementation based on the text annotation platform INCEpTION[1] is made available [2].

1 Introduction

Entity linking (EL) describes the task of disambiguating entity mentions in a text by linking them to a knowledge base (KB), e.g. the text span *Earl of Orrery* can be linked to the KB entry *John Boyle, 5th Earl of Cork*, thereby disambiguating it. EL is highly relevant in many fields like digital humanities, classics, technical writing or biomedical sciences for applications like search (Meij et al., 2014), semantic enrichment (Schlögl and Lejtovicz, 2017) or information extraction (Nooralahzadeh and Øvrelid, 2018).

In these scenarios, the first crucial step is typically to annotate data. Manual annotation is laborious and often prohibitively expensive. To improve annotation speed and quality, we have developed a novel Human-In-The-Loop (HITL) entity linking approach. It helps annotators finding entity mentions in the text and linking them to the correct knowledge base entries. The more mentions get linked over time, the better the annotation support will be.

We demonstrate the effectiveness of our approach with extensive simulation as well as a user study on different, challenging datasets. We have implemented our approach based on the open-source annotation platform INCEpTION (Klie et al., 2018) and publish all datasets and code.

2 Implementation

Entity linking describes the task of disambiguating mentions in a text against a knowledge base. Manual annotation of EL consists of three steps (Shen et al., 2015). First, the annotator selects a span that contains an entity. Then, they search for the correct entity in a KB. These search results are reranked to rank more suitable candidates higher. Each candidate from the knowledge base is assumed to have a label and a description.

To speed up this annotation process, we support users twofold: To find suitable spans, we provide *recommenders* that suggest potential entity spans. They can also classify these entity spans (e.g. as person, location, etc.). These recommenders learn from new annotations and are retrained in the background. For candidate ranking, we follow Zheng et al. (2010) and model it as a learning-to-rank problem: given a marked span, search query and a list of candidates, sort the candidates so that the most relevant candidate is at the top. By selecting an entity label from the candidate list, users express that the selected one was preferred over all other candidates. These preferences are used to train state-of-the-art pairwise learning-to-rank models from the literature: the gradient boosted trees variant `LightGBM` (Ke et al., 2017) and `RankSVM` (Joachims, 2002). The continuously updated models improve over time with an increasing number of annotations. As input features, we use different similarity measures between the marked span and the candidate label, between the spans' context and the candidate description as well as dense word and sentence embeddings of the descriptions.

[1] `https://inception-project.github.io`
[2] `https://github.com/UKPLab/acl2020-interactive-entity-linking`

Proceedings of the 2nd Workshop on Data Science with Human in the Loop: Language Advances, pages 41–43
June 11, 2021. ©2021 Association for Computational Linguistics

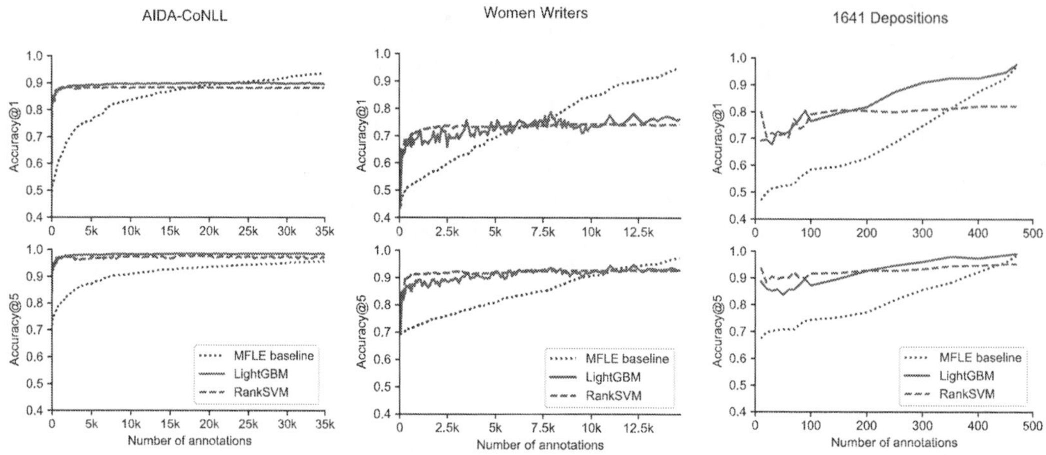

Figure 1: Human-in-the-loop simulation results for our three datasets and models. One can see that the model achieves good Accuracy@5 with only a few annotations, especially for the `RankSVM`.

Datasets We use the following three datasets for validating our approach: 1) the `AIDA-YAGO` state-of-the art dataset introduced by Hoffart et al. (2011). 2) `Women Writers Online`[3] is a collection of texts by pre-Victorian women writers. It includes texts on a wide range of topics and from various genres including poems, plays, and novels. 3) The `1641 Depositions`[4] contain legal texts in form of court witness statements recorded after the Irish Rebellion of 1641.

3 Experiments

To validate our approach, we simulate a user annotating with our HITL ranker. Then, we conduct a user study to test it in a real-life setting. Similar to other work on EL, our main metric for ranking is accuracy. We also measure Accuracy@5, as our experiments showed that users can quickly scan and select the right entity from a list of five elements.

Simulation Fig. 1 depicts the simulation results. All models outperform a majority baseline over most of the annotation process. It can be seen that both of our used models achieve high performance even if trained on very few annotations. The `RankSVM` handles low data better than `LightGBM`, but quickly reaches its peak performance due to it being a linear model. This potentially allows to first use a `RankSVM` for the cold start and when enough annotations are made, `LightGBM`, thereby combining the best of both.

[3]`https://www.wwp.northeastern.edu/wwo`

[4]`http://1641.tcd.ie/`

User Study In order to validate the viability of our approach in a realistic scenario, we conduct a user study. For that, we augmented the already existing annotation tool INCEpTION (Klie et al., 2018) with our Human-In-The-Loop entity ranking and automatic suggestions. We let five users re-annotate parts of the `1641` corpus. We compare two configurations: one uses our reranking, one uses the default ranking. We randomly selected eight documents which we split in two sets of four documents. We measure annotation time, number of suggestions used and search queries performed. The evaluation of the user study shows that using our approach, users on average annotated 35% faster and needed 15% fewer search queries.

4 Conclusion

We presented a domain-agnostic annotation approach for annotating entity linking for low-resource domains. It consists of two main components: recommenders that are algorithms that suggest potential annotations to users and a ranker that, given a mention span, ranks potential entity candidates so that they show up higher in the candidate list, making it easier to find for users. Both systems are retrained whenever new annotations are made, forming the Human-In-The-Loop. In a user study, results show that users prefer our approach compared to the typical annotation process; annotation speed improves by around 35% when using our system relative to using no reranking support.

References

Johannes Hoffart, Mohamed Amir Yosef, Ilaria Bordino, Hagen Fürstenau, Manfred Pinkal, Marc Spaniol, Bilyana Taneva, Stefan Thater, and Gerhard Weikum. 2011. Robust Disambiguation of Named Entities in Text. In *Proceedings of EMNLP'11*, pages 782–792.

Thorsten Joachims. 2002. Optimizing search engines using clickthrough data. In *Proceedings of the eighth ACM SIGKDD international conference on Knowledge discovery and data mining - KDD '02*, pages 133–142.

Guolin Ke, Qi Meng, Thomas Finley, Taifeng Wang, Wei Chen, Weidong Ma, Qiwei Ye, and Tie-Yan Liu. 2017. LightGBM: A Highly Efficient Gradient Boosting Decision Tree. In I. Guyon, U. V. Luxburg, S. Bengio, H. Wallach, R. Fergus, S. Vishwanathan, and R. Garnett, editors, *Advances in Neural Information Processing Systems 30*, pages 3146–3154.

Jan-Christoph Klie, Michael Bugert, Beto Boullosa, Richard Eckart de Castilho, and Iryna Gurevych. 2018. The INCEpTION Platform: Machine-Assisted and Knowledge-Oriented Interactive Annotation. In *Proceedings of the 27th International Conference on Computational Linguistics: System Demonstrations*, pages 5–9.

Edgar Meij, Krisztian Balog, and Daan Odijk. 2014. Entity linking and retrieval for semantic search. In *Proceedings of the 7th ACM international conference on Web search and data mining - WSDM '14*, pages 683–684.

Farhad Nooralahzadeh and Lilja Øvrelid. 2018. SIRIUS-LTG: An Entity Linking Approach to Fact Extraction and Verification. In *Proceedings of the First Workshop on Fact Extraction and VERification (FEVER)*, pages 119–123.

Matthias Schlögl and Katalin Lejtovicz. 2017. APIS - Austrian Prosopographical Information System. In *Proceedings of the Second Conference on Biographical Data in a Digital World 2017*.

Wei Shen, Jianyong Wang, and Jiawei Han. 2015. Entity Linking with a Knowledge Base: Issues, Techniques, and Solutions. *IEEE Transactions on Knowledge and Data Engineering*, 27(2):443–460.

Zhicheng Zheng, Fangtao Li, Minlie Huang, and Xiaoyan Zhu. 2010. Learning to Link Entities with Knowledge Base. In *Prooceedings of NAACL-HLT'10*, pages 483–491.

Bridging Multi-disciplinary Collaboration Challenges in ML Development Workflow via Domain Knowledge Elicitation

Soya Park
MIT CSAIL
soya@mit.edu

Abstract

Building a machine learning model in a sophisticated domain is a time-consuming process, partially due to the steep learning curve of domain knowledge for data scientists. We introduce Ziva, an interface for supporting domain knowledge from domain experts to data scientists in two ways: (1) a `concept creation` interface where domain experts extract important concept of the domain and (2) five kinds of `justification elicitation` interfaces that solicit elicitation how the domain concept are expressed in data instances.

1 Introduction

In recent decades, machine learning (ML) technologies have been sought out by an increasing number of professionals to automate their work tasks or augment their decision-making (Yang et al., 2019). Broad areas of applications are benefiting from integration of ML, such as healthcare (Cai et al., 2019a,b), finance (Culkin and Das, 2017), employment (Manyika et al., 2017), and so on. However, building an ML model in a specialized domain is still expensive and time-consuming for at least two reasons. First, a common bottleneck in developing modern ML technologies is the requirement of a large quantity of labeled data. Second, many steps in an ML development pipeline, from problem definition to feature engineering to model debugging, necessitate an understanding of domain-specific knowledge and requirements (Piorkowski et al., 2021). Data scientists therefore often require input from domain experts to obtain labeled data, to understand model requirements, to inspire feature engineering, and to get feedback on model behavior. In practice, such knowledge transfer between domain experts and data scientists is very much ad-hoc, with few standardized practices or proven effective approaches, and requires significant direct interaction between data scientists and domain experts. Building a high-quality legal, medical, or financial model will inevitably require a data scientist to consult with professionals in such domains. In practice, these are often costly and frustrating iterative conversations and labeling exercises that can go on for weeks and months, which usually still do not yield output in a form readily consumable by a model development pipeline.

In this work, we set out to develop methods and interfaces that facilitate knowledge sharing from domain experts to data scientists for model development. We developed a domain-knowledge acquisition interface **Ziva** (With **Z**ero knowledge, How do **I** de**V**elop **A** machine learning model?). Instead of a data-labeling tool, Ziva intends to provide a diverse set of elicitation methods to gather knowledge from domain experts, then present the results as a repository to data scientists to serve their domain understanding needs and to build ML models for specialized domains. Ziva scaffolds the knowledge sharing in desired formats and allows asynchronous exchange between domain experts and data scientists. It also allows flexible re-use of the knowledge repository for different modeling tasks in the domain.

Specifically, Ziva focuses on eliciting key concepts in the text data of a domain (`concept creation`), and rationale justifying a label that a domain expert gives to a representative data instance (`justification elicitation`). In the current version of Ziva, we provide five different `justification elicitation` methods – bag of words, simplification, perturbation, concept bag of words, and concept annotation.

2 Ziva System

2.1 Concept creation

Creating a taxonomy is an effective way of organizing information (Laniado et al., 2007; Chilton et al., 2013). Ziva provides an interface where SMEs can

Proceedings of the 2nd Workshop on Data Science with Human in the Loop: Language Advances, pages 44–46
June 11, 2021.

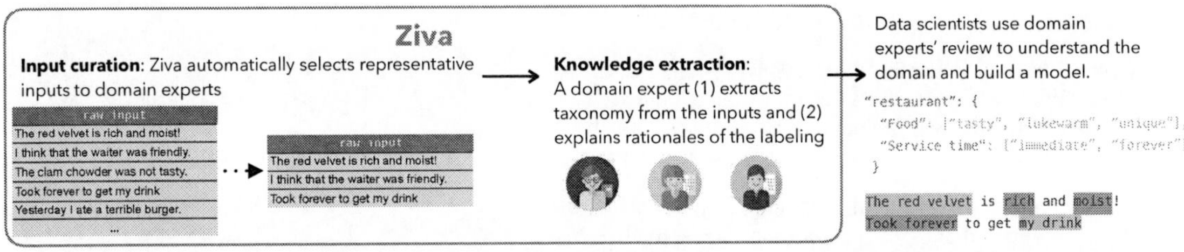

Figure 1: To facilitate domain knowledge sharing, Ziva presents representative instances and to interfaces to review the instances to domain experts, then which will be used by data scientists.

extract domain concepts. Users are asked to categorize each example instance, presented as a card, via a card-sorting activity. Users first group cards by topic (general concepts of the domain such as atmosphere, food, service, price). Cards in each topic are then further divided cards into descriptions referencing specific attributes for a topic (e.g., cool, tasty, kind, high).

2.2 Justification-elicitation interface

Once a domain expert finishes the concept extraction, they review each instance using one of elicitation interfaces, which ask the domain expert to justify an instance's label (this information is then intended for consumption by data scientists).

The `justification elicitation` interfaces were designed through an iterative process of paper prototyping, starting with initial designs inspired by our preliminary interviews. As we conducted paper prototyping, we examined if (1) the answers from different participants were consistent and (2) the information from participants' answers were useful to data scientists.

Bag of words. This base condition reflects the most common current approach. Given an instance and a label (e.g., positive, negative), the domain experts are asked to highlight the text snippets that justify the label assignment.

Instance perturbation. Inspired by one of our data scientists in the formative study, this condition asks a domain expert to *perturb* (edit) the instance such that the assigned label is no longer justifiable by the resulting text. For example, in the restaurant domain, *"our server was kind"*, can be modified to no longer convey a positive sentiment by either negating an aspect (e.g., *"our server was not kind"*) or altering it (e.g., *"our server was rude"*).

Instance simplification. This condition asks domain experts to shorten an instance as much as possible, leaving only text that justifies the assigned label of the original instance. For example, *"That's right. The red velvet cake... ohhhh.. it was rich and moist"*, can be simplified to *"The cake was rich and moist"*, as the rest of the content does not convey any sentiment, and can therefore be judged irrelevant to the sentiment analysis task.

Concept bag of words. This condition incorporates the concept extracted in the prior step. Similar to the Bag of words condition, domain experts are asked to highlight relevant text within each instance to justify the assigned label; however, each highlight must be grouped into one of the concepts. If, during `Concept creation`, the domain expert copied a card to assign multiple topics and descriptions, then the interface prompts multiple times to highlight relevant text for each one. For example, if they classified the instance, *"That's right. The red velvet cake... ohhhh.. it was rich and moist"*, into the concept *"food is tasty"*, they can select *rich*, *moist* and *cake* as being indicative words for that concept.

Concept annotation. This condition is similar to the above Concept bag of words condition. However, when annotating the instance text, domain experts are directed to distinguish between words relevant to the topic and words relevant to the description. Given the above sample instance, the domain expert would need to indicate which part of the sentence applies to *food* (e.g., *cake*) and which to *tasty* (e.g., *rich and moist*). Both this and the previous concept condition are motivated by the well-established knowledge that a variety of NLP tasks, such as relation extraction, question answering, clustering and text generation can benefit from tapping into the the conceptual relationship present in the hierarchies of human knowledge (Zhang et al., 2016). Learning taxonomies from text corpora is a significant NLP research direction, especially for long-tailed and domain-specific knowledge acquisition (Wang et al., 2017).

Details of the interface design and the evaluation can be found in Park et al. (2021).

References

Carrie Jun Cai, Samantha Winter, David Steiner, Lauren Wilcox, and Michael Terry. 2019a. "hello ai": Uncovering the onboarding needs of medical practitioners for human-ai collaborative decision-making.

Carrie Jun Cai et al. 2019b. Human-centered tools for coping with imperfect algorithms during medical decision-making.

Lydia B Chilton, Greg Little, Darren Edge, Daniel S Weld, and James A Landay. 2013. Cascade: Crowdsourcing taxonomy creation. In *Proceedings of the SIGCHI Conference on Human Factors in Computing Systems*, pages 1999–2008.

Robert Culkin and Sanjiv R Das. 2017. Machine learning in finance: The case of deep learning for option pricing. *Journal of Investment Management*, 15(4):92–100.

David Laniado, Davide Eynard, Marco Colombetti, et al. 2007. Using wordnet to turn a folksonomy into a hierarchy of concepts. In *Semantic Web Application and Perspectives-Fourth Italian Semantic Web Workshop*, pages 192–201.

James Manyika, Michael Chui, Mehdi Miremadi, et al. 2017. A future that works: Ai, automation, employment, and productivity. *McKinsey Global Institute Research, Tech. Rep*, 60.

Soya Park, April Yi Wang, Ban Kawas, Q Vera Liao, David Piorkowski, and Marina Danilevsky. 2021. Facilitating knowledge sharing from domain experts to data scientists for building nlp models. In *26th International Conference on Intelligent User Interfaces*, pages 585–596.

David Piorkowski, Soya Park, April Yi Wang, Dakuo Wang, Michael Muller, and Felix Portnoy. 2021. How ai developers overcome communication challenges in a multidisciplinary team: A case study.

Chengyu Wang, Xiaofeng He, and Aoying Zhou. 2017. A short survey on taxonomy learning from text corpora: Issues, resources and recent advances. In *Proceedings of the 2017 Conference on Empirical Methods in Natural Language Processing*, pages 1190–1203. Association for Computational Linguistics.

Qian Yang, Aaron Steinfeld, and John Zimmerman. 2019. Unremarkable ai: Fitting intelligent decision support into critical, clinical decision-making processes. In *Proceedings of the 2019 CHI Conference on Human Factors in Computing Systems*, pages 1–11.

Hao Zhang et al. 2016. Learning concept taxonomies from multi-modal data. In *Proceedings of the 54th Annual Meeting of the Association for Computational Linguistics*, pages 1791–1801. Association for Computational Linguistics.

Active learning and negative evidence for language identification

Thomas Lippincott **Benjamin Van Durme**
Johns Hopkins University
{tom,vandurme}@cs.jhu.edu

Abstract

Language identification (LID), the task of determining the natural language of a given text, is an essential first step in most NLP pipelines. While generally a solved problem for documents of sufficient length and languages with ample training data, the proliferation of microblogs and other social media has made it increasingly common to encounter use-cases that *don't* satisfy these conditions. In these situations, the fundamental difficulty is the lack of, and cost of gathering, labeled data: unlike some annotation tasks, no single "expert" can quickly and reliably identify more than a handful of languages. This leads to a natural question: can we gain useful information when annotators are only able to *rule out* languages for a given document, rather than supply a positive label? What are the optimal choices for gathering and representing such *negative evidence* as a model is trained?

In this paper, we demonstrate that using negative evidence can improve the performance of a simple neural LID model. This improvement is sensitive to policies of how the evidence is represented in the loss function, and for deciding which annotators to employ given the instance and model state. We consider simple policies and report experimental results that indicate the optimal choices for this task. We conclude with a discussion of future work to determine if and how the results generalize to other classification tasks.

1 Background

Language identification (LID) is the task of classifying a document according to the natural language in which it is written (Lui and Baldwin, 2011). It is a special case of *text classification*, where a document is assigned a label l from a finite set of discrete values L. Such problems, and LID as a special case, have been widely studied for decades (Kranig, 2005; Jauhiainen et al., 2018), with recent state-of-the-art methods focusing on neural architectures over character representations (Joulin et al., 2017; Zhang et al., 2015). Most methods share the intuition (verified by many traditional studies) that the signal for LID comes from the character level. This intuition is reinforced by the difficulty that flexible neural architectures have unseating traditional n-gram methods (Lippincott et al., 2019): frequencies of short character-sequences seem to hold most signal for the task.

Negative evidence, for a feature or label, is explicit evidence that it is not present in or does not apply to an instance (Schneider, 2004): in this study, it refers to annotations that say "this document is *not* language X". A given annotator can only know a handful of languages, so in addition to the *positive evidence* when presented with one of them, there may be a much higher volume of implicit negative evidence, i.e. the documents whose language they couldn't recognize. Among text classification tasks, the LID task is a particularly acute, naturally-occurring example of this imbalance, in contrast to specific phenomena like linguistic structure or small-inventory tasks like named-entity recognition or sentiment, where annotators are expected to have a full grasp of the potential label-space.

Our use of model estimates to choose annotators has similarities to work on multi-armed contextual bandits (Riquelme et al., 2018), where the context includes both the new instance and the current model state. Similar to Bayesian last layer optimization (Weber et al., 2018) we focus on the final linear layer in the model, though rather than employing reinforcement learning we directly specify simple policies based on the output distributions. The choice of likeliest annotators is similar to Thompson sampling (Riquelme et al., 2018).

Figure 1[1] shows the performance of a LID model

[1]All figures in this paper show results for four values of *annotations_per_instance*, 2, 4, 8, and 16, indicated by

Proceedings of the 2nd Workshop on Data Science with Human in the Loop: Language Advances, pages 47–51
June 11, 2021.

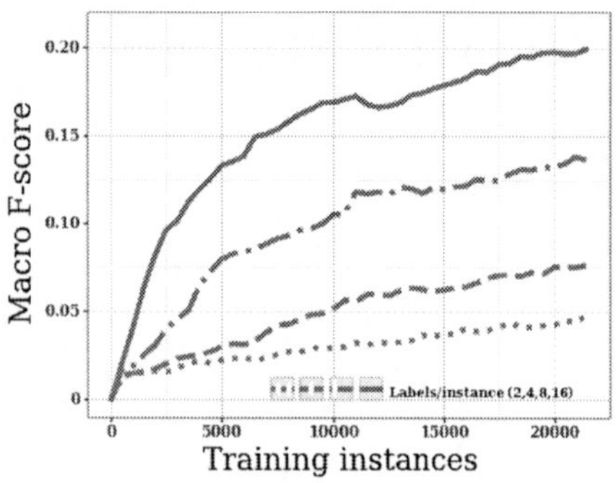

Figure 1: Performance when training **only** on negative evidence ("this is *not* language X") and no use of the model for routing instances to annotators or for estimating probabilities (i.e. the *Random* and *Uniform* policies described in Section 2). As languages are ruled out, probability-mass is shifted to the set containing the correct label. Improvements occur with more labeled instances (x-axis), and with more labels-per-instance.

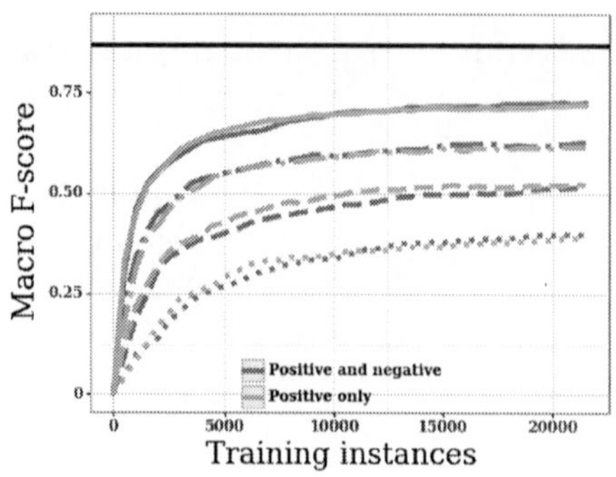

Figure 2: Performance using **positive** evidence, with and without negative evidence, also with no use of the model for routing or estimation. The signal identified in Figure 1 brings no advantages under this simple policy. Here and in subsequent figures, the black line indicates performance under the ideal situation where the full training set is positively labeled.

trained on just negative evidence. The curves clearly demonstrate that negative evidence contains useful information for the task. Figure 2 compares positive evidence with both positive *and* negative evidence, when negative evidence is incorporated naively (see descripions of *Uniform* and *Random* in Section 2). There is no performance gain from including the negative evidence under these conditions. Our goal is to preserve the signal from Figure 1, that is currenly being lost in Figure 2, and determine how to best employ annotation resources as training progresses.

2 Methods

Data The Twitter Language Identification dataset consists of 70k tweet IDs distributed evenly over 70 languages (Twitter, 2015). This provides a significant LID challenge due to the short, idiosyncratic messages and a large label space that includes many less-studied languages. We balance the data by randomly shuffling and keeping the first 400 instances of each language, and discarding seven languages with less than 400 total, as some tweets have become unavailable since the data set was published.

Model Our model truncates and pads input sentences to 128 characters, and maps each character into a randomly initialized 64-dimension embedding space. The $(128x64xBatchSize)$ tensors are fed to a two-dimensional CNN layer with filters of widths $w \in 1:5$ followed by ReLU nonlinearity. The CNN outputs are concatenated, fed to a dense linear layer and softmax to produce distributions over the labels. The choice of character-level CNNs of the given widths gives the model access to the same statistical information employed by traditional n-gram models.

Training We simulate L annotators, one per label, each only capable of recognizing their respective label. Starting with zero instances and a randomly-initialized model, at each step we are provided with 500 new instances, and for each of them, allowed to query $annotators\_per\_instance$ of the annotators, ranked according to an **annotator policy**. Each annotator returns *positive* if the instance is in the language they recognize, *negative* otherwise. This evidence is represented as a target categorical distribution for the model's loss function, according to a **representation policy**. The model is then trained via SGD for a maximum of 500 epochs, with learning rate=0.1, momentum=0.9, maximum iterations=500, minibatch size=32, early stop=20, learning rate reduction of magnitude=0.1 and patience=10, and dropout of 0.5 on the CNN outputs.[2] Note that we are training to convergence *between* receiving each new batch of annotated instances.

Evidence Given the annotations received during the training process, we can selectively employ evi-

increasingly-solid lines: for better readability, we omit this from the legends

[2]This training configuration produced optimal results on dev performance across all experimental conditions

dence: *Positive* and *Positive+Negative* are the most important point of comparison, while *Negative* was used in Figure 1 to illustrate the potential value of the negative annotations.

Annotation policies We experiment with two policies for ranking potential annotators for a new instance: in both cases, the instance is labeled by the first $annotators\_per\_instance$ annotators in the ranked list. The *Random* policy simply shuffles the annotators randomly. The *Likeliest* policy ranks annotators by the probability the model currently assigns to their language for the new instance, from most likely to least. The intuition is that getting annotations for the likeliest languages will either 1) correctly label the instance or 2) remove the maximal amount of misallocated probability mass under the current model parameters.

Representation policies We also experiment with two policies for representing negative evidence as an L-dimensional categorical distribution for input to the loss function (positive evidence is always the corresponding one-hot distribution). The *Uniform* policy, given negative evidence for labels L_{neg}, builds the distribution $P(l) = 0$ if $l \in L_{neg}$, otherwise $P(l) = \frac{1}{|L - L_{neg}|}$. The *Estimated* policy also sets $P(l) = 0$ if $l \in L_{neg}$, but otherwise sets $P(l)$ proportional to the model's current estimate of that language for the instance. We experimented with treating each potential label for each instance as a binary task via binary cross-entropy loss metrics, and with selectively propagating the loss depending on whether an annotation (positive or negative) had been seen for the task, but found that the best approach was to treat it as a categorical, with a KL-divergence loss metric.

```
train = []
for s in 1:S:
  new = get_more_instances(500)
  labeled = label(new, annotator_policy)
  train += encode(labeled, representation_policy)
  continue_training(model, train)
  recordScore(model, test)
```

Figure 3: Training procedure: the model is incrementally fed additional labeled documents, and each time SGD is run until dev set performance stops improving, at which point the test set score is recorded for the current amount of training data.

Measurements We perform five folds of each experiment, in which the full data set is randomly shuffled, and split into train/dev/test sets in 0.8, 0.1, and 0.1 proportions, respectively. Performance on the dev sets was used for early stopping and learning rate decay, while we report test performance averaged over the five folds. Variance was low, and we omit it from figures, but include it in Additional Materials. Figures show macro F1 score as a function of training instance count: line style corresponds to $annotators\_per\_instance$, while color corresponds to the policies being compared. The solid horizontal line at the top of the figures is a reference point of performance with complete, positive annotation of all instances.

We assume that we have access to one annotator per language and route each document as it arrives. In the absence of active learning, a document has a 1/70 chance to be labeled as its *correct* language, and 69/70 chance to be labeled as *not* one of the other languages. We also experiment with a simple policy of routing each document to the annotator for the model's current best-guess language, with the hypothesis this will reassign the most misallocated probability mass.

1. Treat the outputs as a categorical distribution by applying softmax and use standard cross-entropy between this and positive labels, making no use of negative labels. As extreme as this seems, it's not unrealistic in situations that focus on under-represented populations like sub-Saharan Africa or fine-grained distinctions like Arabic dialects to have an acute lack of on-demand expertise, or a large cost associated with it.

2. Treat the outputs and labels as independent Bernoulli distributions, and for each document only back-propagate the error from its explicitly-labeled language (be it a positive or negative label). This focuses the objective on the precise information the annotators have provided.

3. Treat the outputs as a categorical distribution, so identical to 1) for positive labels, but to additionally cast the negative labels as under-specified categorical distributions. With zero additional evidence we can use the maximum entropy distribution subject to the constraints of any negative labels, i.e. the uniform distribution with the negative labels set to zero and renormalized. We could also use external information, such as the population language distribution from another source, or an iterative prior estimation from current estimates, to

inform how the probability mass is distributed across the label space.

3 Results and Discussion

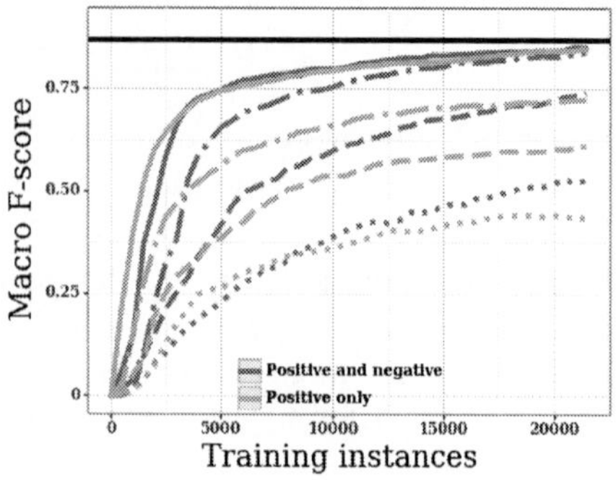

Figure 4: Comparison of the best approach using *Positive* evidence, and the best approach using *Positive+Negative* evidence, both of which use *Likeliest* annotation policy and *Estimated* representation policy. Given the same number of annotations-per-instance (line solidity), negative evidence provides significant performance improvements, after a brief initial delay (see Figure 6).

Figure 4 shows our primary result: the use of negative evidence, in combination with the *Estimated* representation policy and *Likeliest* annotator policy, produces large improvements over the best baseline approach using positive evidence alone. In particular, when the algorithm is given a small number of annotation opportunities per instance (2, 4, 8), it surpasses the baseline at 20k instances by 7, 15, and 10 points, respectively. Positive+negative with 4 annotations per instance exceeds performance of positive with 8 annotations per instance, and with 8 annotations per instance is within 3 points of performance with perfect positive evidence.

On the other hand, the *Positive+Negative* models show performance delays compared to the corresponding positive models. Because the negative instances rely on the quality of the current estimates for constructing target distributions, these are initially quite poor until the model escapes its random initialization. This escape is easier to accomplish with more annotations, which can be seen by comparing where the *Positive+Negative* models start outperforming their *Positive* counterparts.

Figures 6 and 5 compare representation and annotator policies under the simplest configurations. The delayed performance is clearest between the

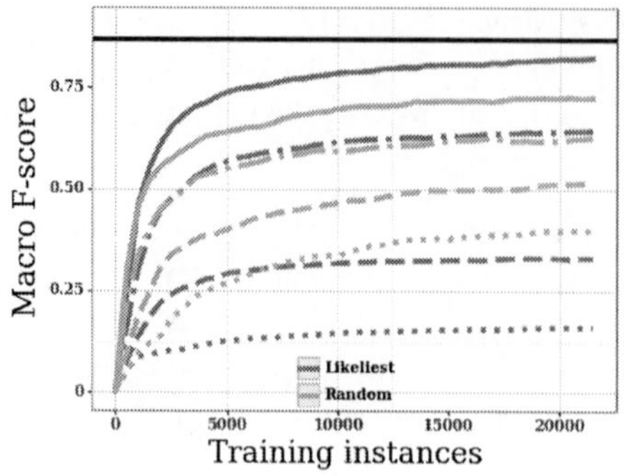

Figure 5: Comparison of *Random* and *Likeliest* annotator policies, both using the *Uniform* representation policy and *Positive+Negative* evidence. The *Likeliest* policy lacks the performance delay seen in Figure 4, but also falls short of the improvement given more training instances.

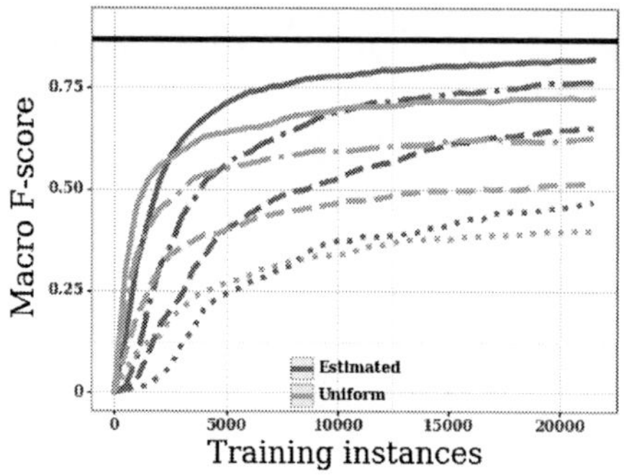

Figure 6: Comparison of *Uniform* and *Estimated* representation policies, both using the *Random* annotator policy and *Positive+Negative* evidence. The *Estimated* policy exhibits the performance delay of Figure 4, indicating this stems from the model's initial poor estimates of unseen label probabilities, but also shows the value of those estimates in the improvements once those estimates are based on sufficient training instances.

representation policies. The *Estimated* representation policy also provides the most performance improvement, eventually providing benefits for every value of $annotators\_per\_instance$. The annotator policies, on the other hand, only provide significant benefits when $annotators\_per\_instance \geq 8$. Referring back to Figure 4 confirms the combination of both policies outperforms either in isolation.

4 Conclusions and future work

We have demonstrated a general method for exploiting negative evidence using an underlying virtuous cycle, where an improved model leads to better annotator selections and more accurate target distributions. These appear to be crucial ingredients for negative evidence to provide benefit: when we remove them, and always select annotators at random and employ CMEDs, the positive+negative models provide no advantage over the positive-only models throughout training. It may be that the benefits would only materialize on larger training sets, but since the models already approach the optimum (black line) this is never seen in practice for this LID task.

Negative evidence can be gathered (and simulated) for any classification task, and it is an open question whether the same approaches will generalize. In particular, we would like to run experiments in speech processing, which has its own language identification problem as well as a number of tasks with even sparser annotation abilities (e.g. speaker identification), and image recognition.

The initial performance delays we observed in Figures 4 and 6 come from the *Estimated* policy's use of the model before it has sufficiently improved. Representation policies that take this into account should be able to shift the early performance curves to the left, similar to work on multi-armed bandits (Weber et al., 2018) emphasizing the importance of uncertainty estimates. The annotation policies we considered can only gather annotations for incoming instances: it may be useful to expand this to include *all* currently-known instances, to allow more flexible shifting of probability mass using the same amount of annotation resources.

References

Tommi Jauhiainen, Marco Lui, Marcos Zampieri, Timothy Baldwin, and Krister Lindén. 2018. Automatic Language Identification in Texts: A Survey. *CoRR*, abs/1804.08186.

Armand Joulin, Edouard Grave, Piotr Bojanowski, and Tomas Mikolov. 2017. Bag of Tricks for Efficient Text Classification. In *Proceedings of the 15th Conference of the European Chapter of the Association for Computational Linguistics: Volume 2, Short Papers*, pages 427–431. Association for Computational Linguistics.

Simon Kranig. 2005. Evaluation of language identification methods. *Bakalárska práca, Universität Tübingen, Nemecko*.

Tom Lippincott, Pamela Shapiro, Kevin Duh, and Paul McNamee. 2019. JHU system description for the MADAR Arabic dialect identification shared task. In *Proceedings of the Fourth Arabic Natural Language Processing Workshop*, pages 264–268, Florence, Italy. Association for Computational Linguistics.

Marco Lui and Timothy Baldwin. 2011. Cross-domain feature selection for language identification. In *Proceedings of 5th international joint conference on natural language processing*, pages 553–561.

Carlos Riquelme, George Tucker, and Jasper Snoek. 2018. Deep Bayesian Bandits Showdown: An Empirical Comparison of Bayesian Deep Networks for Thompson Sampling. In *International Conference on Learning Representations*.

Karl-Michael Schneider. 2004. On word frequency information and negative evidence in Naive Bayes text classification. In *Advances in Natural Language Processing*, pages 474–485. Springer.

Twitter. 2015. Evaluating language identification performance.

Noah Weber, Janez Starc, Arpit Mittal, Roi Blanco, and Lluís Màrquez. 2018. Optimizing over a Bayesian Last Layer. In *Advances in neural information processing systems*.

Xiang Zhang, Junbo Zhao, and Yann LeCun. 2015. Character-level convolutional networks for text classification. In *Advances in neural information processing systems*, pages 649–657.

Towards integrated, interactive, and extensible text data analytics with LEAM

Peter Griggs*
MIT
pgriggs@mit.edu

Çağatay Demiralp*
Sigma Computing
cagatay@sigmacomputing.com

Sajjadur Rahman
Megagon Labs
sajjadur@megagon.ai

Abstract

From tweets to product reviews, text is ubiquitous on the web and often contains valuable information for both enterprises and consumers. However, the online text is generally noisy and incomplete, requiring users to process and analyze the data to extract insights. While there are systems effective for different stages of text analysis, users lack extensible platforms to support interactive text analysis workflows end-to-end. To facilitate integrated text analytics, we introduce LEAM, which aims at combining the strengths of spreadsheets, computational notebooks, and interactive visualizations. LEAM supports interactive analysis via GUI-based interactions and provides a declarative specification language, implemented based on a visual text algebra, to enable user-guided analysis. We evaluate LEAM through two case studies using two popular Kaggle text analytics workflows to understand the strengths and weaknesses of the system.

1 Introduction

The growth of e-commerce has contributed to the proliferation of digital text, particularly user-generated text (reviews, Q&As, discussions), which often contain useful information for improving the services and products on the web. Enterprises increasingly adopt text mining technologies to extract, analyze, and summarize information from such unstructured text data. However, online text collections are incomplete, ambiguous, and often sparse in informational content. Cleaning, featurizing, modeling, visualizing, extracting information from, and identifying topics in such text collections can be daunting and time-consuming without integrated systems that take the whole text analytics pipeline into account.

The characteristics of online text make interactive workflows and visualizations essential for rapid iterative analysis (Ittoo et al., 2016). Therefore we focus on visual interactive text analysis (VITA hereafter) and related systems. Few commercial and open-source tools can support different stages of VITA, *e.g.*, spreadsheets, computational notebooks, and visualization tools (Liu et al., 2018; Smith et al., 2020). Customized visual text analytics tools focus on specific use-cases like review exploration (Zhang et al., 2020a), sentiment analysis (Kucher et al., 2018), and text summarization (Carenini et al., 2006). None of these solutions accommodate the inherently cyclic, trial-and-error-based nature of VITA pipelines end-to-end (Drosos et al., 2020; Wu et al., 2020).

Designing and building VITA systems can be difficult. The primary challenge is the number and diversity of the tasks that need to be supported. Programmatic tools such as computational notebooks can provide extensibility and expressivity to incrementally build such support but they often lack in interactivity and do not facilitate direct data manipulation, impeding analysis.

In response, we propose LEAM , that provides an integrated environment for VITA. LEAM combines the advantages of spreadsheets, computational notebooks, and visualization tools by integrating a Code Editor with interactive views of raw (Data View) and transformed data (Chart View). Figure 1 shows a snapshot of LEAM. A key component in the design of LEAM is the instrumentation of text analysis operations via VITAL, a python API. These built-in operations can also be used directly from the interactive Operations Menu. To evaluate LEAM, we conduct two case studies using two popular Kaggle text analytics workflows. The

DaSH-LA 2021, June 11, 2021, Virtual Conference.

*Work done while authors were at Megagon Labs.

Proceedings of the 2nd Workshop on Data Science with Human in the Loop: Language Advances, pages 52–58
June 11, 2021. ©2021 Association for Computational Linguistics

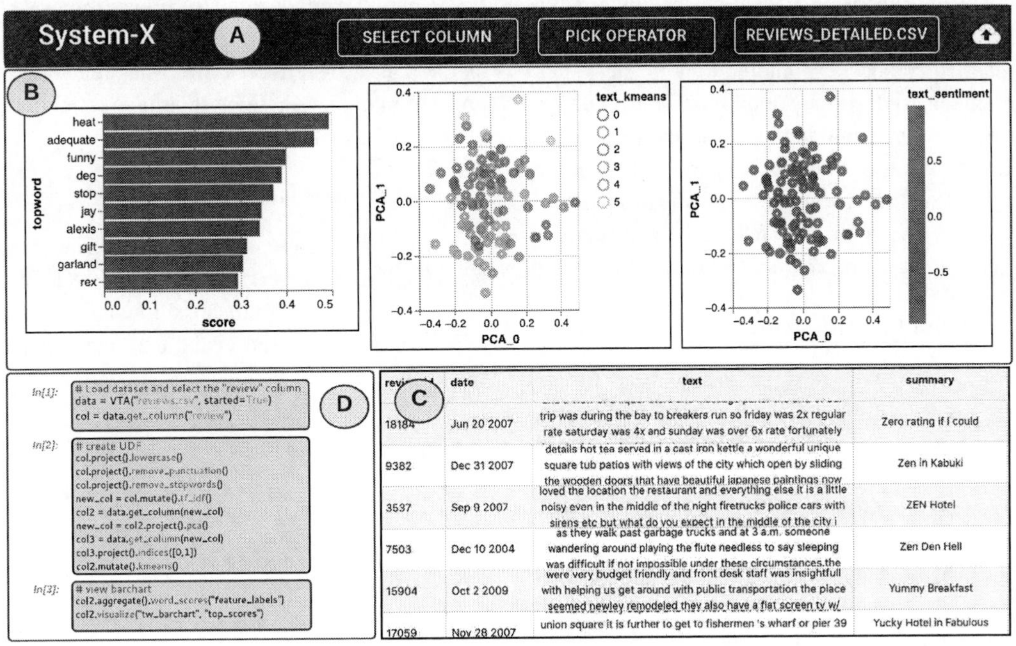

Figure 1: LEAM user interface. (A) Operations Menu enables users to perform visual interactive text analytics (VITA) operations using drop-down menus, (B) Chart View holds a carousel of interactive visualizations created by users, (C) Data View displays the data and its subsequent transformations, and (D) Code Editor allows users to compose and run VITA operations using a declarative specification called VITAL.

study showed that participants preferred the integrated analysis environment and the ability to specify various workflows both interactively (via Operations Menu) and declaratively (via VITAL). However, participants asked for enhanced workflow transparency and consistency of operations. We have released the source-code of LEAM at `https://github.com/megagonlabs/leam`.

2 Related Work

LEAM draws from prior work on interactive text analysis, computational notebook, and declarative specification of analysis workflows.

Interactive visual text analytics. Prior research on visual text analytics have limitations in flexibility and extensibility due to their fixed choices of models, visualizations, and interactions (Kucher et al., 2018; Liu et al., 2018). LEAM adopts the vision of a VITA system outlined in our prior work (Rahman et al., 2020). In this paper, we primarily focus on expressivity (*e.g.*, declarative workflow specification), resusability (*e.g.*, reusing operators and models), on-demand coordination (*e.g.*, linking visualizations and data), and transparency (*e.g.*, GUI interaction logging).

Computational notebooks. Computational notebooks such as Jupyter (Jupyter, 2020) allow programmers to interleave code with visualizations. This linear layout often introduces a physical distance between related charts, limiting an analyst's ability to derives insights by visually comparing different charts. Tools like B2 (Wu et al., 2020) and LUX (Lee, 2020), provide a non-linear interface where charts are placed in a separate visualization pane. While LEAM shares the same principle, it additionally features a Data View and enables coordination between visualization and the data—a desirable property of such interactive programming environments (Chattopadhyay et al., 2020).

Declarative data analysis and visualization. Prior work on data analysis workflow specification focused on several different stages, from data cleaning to exploration. To support data cleaning, Wrangler (Kandel et al., 2011) combines a mixed-initiative interface with a declarative transformation language. Text Extension python library (Codait, 2021) enables users to operate on intermediate data, *e.g.*, spans and tensors, in all phases of an NLP workflow. Grammars of graphics like Vega-Lite (Satyanarayan et al., 2016) and ggplot2 (Wickham, 2016) support visualization specification via abstractions, *e.g.*, JSON. However, users cannot dynamically add new interactions to the visualizations using these abstractions. LEAM enables users to add new interactions to visualizations and create coordination among data and visualizations on-the-fly using declarative specifications developed based on grammar for visual text analysis introduced in our prior work (Rahman et al., 2020).

3 Design Considerations

We now outline our design considerations for creating LEAM. Table 1 shows which of these design considerations are supported by existing tools discussed in Section 2. These design considerations were informed by prior work on identifying challenges related to live programming interfaces (Chattopadhyay et al., 2020; Rule et al., 2018; Kery et al., 2020), studies on exploratory data science practices (Alspaugh et al., 2018; Kery et al., 2018; Zhang et al., 2020b), and guidelines for multiple coordinated view design (Wang et al., 2000), and refined through our experiences working with user-generated text data at MEGAGON LABS:

Design Crietria	Notebooks			Visualization Platforms	VITA (LEAM)
	Jupyter	LUX	B2		
D1/D2. Code	✓	✓	✓	x	✓
D1. Visualization	✓	✓	✓	✓	✓
D1. Data	x	x	x	x	✓
D3. On-demand Coordination	x	x	x	x	x
D4. Reusability	x	x	x	x	✓
D5. Transparency	x	x	✓	x	x

Table 1: Unlike existing tools, LEAM supports all of the design considerations ($D1 - D5$) outlined in Section 3.

D1. Enable integrated analytics. VITA systems should provide a single platform where users can directly manipulate (spreadsheets) and visualize (visualization tools) data while writing codes (notebooks) without context switching between tools.

D2. Specify operations declaratively. VITA systems should provide an expressive specification language to represent and communicate the entire breadth of workflows within the domain.

D3. Facilitate on-demand coordination. Within an integrated environment, VITA systems should enable users to specify coordination between all the available views on demand.

D4. Ensure reusability of operations. Users should be able to craft their analysis pipeline and share and reuse the workflow across use-cases.

D5. Ensure transparency of operations. VITA systems should ensure transparency of interactions on the interface—effect of direct manipulation and programmatic interactions should be immediately visible via visual cues or prompts.

4 LEAM User Interface

The four key components of the interface are a Code Editor, an Operations Menu, a Data View, and a Chart View. We discuss how these components enable integrated visual text analysis (**D1**).

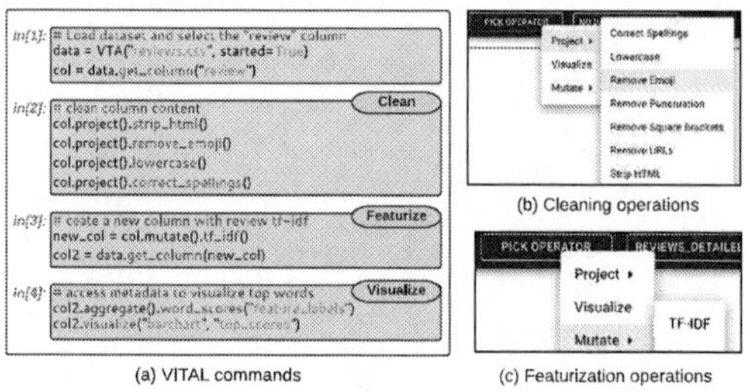

Figure 2: (a) Users writes scripts in Code Editor using the VITAL API for cleaning, featurizing, and visualizing data. Alternatively, users can also utilize the operators in Operations Menu, *e.g.*, cleaning (b) and featurization (c).

Code Editor and Operations Menu. While the Code Editor design (see Figure 1C) is inspired by computational notebooks, it only supports writing, editing, and executing scripts—visualizations and data tables are displayed separately in Chart View and Data View, respectively. The multi-view representation is intended to help users relate their workflows with the underlying data and their visualizations—a benefit of multiple coordinated views. Users can write scripts in the Code Editor in Python. We also implement a Python-based visual interactive text analysis library, VITAL, for issuing various text analysis and visualization operations in the Code Editor (discussed in Section 5). These operations are derived from an algebra for visual text analysis introduced in our prior work (Rahman et al., 2020). Users can also utilize the Operations Menu to execute built-in text analysis and visualization operations. Figure 2a shows an example workflow in the Code Editor consisting of data cleaning, featurization, and visualization operations. Users can also perform these operations from Operations Menu without writing any scripts (see Figure 2b, and 2c).

Data View. Data View (see Figure 1C) shows a tabular representation of the underlying data. The underlying data structure in LEAM is a dataframe. Data View is kept in sync with the dataframe—any changes made to the dataframe is immediately reflected in Data View (**D3**). For example, in Figure 3 when a user cleans the review column in the dataframe, the corresponding cleaned data is displayed in the Data View. In traditional script-based systems like computation notebooks, users are required to explicitly specify a print operation to view and inspect data.

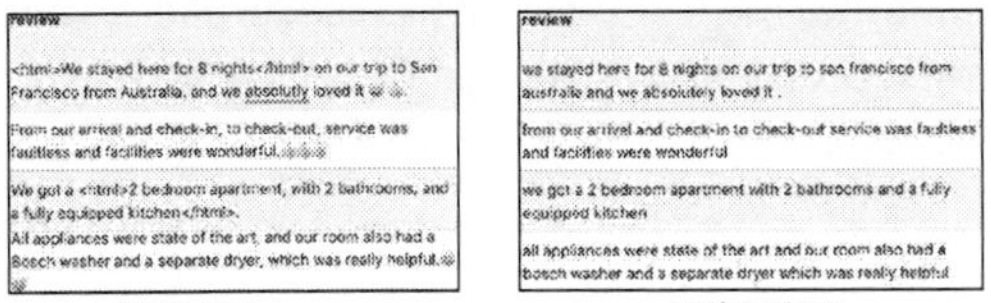

(a) Noisy text (b) Cleaned text

Figure 3: As (a) user performs various cleaning operations on the "review" column as shown in Figure 2, (b) the cleaned column data is immediately displayed in Data View (**D3**).

Chart View. LEAM enables users to generate visualizations either from the Code Editor or Operations Menu and displays those visualizations in the Chart View (see Figure 1B). Unlike computation notebooks, where analyzing visualizations in distant cells can be cumbersome, the side-by-side presentation of charts in Chart View enables users to compare and analyze related visualization without scrolling. We create the visualizations by extending Vega-Lite (Satyanarayan et al., 2016). These visualizations can be generated from Operations Menu or using VITAL commands and can be dynamically updated to add new interactions (discussed in Section 5).

5 Visual Text Analysis Using LEAM

The text analysis operations in LEAM are developed based on a visual text algebra, VTA (Rahman et al., 2020). LEAM provides a Python API called visual interactive text analysis library, VITAL, that enables users to write VTA commands in Code Editor. We now briefly introduce VTA and then demonstrate the corresponding specification library VITAL that we have developed.

5.1 VTA Operators and VITAL

VTA supports various operators for selecting a subset of the data (`selection`), transforming selected data into various representations for analysis (`transformation`), coordinating different views within the interface (`coordination`), and creating new operators by combining existing ones (`composition`). The JSON-style specification format of VTA is quite different from scripting languages widely used by analysts, such as R and Python. Composing operations in VTA can be cumbersome as users are required to specify multiple nested objects. Therefore, we have developed VITAL for declaratively specifying VTA commands in Code Editor of LEAM (**D2**). The VITAL commands are compiled and executed by the backend Python runtime of LEAM. We show several examples of VITAL commands that implement the VTA operators as well as newly introduced features next.

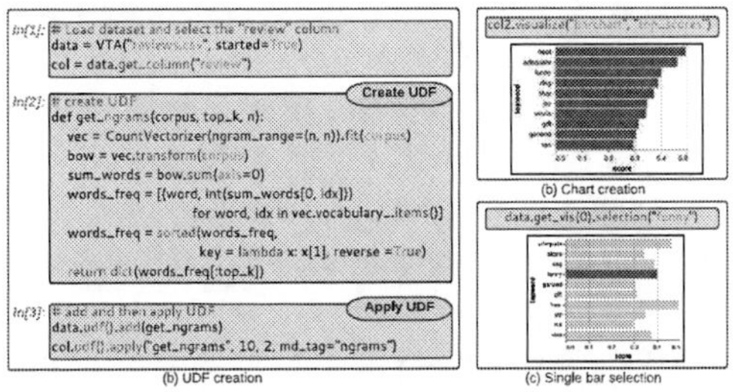

(b) UDF creation (b) Chart creation (c) Single bar selection

Figure 4: Declarative specification (**D2**): (a) using VITAL user creates and applies a UDF to compute top-K n-grams of reviews. Transparency (**D5**): (b) user generates a barchart of top words from Operation Menu which is logged as a VITAL script in Code Editor. Coordination (**D3**): (c) a user selected bar is highlighted on-demand.

5.2 Towards Integrated Text Analysis

We now explain how users can perform text analysis in LEAM.

5.2.1 User-guided Analysis

In Figure 2, we show how a user can analyze a text reviews dataset using various VITAL commands or menu operations like `project` (data cleaning) and `mutate` (featurization). Moreover, users can also combine multiple existing operators to declaratively specify user-defined operators (**D2**). For example, as shown in Figure 4, a user creates a new function to generate top n-grams in a given text corpus and then uses VITAL to load and then apply the UDF. Users can use the `visualize` command to create visualizations of the underlying data (see Figure 4b) and interactions (Figure 4c).

5.2.2 Programmatic Coordination

A key feature of LEAM is the ability to dynamically add coordination to existing visualizations using VITAL (**D3**). Existing libraries like Vega-Lite only allow users to predefine the visualization and corresponding interactions without supporting any dynamic coordination specification.

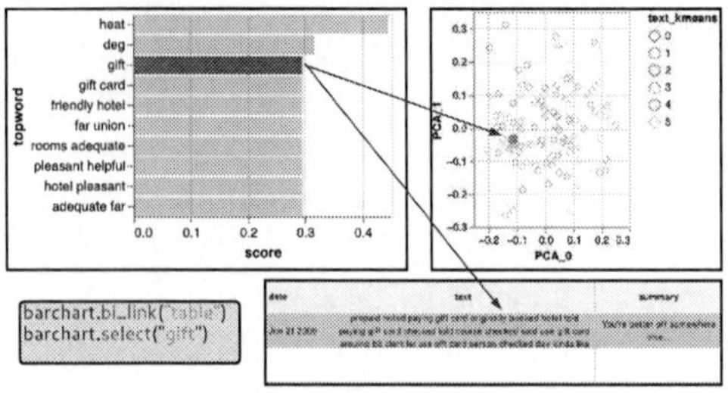

Figure 5: To relate a word in the chart with reviews both in Data View and the scatterplot (**D3**), the user issues a VITAL command in Code Editor (see inset). Clicking a bar in the barchart filters reviews in Data View and highlights relevant reviews in the scatterplot.

As shown in Figure 4c, users can update the selection type of the barchart in Figure 4b to enable single bar selection. Moreover, using VITAL, users can also dynamically specify external coordinations (a) among charts in the Chart View and (b) between Data View and charts. Vega-Lite does not provide a formal interaction grammar for such external coordination. For example, Figure 5 shows how users can enable coordination between the barchart, scatterplots, and data. Such dynamicity allows users to augment the visualizations instead of recreating charts and connect different views on demand to investigate data relationships. LEAM maintains a coordination graph to keep track of the linked views, which we discuss in Section 4.

5.2.3 Reusability and Transparency

Both VITAL and Operation Menu enable users to issue both analysis and coordination operations across different projects and workflows. Moreover, users can add their UDFs as new operators to VITAL and menu operations using the `add_UDF` command (see Figure 4a), thus ensuring reusability (**D4**). Users can also upload pre-trained models (*e.g.*, classification, regression) from Operations Menu and then access and reuse the models using the `get_model` and `predict` commands. To ensure transparency of the user interactions (**D5**) on the Operation Menu, LEAM logs the corresponding VITAL command in a new cell in Code Editor (see Figure 4b). The logging feature enables users to track their interactions, debug the logs if required, and re-execute those interactions.

6 LEAM Architecture

LEAM is developed as a web application and is implemented using ReactJS and Flask framework. We depict the architecture in Figure 6. LEAM client is responsible for capturing user input, and for rendering the views based on results returned by the back-end. Given any user interaction on the front end, the LEAM Request Processor issues a request to the backend LEAM Controller. This controller manages the uploaded data and sessions while propagating user interactions to the *session manager*.

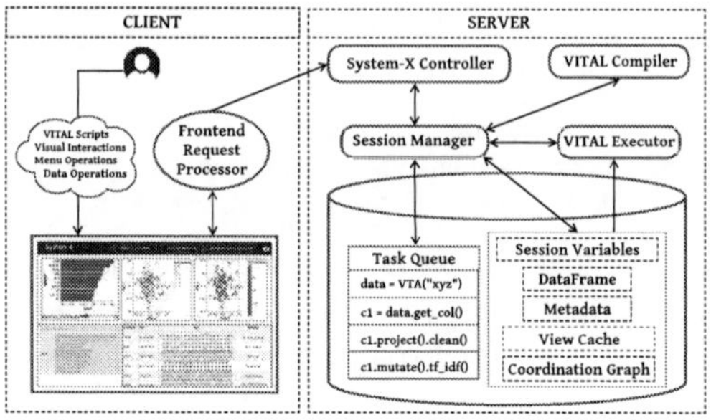

Figure 6: LEAM architecture. The front-end is a web application. The back-end features various components such as task queue, coordination graph, VITAL compiler, and executor to handle and execute user requests.

The session manager interprets the user interaction—any interactions on the Operations Menu is sent to a lightweight VTA Compiler while the VITAL commands on the Code Editor are pushed in a task queue. The VTA compiler translates the user-selected operator to a VITAL command which is then executed by the VTA Executor. LEAM backend employs a Task Queue to keep track of the VITAL commands in Code Editor. LEAM session manager also employs a View Cache to track the states of the front end views. LEAM employs a Coordination Graph to manage coordination among linked views—for any interaction on a view, all the views in its adjacency list are updated. For example, selecting a bar in the barchart in Figure 5 updates the scatterplot and Data View in its adjacency list.

7 Case Studies

To assess the impact of LEAM in performing visual text analysis and collect early feedback, we evaluated it through two case studies.

7.1 Study Design and Tasks

Design. The study consisted of three phases: (a) an introductory phase to help participants familiarize themselves with LEAM, (b) a workflow execution phase where the participants used LEAM to implement a text analysis workflow, and (c) a semi-structured interview to collect qualitative feedback regarding LEAM.

Participants. We recruited two participants within our professional network. Participant P_a was a researcher in natural language processing with extensive experience in review analysis and designing personal assistants and conversational bots. Participant P_b was a software engineer with experience in NLP pipelines and text analysis.

Tasks. We selected a spam detection workflow (Kaggle, 2021b) and a tweet analysis workflow (Kaggle, 2021a) from Kaggle, that are related to analyzing user-generated text as the respective tasks of our use cases. We chose the workflows based on their popularity and relevance to everyday text data analytics workflows in practice. For both the workflows, participants were provided pre-trained models. They were asked first to explore and preprocess a separate test dataset and then classify the data using the respective pre-trained model. For the preprocessing tasks, participants had to create a UDF. Participants were free to use any feature of LEAM or write code in Code Editor.

7.2 Observations

Both participants were able to complete their tasks with varying degrees of help from the experimenters. Participants appreciated the ability to perform the analysis both using Operations Menu (interactive) and Code Editor (declarative). They also found the user interface of LEAM more structured, commenting on the "messiness" of analysis using computational notebooks, also highlighted in prior work (Alspaugh et al., 2018). Moreover, participants found having visualizations within their eyesight without the need for scrolling up and down useful, a benefit of integrating multiple views (Rahman et al., 2021). They appreciated the ability to specify interactive coordination between visualizations and Data View using VITAL. P_a appreciated the ability to reuse operations from Operations Menu for bootstrapping the analysis.

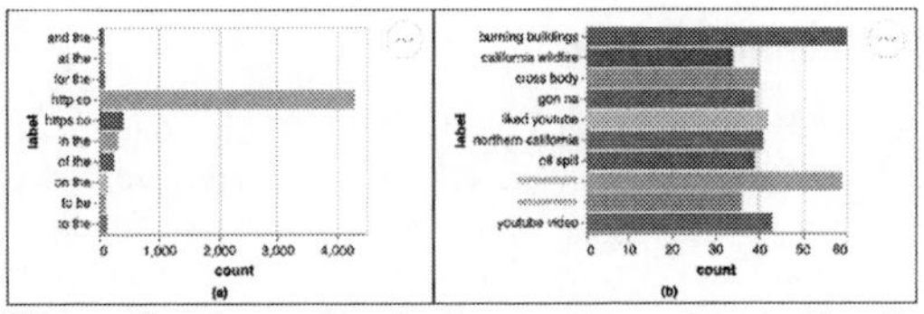

Figure 7: Bigram visualizations on Tweets dataset (Kaggle, 2021a) cleaned with a UDF. Users can immediately see the impact of the cleaning operation: (a) before and (b) after applying the UDF.

Participants also appreciated the ability to visualize the impact of their operations. Figure 7a displays a bi-gram visualization of the unprocessed tweets. After applying the cleaning operator on the tweets, the visualization was automatically updated (see Figure 7b). Such dynamic coordination highlights the importance of supporting context switching between stages in the data science pipeline, such as cleaning and visualization.

Participants also provided feedback for improvement. The most frequently raised issue was the need for improved communication of errors and the support for debugging, a requirement identified in earlier work (Chattopadhyay et al., 2020). Moreover, participants were occasionally confused about the effects of their operations, suggesting the need for visual guidance and better cues. Recent work explores such error detection methods for computational notebooks (Macke et al., 2021). Participants also pointed out a few syntactic inconsistencies of VITAL commands and suggested a more consistent design for ease of learning.

8 Conclusion and Future Work

This paper presents LEAM, a tool that enables users to perform interactive text analysis in-situ. Our declarative specification API VITAL provides support for a suite of operators to author diverse VITA workflows on-demand and enable different modes of interactive coordination among views. Preliminary evaluation of LEAM highlights the benefits of integrating multiple views, supporting both interactive and declarative specification of tasks, enabling reusability of operations, and ensuring transparency of interactions. While the initial results are promising, there is room for improvement in adding more transparency and providing wider operations coverage. LEAM can further benefit from addressing challenges related to scalability, workflow optimization, and version control that related work also explores.

References

Sara Alspaugh, Nava Zokaei, Andrea Liu, Cindy Jin, and Marti A Hearst. 2018. Futzing and moseying: Interviews with professional data analysts on exploration practices. *IEEE transactions on visualization and computer graphics*, 25(1):22–31.

Carenini et al. 2006. Interactive multimedia summaries of evaluative text. In *IUI*, pages 124–131.

Souti Chattopadhyay, Ishita Prasad, Austin Z Henley, Anita Sarma, and Titus Barik. 2020. What's wrong with computational notebooks? pain points, needs, and design opportunities. In *Proceedings of the 2020 CHI Conference on Human Factors in Computing Systems*, pages 1–12.

Codait. 2021. Text extensions for pandas.

Ian Drosos, Titus Barik, Philip J Guo, Robert DeLine, and Sumit Gulwani. 2020. Wrex: A unified programming-by-example interaction for synthesizing readable code for data scientists. In *ACM Human Factors in Computing Systems (CHI)*, pages 1–12.

Ashwin Ittoo, Antal van den Bosch, et al. 2016. Text analytics in industry: Challenges, desiderata and trends. *Computers in Industry*.

Project Jupyter. 2020. Project jupyter.

Kaggle. 2021a. Basic eda, cleaning and glove.

Kaggle. 2021b. Simple eda with data cleaning & glove.

Sean Kandel, Andreas Paepcke, Joseph Hellerstein, and Jeffrey Heer. 2011. Wrangler: Interactive visual specification of data transformation scripts. In *Proceedings of the SIGCHI Conference on Human Factors in Computing Systems*, pages 3363–3372.

Mary Beth Kery, Marissa Radensky, Mahima Arya, Bonnie E John, and Brad A Myers. 2018. The story in the notebook: Exploratory data science using a literate programming tool. In *Proceedings of the 2018 CHI Conference on Human Factors in Computing Systems*, pages 1–11.

Mary Beth Kery, Donghao Ren, Kanit Wongsuphasawat, Fred Hohman, and Kayur Patel. 2020. The future of notebook programming is fluid. In *Extended Abstracts of the 2020 CHI Conference on Human Factors in Computing Systems*, pages 1–8.

Kucher et al. 2018. The state of the art in sentiment visualization. In *Computer Graphics Forum*, volume 37, pages 71–96. Wiley Online Library.

Doris Lee. 2020. Lux: A python api for intelligent visual discovery.

Liu et al. 2018. Bridging text visualization and mining: A task-driven survey. *IEEE TVCG*, 25(7):2482–2504.

Stephen Macke, Hongpu Gong, Doris Lee, Andrew Head, Doris Xin, and Aditya Parameswaran. 2021. Fine-grained lineage for safer notebook interactions. *Proceedings of the VLDB Endowment*, 14(6):1093–1101.

Sajjadur Rahman, Mangesh Bendre, Yuyang Liu, Shichu Zhu, Zhaoyuan Su, Karrie Karahalios, and Aditya Parameswaran. 2021. Noah: Interactive spreadsheet exploration with dynamic hierarchical overviews. *Proceedings of the VLDB Endowment*, 14(6):970–983.

Sajjadur Rahman, Peter Griggs, and Çağatay Demiralp. 2020. Leam: An interactive system for in-situ visual text analysis. In *Conference on Innovative Data Systems Research*.

Adam Rule, Aurélien Tabard, and James D Hollan. 2018. Exploration and explanation in computational notebooks. In *Proceedings of the 2018 CHI Conference on Human Factors in Computing Systems*, pages 1–12.

Satyanarayan et al. 2016. Vega-lite: A grammar of interactive graphics. *IEEE TVCG*, 23(1):341–350.

Smith et al. 2020. The machine learning bazaar: Harnessing the ml ecosystem for effective system development. In *ACM SIGMOD*, pages 785–800.

Wang et al. 2000. Guidelines for using multiple views in information visualization. In *Proceedings of the working conference on Advanced visual interfaces*, pages 110–119. ACM.

Hadley Wickham. 2016. *ggplot2: elegant graphics for data analysis*. springer.

Yifan Wu, Joe Hellerstein, and Arvind Satyanarayan. 2020. B2: Bridging code and interactive visualization in computational notebooks. In *ACM UIST*.

Zhang et al. 2020a. Teddy: A system for interactive review analysis. In *SIGCHI*, pages 1–13.

Ge Zhang, Mike A Merrill, Yang Liu, Jeffrey Heer, and Tim Althoff. 2020b. Coral: Code representation learning with weakly-supervised transformers for analyzing data analysis. *arXiv preprint arXiv:2008.12828*.

Data Cleaning Tools for Token Classification Tasks

Karthik Muthuraman[2], **Frederick Reiss**[1,2], **Hong Xu**[2],
Bryan Cutler[2] and **Zachary Eichenberger**[1,3]
[1]IBM Research – Almaden, San Jose, CA 95120, USA
[2]IBM Center for Open Source Data and AI Technologies (CODAIT),
San Francisco, CA 94105, USA
[3]University of Michigan, Ann Arbor, MI 48109, USA
karthik.muthuraman@ibm.com, frreiss@us.ibm.com, hongx@ibm.com
bjcutler@us.ibm.com, zachary.eichen@gmail.com

Abstract

Human-in-the-loop systems for cleaning NLP training data rely on automated sieves to isolate potentially-incorrect labels for manual review. We have developed a novel technique for flagging potentially-incorrect labels with high sensitivity in named entity recognition corpora. We incorporated our sieve into an end-to-end system for cleaning NLP corpora, implemented as a modular collection of Jupyter notebooks built on extensions to the Pandas DataFrame library. We used this system to identify incorrect labels in the CoNLL-2003 corpus for English-language named entity recognition (NER), one of the most influential corpora for NER model research.

Unlike previous work that only looked at a subset of the corpus's validation fold, our automated sieve enabled us to examine the entire corpus in depth. Across the entire CoNLL-2003 corpus, we identified over 1300 incorrect labels (out of 35089 in the corpus).

We have published our corrections, along with the code we used in our experiments. We are developing a repeatable version of the process we used on the CoNLL-2003 corpus as an open-source library.

1 Introduction

Human-in-the-loop systems for cleaning NLP training data rely on automated sieves to isolate potentially-incorrect labels for manual review. In this work, a full version of which has been presented in (Reiss et al., 2020), we describe how we developed a novel technique for flagging potentially-incorrect labels with high sensitivity in named entity recognition corpora.

We implemented our sieve in the context of a set of extensions to the *Pandas*[1] DataFrame library. In addition to flagging errors, our extensions provide facilities for comparing NLP model results and visualizing model outputs and training data in context.

Because we built these facilities into the primary DataFrame library of the Python data analysis stack, we were able to construct an end-to-end system for NLP data cleaning as a series of Jupyter[2] notebooks. This design gives sophisticated users a view of the internals of the data cleaning process and allows for easy customization.

Our Jupyter notebooks comprises a pipeline that starts with training ensembles of models. Next, the system analyzes the outputs of the ensembles to identify potentially incorrect labels. Additional notebooks provide human annotators with a view of the suspicious labels in context. Later stages of the pipeline merge and analyze the results of manual annotation; then construct a corrected dataset and reports on the nature of the corrections.

We used this system to identify errors in the CoNLL-2003 NER corpus. The English-language portion of the CoNLL-2003 shared task (Tjong Kim Sang and De Meulder, 2003) (henceforth CoNLL-2003) is one of the most widely-used benchmarks for named entity recognition (NER) models. It consists of news articles from the Reuters RCV1 corpus (Lewis et al., 2004). Since its debut, CoNLL-2003 has played a central role in NLP research and continues to do so with more than 2300 citations. While researchers have relied heavily on the CoNLL-2003 corpus as a source of ground truth, few have paid attention to the corpus itself. Errors in the corpus could potentially mislead and even divert the course of future research.

Unlike previous analyses of this dataset that only examined small fractions of the CoNLL-2003 corpus, our work leveraged a high level of automation to analyze the entire corpus. We found over 1300 errors.

[1] https://pandas.pydata.org/

[2] https://jupyter.org

Proceedings of the 2nd Workshop on Data Science with Human in the Loop: Language Advances, pages 59–61
June 11, 2021.

2 Process

Our approach builds on previous work in semi-supervised labeling, with some key differences. Because we were looking for errors in a corpus that already had many high-quality labels, we needed a sieve with especially high sensitivity. We used ensembles of NER models trained on the corpus, and we focused on cases where the models agreed strongly on a particular label, but that label does not appear in the corpus. One of these ensembles was the outputs of the original 16 entries in the 2003 competition. We also trained two other 17-model ensembles ourselves by applying Gaussian random projections to the BERT embeddings space.

We developed extensions to the *Pandas* DataFrame library that enabled us to represent spans within documents as cells within a DataFrame. This facility allowed us to use DataFrames to track the spans of the entities that each of our models produced and to aggregate together the results across models. Using these capabilities, we developed Jupyter notebooks that analyzed our ensembles' outputs to identify labels that appeared in the outputs of multiple models but were not in the corpus.

We used our Pandas extension types' ability to render spans to HTML to view these spans in the context of the original document from within the same Jupyter notebooks.We started with labels that had a strong agreement among models and we progressed to labels with less agreement among models, the fraction of flagged labels that was actually incorrect decreased. When this fraction dropped below 20 percent, we stopped going through the ordered list of flagged labels. We had an inter annotation agreement and audit cycle for each correction made. In total, we made 12 passes (3 ensembles $\times$ 2 sets of labels $\times$ 2 human reviewers) of manual review over the `train` and `test` folds of the corpus and 8 passes over the `test` fold.

When we found that a label was incorrect, we coded the type of error and the required correction so that the error could be corrected automatically later on. We divided errors into several categories as explained in detail in the full version of this paper at (Reiss et al., 2020).

3 Corrections

In total, we examined 3182 labels our ensembles had flagged in the three folds of the corpus. We considered any label where fewer than 7 models

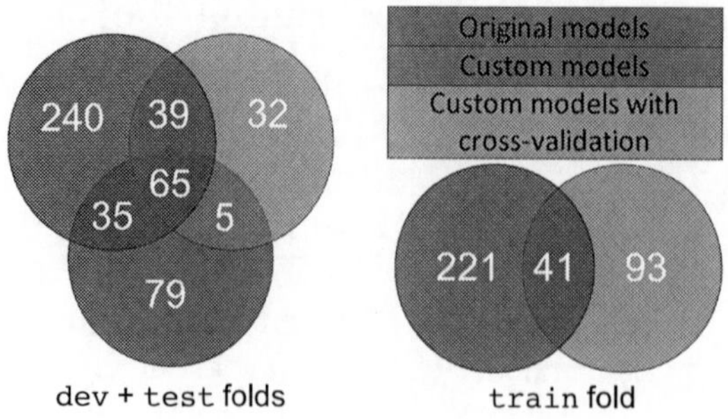

Figure 1: Number of errors flagged by different combinations of ensembles after filtering by human labelers.

agreed with the corpus label to be "flagged". Of these labels, 1274 came from the `test` fold, 854 came from the `dev` fold, and 1054 came from the `train` fold; accounting for 22.6%, 14.3%, and 4.5% of their folds, respectively. Figure 1 shows the split of final errors identified by ensemble and source.

Manual inspection determined that 850 of these 3182 entities (27%) were incorrect. We also found 475 additional incorrect entities in close proximity to the entities that our techniques flagged, for a total of 1320 incorrect labels across the corpus.

After identifying incorrect tags, spans and sentence boundaries, we created a corrected version of the original CoNLL-2003 dataset, which we refer to as the corrected CoNLL-2003 dataset.

4 Ongoing Work

While preparing our dataset of corrections for release, we identified additional improvements to the corrections. We have released a second version of the dataset containing these improvements plus some additional corrections pointed out by members of the open source NLP community.

We have released the code that we used in our experiments so far[3]. To facilitate the reuse of this code on other datasets, we are developing a more refined version of this code. Key changes that we are working on are reducing the number of passes of manual review required, simplifying the creation of ensembles of models, and extending the approach from NER to other token classification tasks like semantic role labeling. We plan to release these improvements.

[3] `https://github.com/CODAIT/text-extensions-for-pandas`

References

David D. Lewis, Yiming Yang, Tony G. Rose, and Fan Li. 2004. Rcv1: A new benchmark collection for text categorization research. *Journal of Machine Learning Research*, 5:361–397.

Frederick Reiss, Hong Xu, Bryan Cutler, Karthik Muthuraman, and Zachary Eichenberger. 2020. Identifying incorrect labels in the CoNLL-2003 corpus. In *Proceedings of the 24th Conference on Computational Natural Language Learning*, pages 215–226. Association for Computational Linguistics.

Erik F. Tjong Kim Sang and Fien De Meulder. 2003. Introduction to the CoNLL-2003 shared task: Language-independent named entity recognition. In *Proceedings of the SIGNLL Conference on Computational Natural Language Learning*, pages 142–147, USA. Association for Computational Linguistics.

Building Low-Resource NER Models Using Non-Speaker Annotations

Tatiana Tsygankova♮, Francesca Marini♮, Stephen Mayhew♭, Dan Roth♮
♮University of Pennsylvania, Philadelphia, PA, 19104
♭Duolingo, Pittsburgh, PA, 15206
ttasya@seas.upenn.edu, fmarini@seas.upenn.edu
stephen@duolingo.com, danroth@seas.upenn.edu

Abstract

In low-resource natural language processing (NLP), the key problems are a lack of target language training data, and a lack of native speakers to create it. Cross-lingual methods have had notable success in addressing these concerns, but in certain common circumstances, such as insufficient pre-training corpora or languages far from the source language, their performance suffers. In this work we propose a complementary approach to building low-resource Named Entity Recognition (NER) models using "non-speaker" (NS) annotations, provided by annotators with no prior experience in the target language. We recruit 30 participants in a carefully controlled annotation experiment with Indonesian, Russian, and Hindi. We show that use of NS annotators produces results that are consistently on par or better than cross-lingual methods built on modern contextual representations, and have the potential to outperform with additional effort. We conclude with observations of common annotation patterns and recommended implementation practices, and motivate how NS annotations can be used in addition to prior methods for improved performance.[1]

1 Introduction

Work in low-resource languages is not only academically compelling, breaking from popular use of massive compute power on unlimited English data, but also useful, resulting in improved digital tools for under-resourced communities. Two common strategies for low-resource NLP include (a) building cross-lingual models, and (b) annotating data in the target language.

Cross-lingual approaches — in which models are trained on some high-resource language, and applied to the target language — have been shown to be surprisingly effective (Wu and Dredze, 2019; Lample and Conneau, 2019). However, in common circumstances, such as when working with languages with insufficient training corpora or those far from the available source languages, cross-lingual methods suffer (Wu and Dredze, 2020; K et al., 2020). Absent sufficient cross-lingual methods, conventional wisdom suggests that only native (or fluent) speakers of a language can provide useful data to train NLP models. But in low-resource scenarios, fluent speakers may not be readily available.

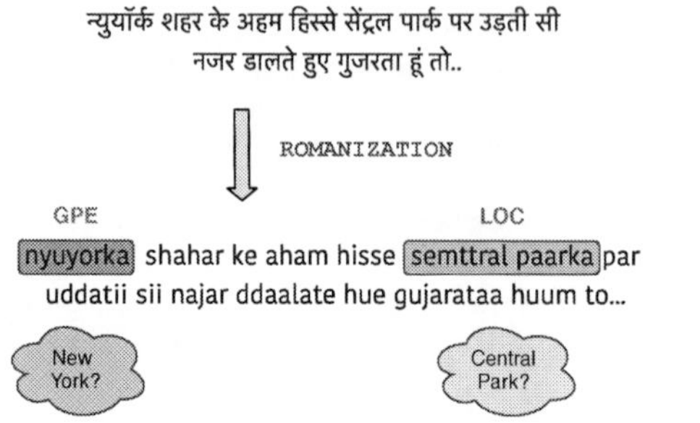

Figure 1: An example of how romanized Hindi text can be annotated without prior language knowledge.

To address this limitation, we hypothesize that the search for annotators can be extended beyond fluent speakers. In this work, we propose an unconventional approach for low-resource named entity recognition (NER) by getting annotations from annotators with no familiarity in the target language, referred to as "non-speaker" (NS) annotation. We posit that annotators are able to use phonetic, syntactic, and even semantic information from their languages of fluency to inform recognition. One example of how phonetic information can be used for NER annotation is shown in Figure 1.

We test our hypothesis in a carefully controlled annotation experiment, comparing the performance of non-speaker (NS) annotators

[1]For more details, see:
http://cogcomp.org/page/publication_view/941

Proceedings of the 2nd Workshop on Data Science with Human in the Loop: Language Advances, pages 62–69
June 11, 2021. ©2021 Association for Computational Linguistics

to that of fluent speakers (FS) in Indonesian, Russian, and Hindi.

Our findings are summarized in two key takeaways: (1) non-speaker annotators are able to produce useful annotations despite having no experience annotating or learning the target language; and (2) non-speaker annotations are on par or better than cross-lingual methods built on modern contextual representations. We conclude with observations over factors that can influence NS annotation quality, such as availability of a good romanization system, or presence of capitalization in the target language.

2 Related Work

Named Entity Recognition (NER) has been studied for many years (Ratinov and Roth, 2009; Lample et al., 2016; Ma and Hovy, 2016), with most focus on English and a few other European languages (Tjong Kim Sang and De Meulder, 2003).

Recently, there has been growing interest in low-resource NLP, with work in part-of-speech tagging (Plank and Agić, 2018), parsing (Rasooli and Collins, 2017), machine translation (Xia et al., 2019), and other fields. Low-resource NER has seen work using Wikipedia (Tsai et al., 2016), self attention (Xie et al., 2018), and multilingual contextual representations (Wu and Dredze, 2019).

There has been a small amount of work using non-speaker annotations (Mayhew et al., 2019a), but mainly as an application of a technique, falling short of the exhaustive study in this paper.

Several interfaces exist for non-speaker annotations in NER, including TALEN (Mayhew, 2018), which we use, ELISA IE (Lin et al., 2018), and Dragonfly (Costello et al., 2020), which performed small-scale experiments with non-speaker annotators.

A similar approach has been proposed for machine translation (Hermjakob et al., 2018b) and speech recognition (Chen et al., 2016). In the former case (assuming the translation direction is Foreign-to-English), it is often sufficient to translate several of the most important content words, then reconstruct the most likely sentence that uses these. In speech recognition, it is possible to listen to a language one does not speak, and produce a phonetic transcriptions that can be aggregated with others into a reasonable transcription, a process referred to as *mismatched crowdsourcing*.

Language	Script	Capitalization	Example
Indonesian	Latin	Yes	Amerika
Russian	Cyrillic	Yes	Америка
Hindi	Devanagari	No	अमेरिका

Table 1: Factors contributing to language difficulty, with examples of the English word "America."

3 Experimental Setup

Our experiment consisted of a series of trials, typically attended by 1–5 participants. Each trial ran for four hours and consisted of three tasks: (1) one-hour instructional training, (2) 20-minute English annotation exercise, and (3) series of five 30-minute sessions annotating documents in the target language.

Language Selection We chose three target languages: Indonesian, Russian, and Hindi. These languages were chosen based on availability of gold-annotated data and fluent speakers, and language difficulty.

The constraint of available fluent speakers for annotation, which we use as a point of comparison on non-speaker annotation performance, led us to choose mid- to high-resource languages for evaluation. To read accounts of similar techniques used on true low-resource languages, see the applications section (§4.3).

We define language difficulty as the task-specific difficulty experienced by an English speaker creating NER annotations in the target language. In practice, this difficulty mainly depends on script and capitalization, but may also depend on other factors such as language family and number of English loanwords. Under this task-specific definition and relevant properties summarized in Table 1, Indonesian is identified as the "easiest" language, Russian is "intermediate," and Hindi is the "hardest."

Participant Selection In total, there were 30 participants involved in the study, selected largely through a network of friends and acquaintances at the University of Pennsylvania. All participants were uniformly paid $10/hour for their time and were preliminarily screened for language exposure. We chose not to use crowd-sourcing platforms, such as Mechanical Turk, to allow flexibility in administration format and recruitment strategy. The methodology for the study was approved by the Institutional Review Board at the university.

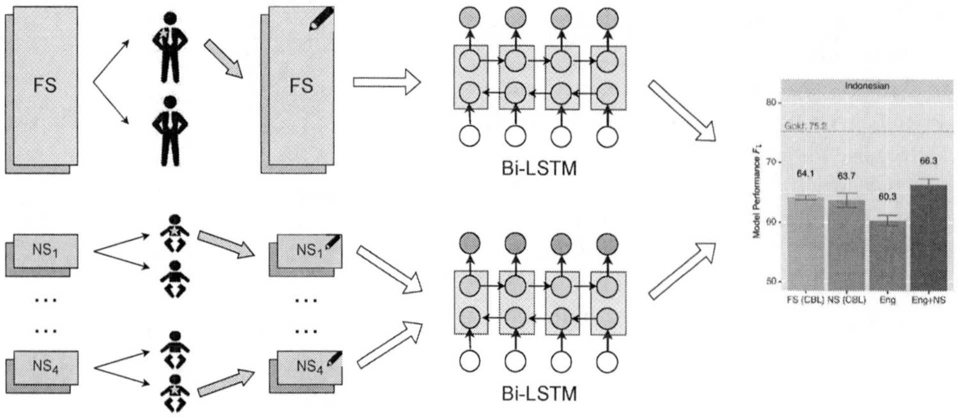

Figure 2: An overview of the data selection process involved in training models on the FS (fluent speaker) and NS (non-speaker) annotations. In each document set, the stars refer to annotators with the higher English exercise score, whose data is used in training. Details on model performance for each language are shown in Figure 3

Language	Train	Dev	Test
Indonesian	76K	18K	16K
Russian	59K	16K	16K
Hindi	72K	18K	20K

Table 2: Size of LORELEI datasets for each language, measured in tokens. Splits were created by the authors.

Language	FS	NS
Indonesian	19K	38K
Russian	28K	38K
Hindi	18K	45K

Table 3: Size of datasets produced by fluent speaker (FS) and non-speaker (NS) annotators, in tokens.

Data We used gold-annotated NER data from the LORELEI project (Strassel and Tracey, 2016; Tracey et al., 2019). This data uses 4 entity tags: Person, Organization, Location, and Geo-political Entity. We created splits of these datasets ourselves, statistics of which can be seen in Table 2. These corpora are not parallel.

Accounting for annotation speed differences, FS and NS annotators were given document sets of different sizes to annotate during the same time frame. Each document set used in the experiment was annotated by at least two participants. (visual reference in Figure 2).

Task 1: Instructional Training In total, two instructional documents were used – one providing an overview of the task goals and annotation software, and the other outlining key annotation principles in the form of an interactive annotation guideline quiz. The annotation software used was TALEN (Mayhew, 2018), a tool designed for annotating named entities when the annotators don't speak the target language.

Task 2: English Annotation Exercise After the quiz, participants were asked to annotate English LORELEI data for 20 minutes. The goal of this exercise was both to familiarize the participants with the software interface and provide an indicator of their annotator potential and understanding of the annotation guidelines, used later to filter out low-quality annotators.

Task 3: Target Language Annotation Sessions Participants completed their 2.5 hours of annotation in 5 sessions of 30 minutes each. All FS annotators spent their time annotating documents in their native language, while NS annotators worked with foreign languages that they had no prior exposure to. Given that all of the languages used in the study were high- to mid-resource, annotators were given explicit instructions not to use external model resources such as Google Translate, but were allowed to use internet search to determine the nature of the entities. For Russian and Hindi, which do not use Latin script, we provided uroman (Hermjakob et al., 2018a) romanization, so that the script was not a barrier to successful annotation (Figure 1).

Summary statistics of the annotated documents can be found in Table 3. Note that the larger annotated data size from the NS annotators reflects the fact that there were more NS annotators than FS annotators, a choice we deliberately made.

Language	FS P	FS R	FS F_1	NS P	NS R	NS F_1
Indonesian	80.6	75.6	78.0	59.8	55.7	57.7
Russian	69.0	67.3	68.1	57.0	45.9	50.9
Hindi	85.5	80.4	82.9	59.8	33.4	42.8

Table 4: Annotation quality of annotations collected from fluent speaker (FS) and non-speaker (NS) annotators against the gold data.

	Annotation Time (hr)				
Language	0.5	1	1.5	2	2.5
Indonesian	55.5	54.7	57.8	57.3	57.5
Russian	42.5	47.5	47.5	49.7	50.6
Hindi	24.5	32.3	41.1	40.3	41.8

Table 5: Changes in mean annotation quality of non-speaker (NS) annotations over time show an upwards trajectory that steepens with language difficulty.

4 Experiments & Analysis

This section describes the analysis done on the gathered FS and NS annotations, through the setup of our models and metrics used and key experimental takeaways.

4.1 Models & Metrics

Two Performance Measures In this work, we report two distinct F_1 performance measures: *Annotation Quality* and *Model Performance*.

Annotation Quality refers to the results of participant annotation compared to the existing gold annotations on the same documents. In this evaluation, no model is trained, and we simply calculate the F_1 scores by treating NS annotations as predictions themselves (results reported in Tables 3 and 5).

In contrast, *Model Performance* refers to the more traditional NER setup, in which we train a model over obtained annotations, and predict on some held out test set. The following sections outline the results of this performance metric (results reported in Figure 3).

Data Preparation To account for random errors, we prioritized recruiting at least two participants to annotate each document set. We then used English exercise scores to choose between the resulting conflicting annotations for the same document sets. A summary of the data selection process is shown in Figure 2.

In order to ensure that documents lacking annotations were considered to be NS annotator mistakes rather than negative training examples, we removed all empty documents from the NS data before training. No other pre-processing was done.

Machine Learning Models For all experiments, we used a standard BiLSTM-CRF model (Ma and Hovy, 2016) implemented in AllenNLP (Gardner et al., 2018), and used multilingual BERT embeddings (Devlin et al., 2019), which have been shown to exhibit surprising cross-lingual properties (Wu and Dredze, 2019). For the sake of speed and simplicity, we use BERT embeddings as features, and do not fine-tune the model. For each dataset, we train with 5 random seeds (Reimers and Gurevych, 2017) and report the average.

We recognize that these annotations are missing many entities. Following recent work on partial annotations, we use an iterative method from (Mayhew et al., 2019a) called Constrained Binary Learning (CBL) that detects unmarked tokens likely to be entities and down-weights them in training. Subsequent results reported use this method on all FS and NS annotations.

Baseline Comparisons Given that there is little prior work on this subject, it's hard to compare our results against an established baseline. To contextualize our results, we compare NS models against FS models and cross-lingual methods. However, both are imperfect comparisons and should be interpreted with caution.

In our comparison with FS models, the main difficulty is unequal training data size. Our experimental design intentionally left us with more NS annotations than FS annotations (see Table 3). It might be tempting to address this difficulty by balancing data sizes, however constraining the NS annotations to the sizes of the FS data would not give a fair comparison: the imbalance reflects the real-life scenario in which non-speakers of a language are far easier to find than speakers of the language, who may not be available at all.

In our comparison with cross-lingual models, the main difficulty is the strength of pre-trained embeddings for the baseline models. As a strong language-independent baseline for existing cross-lingual methods, we trained models on English NER data and evaluated on the target language test data (experiments with related languages showed similar results, and were omitted for space constraints). Our experimental decision

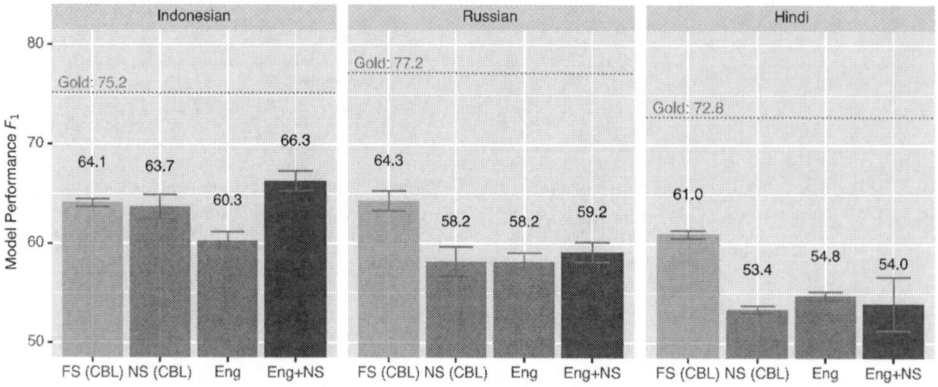

Figure 3: Comparison of models trained on fluent speaker (FS) and non-speaker (NS) annotations to English cross-lingual models, showing comparable or improved performance across all languages. Error bars show one standard deviation calculated over five trials. CBL refers to Constrained Binary Learning. The Eng+NS model is trained on the concatenation of English and NS data. The dashed lines refer to the performance of models trained on the gold annotated training set.

to use relatively high-resource languages meant that mBERT models had access to reasonably large amounts of pre-training data (each language was in the top 50 by Wikipedia size), and are therefore unfairly strong. One would expect cross-lingual performance to decrease on lower resource languages (Wu and Dredze, 2020).

4.2 Main Results

Figure 3 summarizes the results of this experiment by providing a comparison of models trained on non-speaker (NS) and fluent speaker (FS) annotations to cross-lingual models. From these results we distill two main takeaways.

Takeaway 1: NS Annotation Works

The results of our experiments show that across all languages, non-speaker annotations have produced meaningful results. In Indonesian, NS models are evidently strong and perform at a similar level to models trained on fluent-speaker annotations. This is likely attributable to the high entity overlap between English and Indonesian and limited language-specific information required for successful annotation. In practice, this indicates that 2.5 hours of language exposure was enough for NS annotators to produce annotations with quality sufficient enough to be useful.

The gap between NS and FS model performance widens on other languages, and correlates with an annotation quality drop. This suggests that 2.5 hours are not sufficient to produce NS annotations rivaling FS models (however, as we will see in Takeaway 2, this is sufficient to rival cross-lingual baselines). One reason is that in more difficult languages, annotators need more time to become acquainted with the language, so we could expect more substantial improvements over time. To test this hypothesis, we examined mean annotation quality trends of NS annotators, summarized in Table 5. Across all languages, we see annotators improving over time. For Russian and Hindi in particular, we observe a more overt learning curve indicating that there are more nuances to these languages which must be noticed by annotators over time. This upwards positive trend in annotation quality suggests that the NS results reported here are not the peak results that could be achieved. With additional training and experience, NS annotators can produce stronger results even in more difficult languages.

Takeaway 2: NS Remains On Par With Cross-Lingual Baselines

In Figure 3, across all languages performance of models built on NS annotations (blue bars) consistently matches or exceeds the performance of cross-lingual models (red bars). Again, in a low-resource scenario we might expect cross-lingual model performance to drop substantially, so the fact that they are comparable in this situation is encouraging. Additional experiments combining NS and English data (purple bars) shows improvements in Indonesian and Russian, but inconclusive changes in Hindi. Altogether, these results demonstrate that using NS annotations is one of the most effective available ways of building an NER model in a low-resource scenario.

While an unexpected observation shows that FS scores are always 15–20 points below models trained on gold-annotated data, we hypothesize that this difference is mainly attributed to training level and not language ability (Geva et al., 2019).

4.3 Low-resource Applications

Although the use of non-speaker annotators has little representation in the research community, there have been several projects that lean on this idea heavily. In the LORELEI evaluations,[2] research groups were tasked with producing NLP tools on truly low-resource languages (including Kinyarwanda, Sinhalese, Ilocano, and Odiya) within a short time frame. A number of new techniques came out of these evaluations, and many groups resorted to using non-speaker annotators (Cheung et al., 2017; Mayhew et al., 2017, 2018, 2019b). In each group, annotators were trained more thoroughly than in the empirical study here, and exhibited a more focused and long-term effort. However, in these projects, the goal was to maximize the final score, not make careful observations of the annotation process. This paper fulfills that need.

5 Discussion

While Section 4 showed quantitative outcomes of experimental processes, this section explores the many factors that can contribute to obtaining high quality NS annotations.

NS Annotation Practices & Strengths When capitalization is available in the target language, it is a strong indicator for named entities. Analyzing NS annotations over languages with capitalization – Indonesian and Russian – shows that over 90% of annotated tokens are capitalized, a rate similar to what we would expect in English.

For languages with non-Latin scripts – Russian and Hindi – NS annotators often relied on phonetic clues and always annotated on romanized versions of the text. Having access to well-romanized text is critical, as it helps NS annotators make connections between English cognates or previously tagged entities. Some real examples of phonetically recognizable entities from Hindi are:

paakistaan, biibiisii hindii, baamglaadesh

A majority of entities tagged in languages with no capitalization are either geo-political entities (i.e. Pakistan, America) or well-known Western names (i.e. Obama, Twitter, BBC). Once an annotator learns a word representation in the target language, they tend to tag every instance as an entity. As a result, we found that NS annotators tend to tag a proportionally less diverse set of entities than FS annotators.

What makes a good annotator? Analyzing participant language familiarity and instructional quiz scores shows that neither multilingualism nor initial guideline understanding present a clear predictor for good annotators. Participants who performed best were detail-oriented, patient, and often proactively vocalized their interest in the task or the top annotator award incentive.

One strength of human non-speaker annotators to annotate NER is that, unlike an automatic system, they are able to make inferences over common sense world knowledge. For example, they may use a header to pick out the domain of a document, or use neighboring entities to inform decisions, as in Figure 1, where the presence of *New York* suggests *Central Park* as an entity.

How does this generalize to other tasks? Looking to other NLP tasks, it seems clear that NS annotations of conceptually in-depth tasks such as dependency parsing or textual entailment are unlikely to have usable quality. However, for tasks such as part of speech tagging, it could be possible, especially with the help of a tag lexicon and an elementary grammar.

6 Conclusion

We demonstrate the effectiveness of using non-speaker annotations as an alternative to cross-lingual methods for building low-resource NER models. A qualitative exploration of the resulting data provides insights about what makes NS annotators so unintuitively successful. One avenue for future exploration is with active learning (Settles, 2009), which has been shown to help in low-resource situations (Chaudhary et al., 2019). Further work may also explore optimal ways to combine NS annotators with FS annotators, should they be available.

[2]https://www.nist.gov/itl/iad/mig/lorehlt-evaluations

7 Acknowledgement

This work was supported by Contract HR0011-18-2-0052 and Contract HR0011-15-C-0113 with the US Defense Advanced Research Projects Agency (DARPA). Approved for Public Release, Distribution Unlimited. The views expressed are those of the authors and do not reflect the official policy or position of the Department of Defense or the U.S. Government.

References

Aditi Chaudhary, Jiateng Xie, Zaid Sheikh, Graham Neubig, and Jaime Carbonell. 2019. A little annotation does a lot of good: A study in bootstrapping low-resource named entity recognizers. In *Proceedings of the 2019 Conference on Empirical Methods in Natural Language Processing and the 9th International Joint Conference on Natural Language Processing (EMNLP-IJCNLP)*, pages 5164–5174, Hong Kong, China. Association for Computational Linguistics.

Wenda Chen, Mark Hasegawa-Johnson, and Nancy F Chen. 2016. Mismatched crowdsourcing based language perception for under-resourced languages. *Procedia Computer Science*, 81:23–29.

Leon Cheung, Thamme Gowda, Ulf Hermjakob, Nelson Liu, Jonathan May, Alexandra Mayn, Nima Pourdamghani, Michael Pust, Kevin Knight, Nikolaos Malandrakis, et al. 2017. ELISA system description for LoReHLT 2017.

Cash Costello, Shelby Anderson, Caitlyn Bishop, James Mayfield, and Paul McNamee. 2020. Dragonfly: Advances in non-speaker annotation for low resource languages. In *LREC*.

Jacob Devlin, Ming-Wei Chang, Kenton Lee, and Kristina Toutanova. 2019. BERT: Pre-training of deep bidirectional transformers for language understanding. In *Proceedings of the 2019 Conference of the North American Chapter of the Association for Computational Linguistics: Human Language Technologies, Volume 1 (Long and Short Papers)*, pages 4171–4186, Minneapolis, Minnesota. Association for Computational Linguistics.

Matt Gardner, Joel Grus, Mark Neumann, Oyvind Tafjord, Pradeep Dasigi, Nelson F. Liu, Matthew Peters, Michael Schmitz, and Luke Zettlemoyer. 2018. AllenNLP: A deep semantic natural language processing platform. In *Proceedings of Workshop for NLP Open Source Software (NLP-OSS)*, pages 1–6, Melbourne, Australia. Association for Computational Linguistics.

Mor Geva, Yoav Goldberg, and Jonathan Berant. 2019. Are we modeling the task or the annotator? an investigation of annotator bias in natural language understanding datasets. In *Proceedings of the 2019 Conference on Empirical Methods in Natural Language Processing and the 9th International Joint Conference on Natural Language Processing (EMNLP-IJCNLP)*, pages 1161–1166, Hong Kong, China. Association for Computational Linguistics.

Ulf Hermjakob, Jonathan May, and Kevin Knight. 2018a. Out-of-the-box universal Romanization tool uroman. In *Proceedings of ACL 2018, System Demonstrations*, pages 13–18, Melbourne, Australia. Association for Computational Linguistics.

Ulf Hermjakob, Jonathan May, Michael Pust, and Kevin Knight. 2018b. Translating a language you don't know in the Chinese room. In *Proceedings of ACL 2018, System Demonstrations*, pages 62–67, Melbourne, Australia. Association for Computational Linguistics.

Karthikeyan K, Zihan Wang, Stephen Mayhew, and Dan Roth. 2020. Cross-Lingual Ability of Multilingual BERT: An Empirical Study.

Guillaume Lample, Miguel Ballesteros, Sandeep Subramanian, Kazuya Kawakami, and Chris Dyer. 2016. Neural architectures for named entity recognition. In *Proceedings of the 2016 Conference of the North American Chapter of the Association for Computational Linguistics: Human Language Technologies*, pages 260–270, San Diego, California. Association for Computational Linguistics.

Guillaume Lample and Alexis Conneau. 2019. Cross-lingual language model pretraining. *arXiv preprint arXiv:1901.07291*.

Ying Lin, Cash Costello, Boliang Zhang, Di Lu, Heng Ji, James Mayfield, and Paul McNamee. 2018. Platforms for non-speakers annotating names in any language. In *Proceedings of ACL 2018, System Demonstrations*, pages 1–6, Melbourne, Australia. Association for Computational Linguistics.

Xuezhe Ma and Eduard Hovy. 2016. End-to-end sequence labeling via bi-directional LSTM-CNNs-CRF. In *Proceedings of the 54th Annual Meeting of the Association for Computational Linguistics (Volume 1: Long Papers)*, pages 1064–1074, Berlin, Germany. Association for Computational Linguistics.

Stephen Mayhew. 2018. TALEN: Tool for Annotation of Low-resource ENtities. In *ACL Demonstrations*.

Stephen Mayhew, Snigdha Chaturvedi, Chen-Tse Tsai, and Dan Roth. 2019a. Named Entity Recognition with Partially Annotated Training Data. In *Proc. of the Conference on Computational Natural Language Learning (CoNLL)*.

Stephen Mayhew, Chase Duncan, Mark Sammons, Chen-Tse Tsai, Dan Roth, Xin Li, Haojie Pan, Sheng Zhou, Jennifer Zou, and Yangqiu Song. 2017. University of Illinois LoReHLT17 Submission. Technical report.

Stephen Mayhew, Tatiana Tsygankova, Francesca Marini, Zihan Wang, Jane Lee, Xiaodong Yu, Xingyu Fu, Weijia Shi, Zian Zhao, Wenpeng Yin, Karthikeyan K, Jamaal Hay, Michael Shur, Jennifer Sheffield, and Dan Roth. 2019b. University of Pennsylvania LoReHLT 2019 Submission. Technical report.

Stephen Mayhew, Shyam Upadhyay, Wenpeng Yin, Lucia Huo, Devanshu Jain, Prasanna Poudyal, Tatiana Tsygankova, Yihao Chen, Xin Li, Nitish Gupta, Chase Duncan, Mark Sammons, Jennifer Sheffield, and Dan Roth. 2018. University of Pennsylvania LoReHLT 2018 Submission. Technical report.

Barbara Plank and Željko Agić. 2018. Distant supervision from disparate sources for low-resource part-of-speech tagging. In *Proceedings of the 2018 Conference on Empirical Methods in Natural Language Processing*, pages 614–620, Brussels, Belgium. Association for Computational Linguistics.

Mohammad Sadegh Rasooli and Michael Collins. 2017. Cross-lingual syntactic transfer with limited resources. *Transactions of the Association for Computational Linguistics*, 5:279–293.

Lev Ratinov and Dan Roth. 2009. Design Challenges and Misconceptions in Named Entity Recognition. In *Proc. of the Conference on Computational Natural Language Learning (CoNLL)*.

Nils Reimers and Iryna Gurevych. 2017. Reporting score distributions makes a difference: Performance study of LSTM-networks for sequence tagging. In *Proceedings of the 2017 Conference on Empirical Methods in Natural Language Processing*, pages 338–348, Copenhagen, Denmark. Association for Computational Linguistics.

Burr Settles. 2009. Active learning literature survey. Technical report, University of Wisconsin-Madison Department of Computer Sciences.

Stephanie Strassel and Jennifer Tracey. 2016. LORELEI language packs: Data, tools, and resources for technology development in low resource languages. In *Proceedings of the Tenth International Conference on Language Resources and Evaluation (LREC 2016)*, pages 3273–3280, Portorož, Slovenia. European Language Resources Association (ELRA).

Erik F. Tjong Kim Sang and Fien De Meulder. 2003. Introduction to the CoNLL-2003 shared task: Language-independent named entity recognition. In *Proceedings of the Seventh Conference on Natural Language Learning at HLT-NAACL 2003*, pages 142–147.

Jennifer Tracey, Stephanie Strassel, Ann Bies, Zhiyi Song, Michael Arrigo, Kira Griffitt, Dana Delgado, Dave Graff, Seth Kulick, Justin Mott, and Neil Kuster. 2019. Corpus building for low resource languages in the DARPA LORELEI program. In *Proceedings of the 2nd Workshop on Technologies for MT of Low Resource Languages*, pages 48–55, Dublin, Ireland. European Association for Machine Translation.

Chen-Tse Tsai, Stephen Mayhew, and Dan Roth. 2016. Cross-Lingual Named Entity Recognition via Wikification. In *Proc. of the Conference on Computational Natural Language Learning (CoNLL)*.

Shijie Wu and Mark Dredze. 2019. Beto, bentz, becas: The surprising cross-lingual effectiveness of BERT. In *Proceedings of the 2019 Conference on Empirical Methods in Natural Language Processing and the 9th International Joint Conference on Natural Language Processing (EMNLP-IJCNLP)*, pages 833–844, Hong Kong, China. Association for Computational Linguistics.

Shijie Wu and Mark Dredze. 2020. Are all languages created equal in multilingual bert? In *Proceedings of the 5th Workshop on Representation Learning for NLP*. Association for Computational Linguistics.

Mengzhou Xia, Xiang Kong, Antonios Anastasopoulos, and Graham Neubig. 2019. Generalized data augmentation for low-resource translation. In *Proceedings of the 57th Annual Meeting of the Association for Computational Linguistics*, pages 5786–5796, Florence, Italy. Association for Computational Linguistics.

Jiateng Xie, Zhilin Yang, Graham Neubig, Noah A. Smith, and Jaime Carbonell. 2018. Neural cross-lingual named entity recognition with minimal resources. In *Proceedings of the 2018 Conference on Empirical Methods in Natural Language Processing*, pages 369–379, Brussels, Belgium. Association for Computational Linguistics.

Evaluating and Explaining Natural Language Generation with GenX

Kayla Duskin
Data Science and Analytics Group
Pacific Northwest National Laboratory
kayla.duskin@pnnl.gov

Shivam Sharma
Department of Computer Science
New Jersey Institute of Technology
ss4354@njit.edu

Ji Young Yun
Visual Analytics Group
Pacific Northwest National Laboratory
jiyoung.yun@pnnl.gov

Emily Saldanha
Data Science and Analytics Group
Pacific Northwest National Laboratory
emily.saldanha@pnnl.gov

Dustin Arendt
Visual Analytics Group
Pacific Northwest National Laboratory
dustin.arendt@pnnl.gov

Abstract

Current methods for evaluation of natural language generation models focus on measuring text quality but fail to probe the model creativity, i.e., its ability to generate novel but coherent text sequences not seen in the training corpus. We present the GenX tool which is designed to enable interactive exploration and explanation of natural language generation outputs with a focus on the detection of memorization. We demonstrate the tool on two domain-conditioned generation use cases — phishing emails and ACL abstracts.

1 Introduction

The capabilities of natural language generation (NLG) models have grown rapidly in recent years, with state-of-the-art models such as GPT-3 (Brown et al., 2020) able to produce text that is often indistinguishable from human-written text. Despite this progress, there are many remaining challenges in effectively evaluating the quality of machine text generations. Most existing evaluation approaches rely on human evaluation of the quality, fluency, and realism of a sample of generated outputs in combination with automated metrics that attempt to replicate these human judgements. However, this focus on text *quality* disregards several other key evaluation dimensions such as the *creativity* of the model and the degree of training set *memorization*.

An NLG model that simply reproduces long text snippets from the training data is likely to achieve high quality, but does not represent the ability of the model to creatively generate novel text sequences. This can contribute to an inappropriate belief in the model's sophistication if users are not aware the generated text is copied wholesale from the training data. Data scientists developing NLG models are not likely to be familiar enough with a given training corpus to detect this problem from the NLG model output without additional tool support.

A second related issue arises more generally when text datasets collected from multiple sources are used to train machine learning models. In this case, identical text substrings can inadvertently end up on both sides of a train-test split. This can lead to artificially inflated model performance metrics, especially in deep learning models, having sufficient parameters to enable input memorization and shortcut generalization. While detection of exact duplicates is straightforward, detection of partial, sub-document duplication is more challenging.

To address these issues, we present the GenX [1] tool which is designed to enable data scientists to understand the provenance of the output of a text generation model. Specifically, GenX lets users understand which sentences or passages from a generated text output are very similar to sentences in the model's training input. It compares sentences in the output text to text that the model was trained on and renders a marked up version of the text to indicate what parts of the text may have been memorized from the training data. The tool also lets the user find interesting text based on pre-computed statistics related to this potential memorization.

[1] Source: https://github.com/pnnl/genx

Proceedings of the 2nd Workshop on Data Science with Human in the Loop: Language Advances, pages 70–78
June 11, 2021.

2 Related Work

Language generation metrics Many NLG tasks are framed as supervised sequence-to-sequence problems, such as in the case of machine translation. Metrics for such tasks evaluate the similarity between a candidate sentence and a set of reference sentences. There are wide range of automated metrics including BLEU (Papineni et al., 2002), SARI (Xu et al., 2016), BLUERT (Sellam et al., 2020), and GLEU (Wu et al., 2016). These metrics have been shown to have mixed success in terms of replicating the intuition of humans regarding text quality (Novikova et al., 2017).

For open domain NLG models, datasets such as Penn Tree Bank (Marcus et al., 1994) or LAMBADA (Paperno et al., 2016) are commonly used for evaluation. However, these datasets cannot help when models are meant to be constrained to a certain domain, and they do not consider long-form text generation, only text completion tasks. Another common method is to leverage the trained model for downstream tasks to assess the quality of the language model (Radford et al., 2019). Work by (Hashimoto et al., 2019) has proposed combining human and statistical evaluation to measure the quality and diversity of generated text.

Domain-conditioned text generation NLG models can be evaluated by their perplexity calculated on a held out data set. While perplexity is useful for measuring model performance, it has limitations in measuring quality (Theis et al., 2015) and is typically is calculated at the model level, without taking in to consideration differences in generated text that result from different decoding strategies that affect the quality of the output.

Evaluating memorization in language generation In comparison to work related to text quality measures, less work has been dedicated to the evaluation of memorization in NLG models. In addition to its direct bearing on model creativity, memorization of training data in generation models has significant privacy implications, especially in domains that include sensitive information such as social media data or clinical notes. Previous efforts to evaluate memorization have focused on the leakage of sensitive information by adding "secret" information to the training data and evaluating the perplexity of the inserted secret during generation (Carlini et al., 2019). There as been little previous work on looking for memorization more generally in order to evaluate model creativity.

Evaluating test set contamination A number of recent works have identified issues in natural language processing datasets with text overlap and near-duplication in training and testing sets leading to artificially inflated performance metrics. Such issues have been identified in question answering datasets (Lewis et al., 2020) and large software and code corpora (Allamanis, 2019). Language modeling benchmarks have also been shown to exhibit this issue. For instance, the Billion Word Benchmark has a 13% overlap between train and test 8 grams (Radford et al., 2019). Language models trained on large datasets scraped from the web also pose a risk for test set contamination. Brown et al. (2020) evaluate the impact of test example presence in the pre-training set on GPT-3 for some of their benchmark test sets using 13-gram overlap. They find a substantial amount of overlap between their pretraining data and test data (>50% for a quarter of the benchmarks), but noted that manual inspection of the overlapping examples showed a significant number of false positives.

Interactive/explanation tools Previous work has largely focused on developing methods for automated quantitative evaluation of generation quality, but fewer efforts have been applied to the development of interactive tools to explain and understand the generation of individual examples. The *compare-mt* tool automates the comparison of multiple NLG models according to traditional BLEU-type metrics as well as providing more detailed breakdowns of accuracies by word or sentence type (Neubig et al., 2019). The *VizSeq* tool provides an interactive interface to explore metric performance on the full corpus, groups of instances, and individual examples (Wang et al., 2019). The existing tools are largely focused on text quality evaluation rather than memorization evaluation and are designed specifically for supervised generation tasks such as translation rather than open-domain or domain-conditioned generation tasks.

Anti-plagiarism software Anti-plagiarism tools also aim at quantifying similarity between texts. Many such tools are proprietary, reference against an existing database of published work, and consider each document on an individual basis. In contrast, GenX allows for referencing against specific training text and is meant to assess a collection of generated documents as a whole. Additionally, in NLG not all "copying" is bad, and GenX characterizes any matching text segments through metrics that go beyond a binary classification.

3 GenX Tool & Implementation

GenX is implemented as a Jupyter Notebook[2] widget[3], which allows for an interactive user experience that is tightly integrated with a popular computational environment for data science. The widget is implemented in two parts: a Python side, which performs preprocessing and integration with the Jupyter environment, and a JavaScript side, which handles rendering user interaction. The inputs to GenX are Pandas[4] DataFrames for the raw text (each row in the data frame corresponds a sentence), the corresponding sentence-level embedding representation of that text, and an identifier for which document the sentence belongs to. GenX requires that the raw text and embeddings are also split into train and test sets. The test set may either be text generated from an NLG model or the test split of the real data. Thus GenX inputs are *train text*, *train embedding*, *test text*, and *test embedding* DataFrames. By design, GenX does not assume a particular embedding technique and requires the user to compute the embeddings. This allows the user to employ whatever method is appropriate for their use-case (e.g. TF-IDF, neural network) and does not preclude the adoption of new state-of-the-art embeddings methods in the future. For our demonstrations, we use Sentence BERT (Reimers and Gurevych, 2019) to create the embeddings used in the tool.

During preprocessing, i.e., after input but before rendering, the Python half of GenX computes the cosine distance between each sentence in the train and test embeddings. The 10 nearest neighbors of each sentence in the test split and their respective distances are passed to the JavaScript half of the widget along with the test sentence DataFrame. The tool passes the rows of the train text DataFrame that were among the neighbors of any sentence in the test set. When a test sentence is rendered, its nearest neighbor distances are visualized in a bar graph following that sentence. The bars are sorted by distance, with the first nearest neighbor placed on the left, and the last nearest neighbor on the right, so the bars always increase monotonically. They allow the user to get a better understanding of the nearest neighbor distribution, e.g., whether the first nearest neighbor is unique or there are other semantically similar sentences in the train set.

Furthermore, the tool indicates which parts of the sentences are copied verbatim, or nearly so from the training data. To do so, we align each test sentence against its nearest neighbor in the train set using dynamic time warping (Sakoe and Chiba, 1978) at the token level. We use Levenshtein distance (Levenshtein, 1966) as the token-token distance function[5]. We highlight the tokens in the test sentence that are exactly matched to tokens in their nearest neighbor sentence with a strong underline. Tokens that are partially matched, i.e. with a Levenshtein distance less than 5, have a weaker underline. The remaining tokens are not underlined. The user can mouse over a bar to compare the text of each nearest neighbor against the test sentence.

When reading a document, the user may want to get a sense of what documents the nearest neighbor sentences are sourced from. For example, when repeats occur, do they occur together in the same source document? We include a step line chart visualization above the text to illustrate this. The x-axis is the sentence number of the generated sentence, and the y-axis is the source document identifier of the nearest neighbor of that sentence. The y-axis is sorted by first occurrence, so that the chart will increase monotonically unless a source document is revisited, which is clearly visible as dip in the chart. The line chart is also brushable allowing the user find corresponding sentences in the text below.

The tool also contains an interactive scatter plot to help the user focus on interesting or problematic examples of generated text and avoid having to page through every document. The axes of the scatter plots are two novel document-level metrics which we refer to as *distinctiveness* and *diversity*.

For a given document in the test data, Distinctiveness is the distance of the first nearest neighbor to each test sentence in a document, averaged across the generated sentences in the document. Low distinctiveness means that many sentences in that document were semantically similar to sentences in the training set, and indicate copying for specific phrases and may be symptomatic of memorizing repeated phrases. Low distinctiveness for the training set overall may be indicative of broader model

[2] https://jupyter.org

[3] https://github.com/jupyter-widgets/widget-cookiecutter

[4] https://pandas.pydata.org

[5] We tried a simpler approach of using Dynamic Time Warping at the character level, but this produced difficult to interpret highlighting for sentences with low alignment.

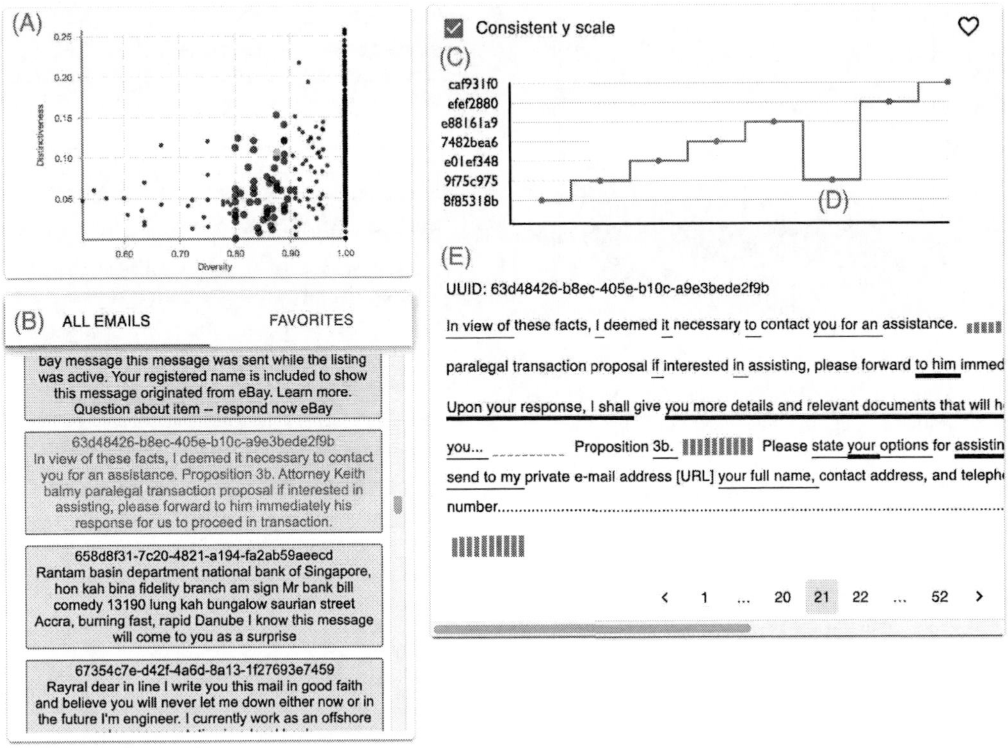

Figure 1: GenX interface with the distinctiveness/diversity overview of the corpus (A), the document navigation tool (B), and the individual document view containing the step line chart for diversity visualization (C) with an interesting dip indicating revisiting of a training document (D) and the document text with train data overlap and similarity annotations (E).

issues impacting creativity, potentially caused by sub-optimal parameter settings.

Each sentence in the training data is found within a particular source document. For a given document in the test data, Diversity is the number of unique corresponding source documents for the nearest neighbor of each test sentence in the generated document divided by the number of test sentences. Low diversity means the test document has similarity to a single source document, and is indicative of longer length copying from the training set, while a maximum diversity value of 1.0 indicates that the nearest neighbor of each generated sentence is from a different document in the training set. Because of the limited prior work on model memorization and lack of existing metrics, we introduce these two new metrics to quantitatively capture the patterns of sentence-level (distinctiveness) and document-level (diversity) memorization by the models. We also average these metrics across documents in the test corpus for corpus-level analysis (see Table 1).

4 Use Case: Phishing Email Generation

Phishing Emails We initially developed the GenX tool when working with a composite dataset of publicly available phishing datasets that contained many duplicates and near-duplicates. This dataset was initially comprised of the aggregation of data made available by (Azunre, 2019), and (Nazario, 2011) as well as phishing emails provided by industry partners. The initial dataset contained a total of 60,705 emails, however after initial de-duplication efforts using exact string matching only 9,234 emails remained which was split into a train set of 8,311 and a test set of 923. After further de-duplication efforts, aided by GenX, the final dataset consists of 5,634 emails in the training set and held out validation and test sets of size 500 each. While we have been rigorous in our efforts to remove emails that are duplicated, the formulaic nature of phishing emails leads to many commonly repeated phrases, sentences, or paragraphs.

Phishing Test/Train split While the GenX tool was originally designed for the evaluation of mem-

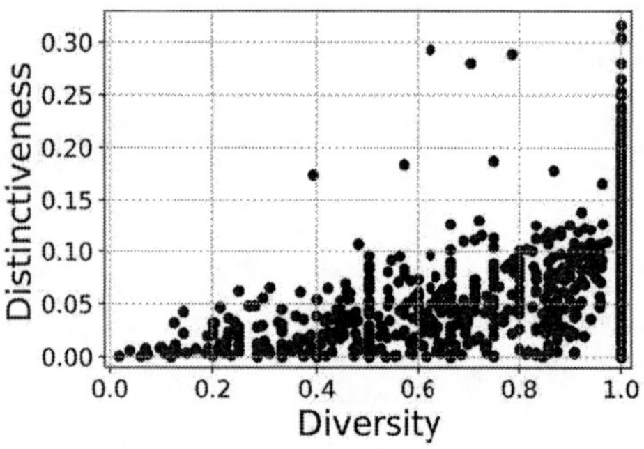

Figure 2: Distinctiveness and diversity scores for emails in the train and test sets of the phishing dataset reveal that there is significant test set contamination

[BOS] new contracting software hey stacie , our dev team has found a new contract management system and were trying to decide if its better than what youre using now . weve sent you a test contract at url so you can test out the new system . if you wouldnt mind giving us some feedback afterward , it would be appreciated . thanks , jeff bingum it engineer , xorg url xorg [EOS]

Figure 3: Example email from the phishing test set with high overlap with an email from the training set, differing only in the name of the recipient.

orization in NLG models, its ability to explore text overlap makes it well suited to the task of looking for test set contamination. To test this use case, we use GenX to look for text duplication across the train/test split of our 9k email phishing data set. Figure 2 shows the distinctiveness/diversity scatter plot which reveals a large number of of low-distinctiveness, low-diversity pairs between the training and test set which is indicative of significant levels of text duplication. Additionally, the example shown in Figure 3 demonstrates how GenX allows for qualitative analysis of the text in question. We can see from the underlining that almost all of the text in the example test set email appeared verbatim in a training set email, with the only difference being the name of the recipient. We identified this as a common pattern within the dataset because attackers duplicate popular phishing emails, making minor edits for personalization.

Phishing generation To build a phishing domain-conditioned generation model, we fine-tuned a GPT-2 small model (Radford et al., 2019) on the phishing training set using a learning rate of $5 * 10^{-5}$ and a batch size of 8. We chose two models to illustrate the use of GenX for qualitative

Paypal Protect your account info make sure you never provide your password to fraudulent persons. Paypal automatically encrypts your confidential information using the secure sockets layer protocol (SSL) with an encryption key length of 128-bits (the highest level commercially available). Paypal will never ask you to enter your password in an email. For more information on protecting yourself from fraud, please review our security tips at [URL] protect your password you should never give your PayPal password to anyone, including PayPal employees.

(a) High memorization, highly coherent example

Annie so, Paul. I feel sorry for you, Paul, I wonder if she'd grown old enough to keep track of her own chores. You must have noticed that droplets of ink glimmered around her necker and chin as well as around her temples. Like forgotten keys. You must also have noticed that droplets of ink glimmered around her necker and chin as well as around her temples. As if some forgotten page of forgotten Shakespearean tragedy had written it down Paul, Paul. Like probably the case of his head and neck and face. He lay in a very uncomfortable stupor for a while, then came the complete opposite: a perfect circle of bright moo and blue earth. Creosote

(b) Low memorization, incoherent example

Figure 4: Example generations from the phishing models showing the memorization/coherence trade-off

analysis of different models. Model 1 was trained for 10 epochs, while Model 2 was trained for 20 epochs. For each model we generate 500 unique emails, using a decoding temperature of 1.1.

We leverage GenX to perform qualitative evaluation of the levels of memorization in generations by these models. We find an overall high level of training email memorization, with the generation models producing emails that are nearly word-for-word replications of emails from the training set. In the distinctiveness-diversity plots (Figure 5), we observe that while there are many generated emails with high diversity, there still a significant population of emails with low distinctiveness and diversity scores. Using these plots to identify emails with lower and higher levels of memorization and then observing the corresponding email text in the individual document view, we are able to discover the interesting pattern that lower levels of memorization seem to be correlated with lower levels of coherence as determined by the human. In other words, the models are unable to creatively produce novel phishing emails and must rely on rote copying from the training data for reasonable human-evaluated performance. We can also use the tool to perform relative comparisons between memorization across different modeling choices. In this case, we find that increasing the number of train-

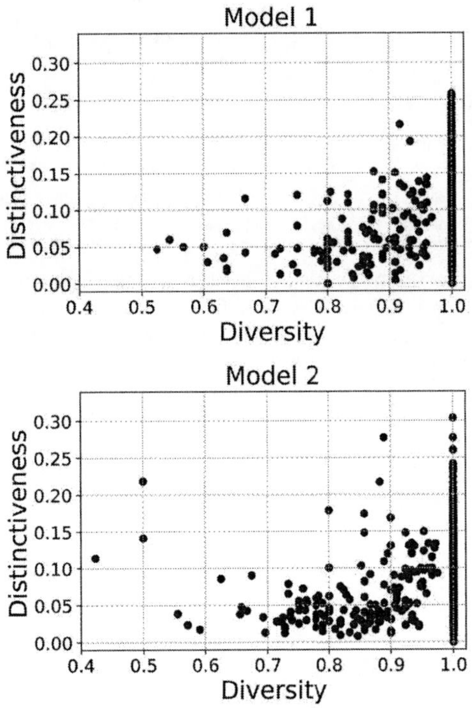

Figure 5: Diversity vs. distinctiveness for the two phishing NLG models. Both show training data memorization, but Model 2 contains more low-distinctiveness, lower-diversity examples).

We study the task of transliteration restoration for languages without a standard orthography. We propose a method that trains a neural encoder-decoder model to restore words that were erroneously transliterated. We evaluate our system on five different languages: Bengali, Cantonese, Chinese, English, German, and Spanish. We show that it outperforms strong encoders such as USE and CBOW. Furthermore, we propose an approach to preserve morphology and fluency of transliteration by preserving the orthography.

(a) ACL Model 1: Low memorization, highly coherent example

Lexical complexity often impacts readability and marks difficulty for learners, often requiring appropriate approaches to express the information. To facilitate grounded learning, we present a method for determining lexical complexity using gradient descent neural networks. By modeling complexity explicitly via gradient descent, the resulting model is simple, yet capable of finding lexical complexity patterns across a range of variables. Moreover, we empirically show the benefit of gradient descent and show that it greatly outperforms previously published techniques on large standard corpora.

(b) ACL Model 2: Low memorization, highly coherent example

Figure 6: Generated abstracts with low memorization and high creativity of the generative models.

ing epochs increases the level of memorization. We show several examples of generated emails from these models in Figure 4, which highlight the memorization-coherence trade off.

5 Use Case: ACL Abstract Generation

ACL Abstract Data The second dataset is the set of abstracts available from the ACL anthology [6], chosen simply because we considered it a relevant corpus for demonstration. We employed 17,903 abstracts as the training data for our generative model and withheld 2,000 abstracts for validation and 2,000 abstracts as the test set, whose NLG model perplexity is reported in in Table 1.

ACL generation We fine-tuned a GPT-2 small model (Radford et al., 2019) on the ACL training set with a learning rate of $5 * 10^{-5}$ and a batch size of 8. For this comparison we used a model that had been trained for 25 epochs, but created two sets of generated examples using different decoding temperatures, 0.8 for Set 1 and 1.1 for Set 2. Each set contains 600 generated abstracts.

In contrast with the phishing data set, the exploration of model outputs for the ACL data with the GenX tool reveal that these models achieve low levels of memorization and high levels of coherence overall. We show several example abstracts generated from the ACL models in Figure 6. We can observe the low level of memorization in these abstracts because the only words underlined in the generated text are common words like "the" or "an" indicating that the nearest neighbor sentences in the training data only overlap in an insignificant way with the generated text. Additionally, we observe the uniformly high distinctiveness values of the nearest neighbor distance bar charts. We use the distinctiveness/diversity scatter plots (Figure 7) to explore generations with higher and lower metric values. In contrast with the phishing models, our qualitative examination reveals that even generated abstracts with no indications of memorization have high coherence, indicating that the models can generate creative and novel outputs without resorting to copying from the training data. Comparison of the two different decoding temperatures, reveals that lower temperature does not result in increased memorization but it does have slightly improved coherence than the higher temperature model.

[6] https://www.aclweb.org/anthology/

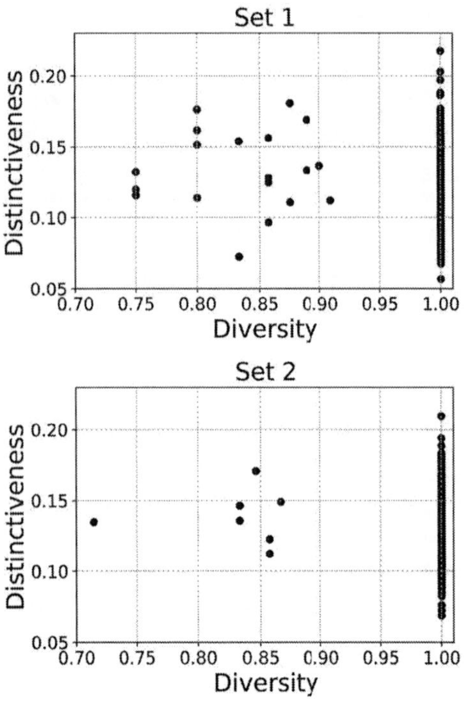

Figure 7: Diversity vs. distinctiveness for ACL NLG models. Both sets show high levels of high-diversity examples, with almost no low-diversity, low-distinctiveness generations

Task	Model	Perplexity	Average Distinctiveness	Average Diversity
Phishing Train Vs Test	-	-	0.08	0.80
Phishing Generations	Model 1	8.08	0.10	0.96
	Model 2	8.01	0.10	0.95
ACL Generations	Set 1	21.11	0.12	0.99
	Set 2	21.11	0.13	1.0

Table 1: The perplexity, average distinctiveness score, and average diversity score for each set of texts. We report the average scores here but in practice find that the average values are not as useful for diagnosing memorization and recommend using the interactive tool or scatter plots to identify specific low-quality examples.

6 Discussion & Limitations

GenX is a tool for incorporating human judgement with the analysis of generated text, without placing the full burden on human annotators to locate instances where the model is copying from the training data. The distinctiveness and diversity scores provide quantitative context to the qualitative interpretation of the highlighted text. When used on a model with high levels of duplication in the training set, the tool helped us establish a threshold of acceptable memorization. When used on a model with low levels of duplication the tool helped us identify compelling examples of creatively generated text not copied from the training data.

A key contribution of this work is going beyond the typical evaluation metrics such as perplexity. Table 1 shows that perplexity alone does not reveal the nuanced behavior of generative models. Looking at perplexity scores on the held out data alone, the ACL NLG model seems to perform worse than the phishing NLG model when in reality the ACL NLG model produces coherent examples with low levels of memorization. Additionally, GenX highlights differences between models where the perplexity is similar but there are qualitative differences in the generation, especially when the interactive components of the tool are used to understand the distribution of the memorization levels of individual emails and identify specific patterns and examples of memorization.

GenX has challenges scaling to large datasets. While we demonstrated utility on datasets with tens of thousands of text examples, the nearest neighbor approach used would become intractable on massive text corpora such as CommonCrawl [7]. This limits GenX to scenarios where training data is a manageable size, but does not yet help address the issue of test set contamination from large-scale web scrapes. As future work, we plan to incorporate approximate neighbor techniques (Dong et al., 2011) to mitigate this issue.

In the phishing use case, identical sentences were found across many training documents, making diversity measurements artificially high, due to the arbitrary choice of nearest neighbors. We plan to use a minimum set cover algorithm to improve diversity score accuracy to break ties by selecting the smallest number of training documents that cover the nearest neighbors in the test document.

7 Conclusion

GenX provides a unique capability for interactive evaluation and explanation of NLG model output. The tool goes beyond typical aggregate performance metrics and provides new insight into domain-conditioned NLG model creativity and memorization. Across two use cases, we showed this helped distinguish models in situations where aggregate evaluation metrics did not.

[7] https://commoncrawl.org/the-data/

Broader Impact and Ethical Statement

Natural language generation (NLG) models have received much attention beyond their research community. However such attention can be harmful when it inappropriately attributes human-level intelligence and creativity to clever statistical processes. Increased transparency and explainability of NLG models can help to prevent societal harm that arises from over-estimating model ability. Furthermore, the applicability of GenX to ensure more distinct train/test splits also helps to create more robust language models (by decreasing overestimated F-scores) that have similar performance "in the wild" and in the laboratory.

There are ethical considerations around conditioning NLG models on phishing emails. These emails are malicious by nature, and our models could provide bad actors a means to cause greater harm. However, the research described in this paper is part of a broader effort to generate realistic phishing emails for educational purposes to mitigate users susceptibility to phishing. Our work can reduce the burden on analysts who currently painstakingly craft these training emails by hand. We are also encouraged by the positive results in fake-news detection (Zellers et al., 2019) and believe that the insights from phishing generators can inform more robust phishing detection models. We do not plan to publicly release the phishing domain conditioned models or source code used in this specific use case.

References

Miltiadis Allamanis. 2019. The adverse effects of code duplication in machine learning models of code. In *Proceedings of the 2019 ACM SIGPLAN International Symposium on New Ideas, New Paradigms, and Reflections on Programming and Software*, Onward! 2019, page 143–153, New York, NY, USA. Association for Computing Machinery.

Paul Azunre. 2019. Fraudulent email bodies. `https://www.kaggle.com/azunre/fraudulent-email-bodies`.

Tom B Brown, Benjamin Mann, Nick Ryder, Melanie Subbiah, Jared Kaplan, Prafulla Dhariwal, Arvind Neelakantan, Pranav Shyam, Girish Sastry, Amanda Askell, et al. 2020. Language models are few-shot learners. *arXiv preprint arXiv:2005.14165*.

Nicholas Carlini, Chang Liu, Úlfar Erlingsson, Jernej Kos, and Dawn Song. 2019. The secret sharer: Evaluating and testing unintended memorization in neural networks. In *28th USENIX Security Symposium (USENIX Security 19)*, pages 267–284.

Wei Dong, Charikar Moses, and Kai Li. 2011. Efficient k-nearest neighbor graph construction for generic similarity measures. In *Proceedings of the 20th international conference on World wide web*, pages 577–586.

Tatsunori B Hashimoto, Hugh Zhang, and Percy Liang. 2019. Unifying human and statistical evaluation for natural language generation. *arXiv preprint arXiv:1904.02792*.

Vladimir I Levenshtein. 1966. Binary codes capable of correcting deletions, insertions, and reversals. In *Soviet physics doklady*, volume 10, pages 707–710.

Patrick Lewis, Pontus Stenetorp, and Sebastian Riedel. 2020. Question and answer test-train overlap in open-domain question answering datasets. *arXiv preprint arXiv:2008.02637*.

Mitch Marcus, Grace Kim, Mary Ann Marcinkiewicz, Robert MacIntyre, Ann Bies, Mark Ferguson, Karen Katz, and Britta Schasberger. 1994. The penn treebank: annotating predicate argument structure. In *HUMAN LANGUAGE TECHNOLOGY: Proceedings of a Workshop held at Plainsboro, New Jersey, March 8-11, 1994*.

Jose Nazario. 2011. PhishingCorpus. `https://monkey.org/~jose/phishing/`.

Graham Neubig, Zi-Yi Dou, Junjie Hu, Paul Michel, Danish Pruthi, and Xinyi Wang. 2019. compare-mt: A tool for holistic comparison of language generation systems. In *Proceedings of the 2019 Conference of the North American Chapter of the Association for Computational Linguistics (Demonstrations)*, pages 35–41, Minneapolis, Minnesota. Association for Computational Linguistics.

Jekaterina Novikova, Ondřej Dušek, Amanda Cercas Curry, and Verena Rieser. 2017. Why we need new evaluation metrics for NLG. In *Proceedings of the 2017 Conference on Empirical Methods in Natural Language Processing*, pages 2241–2252, Copenhagen, Denmark. Association for Computational Linguistics.

Denis Paperno, Germán Kruszewski, Angeliki Lazaridou, Quan Ngoc Pham, Raffaella Bernardi, Sandro Pezzelle, Marco Baroni, Gemma Boleda, and Raquel Fernández. 2016. The lambada dataset: Word prediction requiring a broad discourse context. *arXiv preprint arXiv:1606.06031*.

Kishore Papineni, Salim Roukos, Todd Ward, and Wei-Jing Zhu. 2002. Bleu: a method for automatic evaluation of machine translation. In *Proceedings of the 40th Annual Meeting of the Association for Computational Linguistics*, pages 311–318, Philadelphia, Pennsylvania, USA. Association for Computational Linguistics.

Alec Radford, Jeffrey Wu, Rewon Child, David Luan, Dario Amodei, and Ilya Sutskever. 2019. Language models are unsupervised multitask learners. *OpenAI blog*, 1(8):9.

Nils Reimers and Iryna Gurevych. 2019. Sentence-bert: Sentence embeddings using siamese bert-networks. *arXiv preprint arXiv:1908.10084*.

Hiroaki Sakoe and Seibi Chiba. 1978. Dynamic programming algorithm optimization for spoken word recognition. *IEEE transactions on acoustics, speech, and signal processing*, 26(1):43–49.

Thibault Sellam, Dipanjan Das, and Ankur P Parikh. 2020. Bleurt: Learning robust metrics for text generation. *arXiv preprint arXiv:2004.04696*.

Lucas Theis, Aäron van den Oord, and Matthias Bethge. 2015. A note on the evaluation of generative models. *arXiv preprint arXiv:1511.01844*.

Changhan Wang, Anirudh Jain, Danlu Chen, and Jiatao Gu. 2019. Vizseq: A visual analysis toolkit for text generation tasks. In *In Proceedings of the 2019 Conference on Empirical Methods in Natural Language Processing: System Demonstrations*.

Yonghui Wu, Mike Schuster, Zhifeng Chen, Quoc V Le, Mohammad Norouzi, Wolfgang Macherey, Maxim Krikun, Yuan Cao, Qin Gao, Klaus Macherey, et al. 2016. Google's neural machine translation system: Bridging the gap between human and machine translation. *arXiv preprint arXiv:1609.08144*.

Wei Xu, Courtney Napoles, Ellie Pavlick, Quanze Chen, and Chris Callison-Burch. 2016. Optimizing statistical machine translation for text simplification. *Transactions of the Association for Computational Linguistics*, 4:401–415.

Rowan Zellers, Ari Holtzman, Hannah Rashkin, Yonatan Bisk, Ali Farhadi, Franziska Roesner, and Yejin Choi. 2019. Defending against neural fake news. In *Advances in neural information processing systems*, pages 9054–9065.

CrossCheck: Rapid, Reproducible, and Interpretable Model Evaluation

Dustin Arendt* **Zhuanyi Shaw***
Prasha Shrestha† **Ellyn Ayton†** **Maria Glenski†** **Svitlana Volkova***
*Visual Analytics Group, †Data Sciences and Analytics Group
Pacific Northwest National Laboratory
`{first}.{last}@pnnl.gov`

Abstract

Evaluation beyond aggregate performance metrics, e.g. F1-score, is crucial to both establish an appropriate level of trust in machine learning models and identify avenues for future model improvements. In this paper we demonstrate `CrossCheck`, an interactive capability for rapid cross-model comparison and reproducible error analysis. We describe the tool, discuss design and implementation details, and present three NLP use cases – named entity recognition, reading comprehension, and clickbait detection that show the benefits of using the tool for model evaluation. `CrossCheck` enables users to make informed decisions when choosing between multiple models, identify when the models are correct and for which examples, investigate whether the models are making the same mistakes as humans, evaluate models' generalizability and highlight models' limitations, strengths and weaknesses. Furthermore, `CrossCheck` is implemented as a Jupyter widget, which allows for rapid and convenient integration into existing model development workflows.

1 Motivation

AI models are often imperfect, opaque, and brittle. Gaining actionable insights about model strengths and weaknesses is challenging because simple metrics like accuracy or F1-score are not sufficient to capture the complex relationships between model inputs and outputs. Many researchers agree that ML models have to be optimized not only for expected task performance but for other important criteria such as explainability, interpretability, reliability, and fairness that are prerequisites for trust (Lipton, 2016; Doshi-Velez and Kim, 2017; Poursabzi-Sangdeh et al., 2018). Standard performance metrics can be augmented with exploratory model performance analysis, where a user can interact with inputs and outputs to find patterns or biases in the way the model makes mistakes to answer the questions of when, how, and why the model fails.

To support ML model evaluation beyond standard performance metrics, we developed a novel interactive tool `CrossCheck`[1]. Unlike several recently developed tools for analyzing model errors (Agarwal et al., 2014; Wu et al., 2019), understanding model outputs (Lee et al., 2019; Hohman et al., 2019), and model interpretation and diagnostics (Kahng et al., 2017, 2016; Zhang et al., 2018), `CrossCheck` is designed to allow rapid prototyping and cross-model comparison iteratively during model development to support comprehensive experimental setup and gain interpretable and informative insights into model performance.

Many visualization tools have been developed recently, *e.g.*, ConvNetJS[2], TensorFlow Playground[3], that focus on structural interpretability (Kulesza et al., 2013; Hoffman et al., 2018) and operate in the neuron activation space to explain models' internal decision making processes (Kahng et al., 2017) or focus on visualizing a model's decision boundary to increase user trust (Ribeiro et al., 2016). Instead, `CrossCheck` targets functional interpretability and operates in the model output space to diagnose and contrast model performance.

Similar work to `CrossCheck` includes AllenNLP Interpret (Wallace et al., 2019) and Errudite (Wu et al., 2019). AllenNLP Interpret relies on saliency map visualizations to uncover model biases, find decision rules, and diagnose model errors. Errudite implements a domain specific language for counterfactual explanations. Errudite and AllenNLP Interpret focus primarily on error analysis for a single model, while our tool is specifically designed for contrastive evaluation across multiple models *e.g.*, neural architectures with different parameters.

Manifold (Zhang et al., 2018) supports cross-

[1] `https://github.com/pnnl/crosscheck`
[2] `https://github.com/karpathy/convnetjs`
[3] `https://playground.tensorflow.org/`

Proceedings of the 2nd Workshop on Data Science with Human in the Loop: Language Advances, pages 79–85
June 11, 2021.

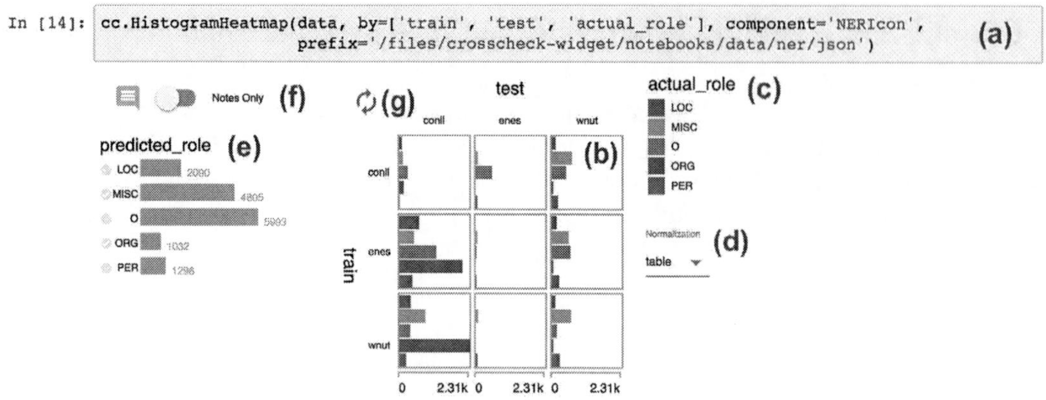

Figure 1: `CrossCheck` embedded in a Jupyter Notebook cell: (a) code used to instantiate the widget (b) the histogram heatmap shows the distribution of the third variable for each combination of the first two (c) the legend for the third variable (d) normalization controls (e) histogram & filter for remaining variables (f) controls for notes (g) button to transpose the rows and columns.

model evaluation, however the tool is narrowly focused on model confidence and errors via pairwise model comparison with scatter plots which is quite limited and does not satisfy the needs of complex NLP tasks. `CrossCheck` enables users to investigate "where" and "what" types of errors models make and, most importantly, assists the user with answering the question of "why" a model makes that error by relying on a set of derived attributes from the input like inter-annotator agreement, question type, answer length, the input paragraph, *etc.*

We built `CrossCheck` to make our existing error analysis workflow faster and reproducible, reducing human effort to replicate exploratory analyses of new models. `CrossCheck` helps calibrate trust by enabling users to:

- contrast multiple models,
- see when the model is right (or wrong), understand the relationship between correctness and confidence, and examine those examples,
- investigate whether the model makes the same mistakes as humans,
- highlight model limitations, and
- understand how models generalize across domains, languages, and datasets – which has pervasive demand across NLP.

2 CrossCheck

`CrossCheck` is embedded in a Jupyter[4] notebook and input is a single mixed-type table, *i.e.* a pandas DataFrame[5], allowing for tight integration with data scientists' workflows (see Figure 1a). Below we outline the features of `CrossCheck` in detail.

`CrossCheck`'s main view (see Figure 1b) extends the *confusion matrix* visualization technique by replacing each cell in the matrix with a histogram — we call this view the histogram heatmap. Each cell shows the distribution of a third variable conditioned on the values of the corresponding row and column variables. Every bar represents a subset of instances, *i.e.,* rows in the input table, and encodes the relative size of that group. This view also contains a legend showing the bins or categories for this third variable (see Figure 1c).

The histograms in each cell in `CrossCheck` are drawn horizontally to encourage comparison across cells in the vertical direction. `CrossCheck` supports three normalization schemes (see Figure 1d), *i.e.,* setting the limit of the x-axis in each cell: (1) normalizing by the maximum count within the entire matrix, (2) within each column, or (3) within each cell. We hide certain axes and adjust the padding between cells to emphasize the selected normalization. Figure 2 illustrates how these different normalization options appear in `CrossCheck`. By design, there is no equivalent row normalization option, but the matrix can be transposed (see Figure 1g) for an equivalent effect.

Any variables not directly compared in the histogram heatmap are visualized on the left side of the widget as histograms (see Figure 1e). These histograms also allow the user to filter data when it is rendered in the main view by clicking on the bar(s) corresponding to the data they want to keep.

[4]`https://jupyter.org`
[5]`http://pandas.pydata.org`

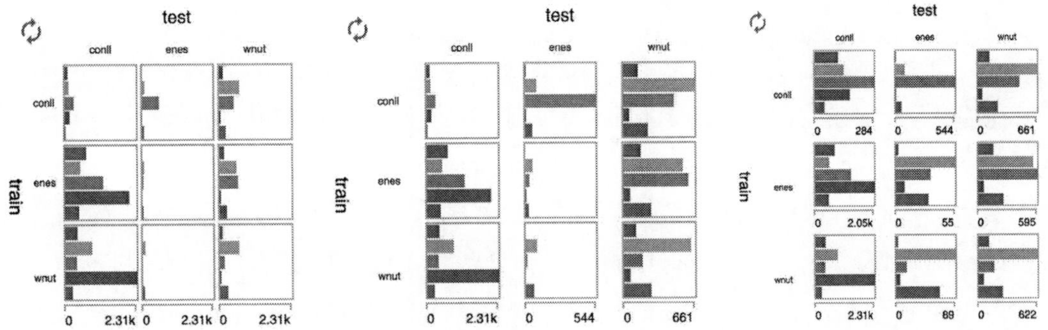

(a) by table (b) by column (c) by cell

Figure 2: CrossCheck supports three histogram normalization options that affect how axes and padding are rendered to improve the readability and interpretation of the view (a) by table: minimal padding, the same x-axes are shown on the bottom row (b) by column: extra padding between columns, different x-axes are shown on the bottom row (c) by cell: extra padding between rows and columns, different x-axes are shown for each cell.

Users can click on any bar in the histogram heatmap to view those instances in a sidebar where they can annotate noteworthy findings. Enabling "Notes Only" (see Figure 1f) shows only instances that have been annotated in the histogram heatmap, revealing what has been annotated in the context of the current variable groupings.

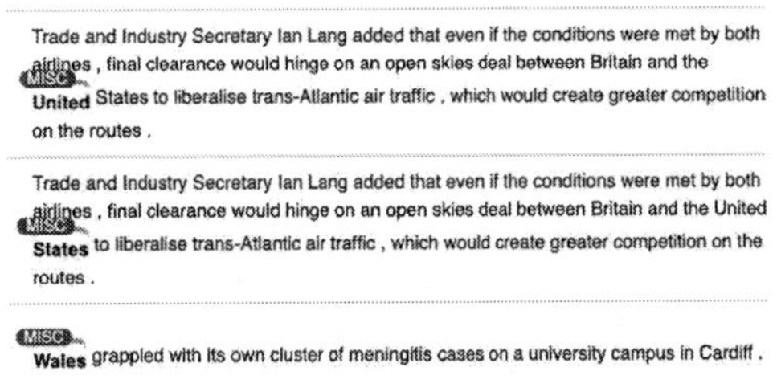

(a) Named Entity Recognition

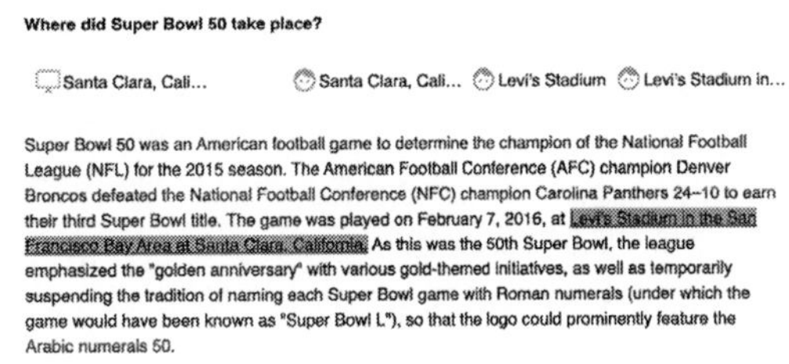

(b) Reading Comprehension

Figure 3: Examples of model outputs in CrossCheck for core NLP tasks – for the NER task (above), predicted named entities are highlighted, and for the RC task (below), predicted answer span is highlighted.

3 Use Cases and Evaluation

In this section, we highlight how CrossCheck can be used in core NLP tasks such as named entity recognition (NER) and reading comprehension (RC) or practical applications of NLP such as clickbait detection (CB). We present an overview of the datasets used for each task below:

- NER: CoNLL (Sang, 2003), ENES (Aguilar et al., 2018), WNUT 17 Emerging Entities (Derczynski et al., 2017)[6],
- MC: Stanford Question Answering Dataset (SQuAD) (Rajpurkar et al., 2016)[7],
- CB: Clickbait Challenge 2017 (Potthast et al., 2018)[8].

3.1 Named Entity Recognition (NER)

To showcase CrossCheck, we trained and evaluated the AllenNLP NER model (Peters et al., 2017) across three benchmark datasets – CoNLL, WNUT, and ENES, producing nine different evaluations. The model output includes, on a per-token level, the model prediction, the ground truth, the original sentence (for context), and what the training and testing datasets were as shown in Figure 3a.

This experiment was designed to let us understand how models trained on different datasets generalize to the same test data (shown in columns) and how models trained on the same training data transfer to perform across different test datasets (shown in rows). Figure 2 illustrates the CrossCheck grid of train versus test datasets. The data has been filtered so that only errors contribute to the bars so we see a distribution of errors per train-test combination across the actual role. The CoNLL dataset is much larger so we normalize within columns in Figure 2b to find patterns within those sub-groups.

[6]github.com/leondz/emerging_entities_
17

[7]rajpurkar.github.io/SQuAD-explorer/

[8]www.clickbait-challenge.org/#data

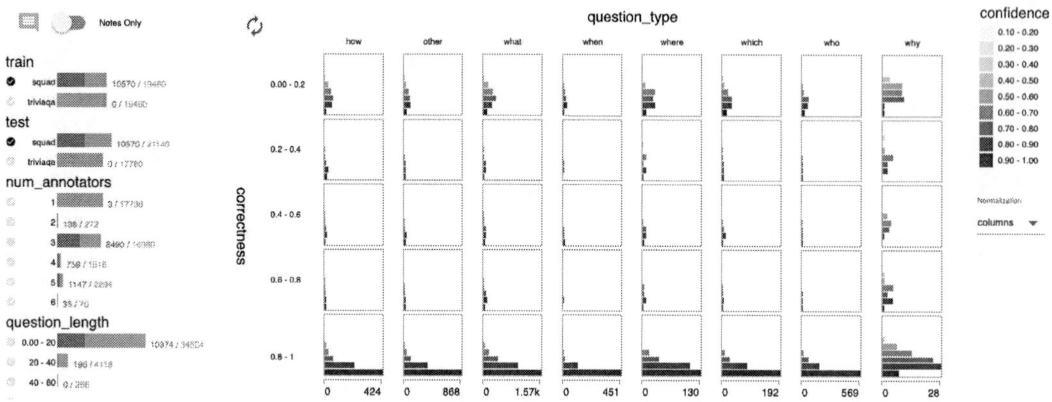

Figure 4: `CrossCheck` for evaluation of reading comprehension models to understand the relationship between correctness, confidence and question types. This highlight models limitations and shows for what examples the model answers correctly.

Table 1: Traditional evaluation: F1-scores for the NER models trained and tested across domains.

Train \ Test	CoNLL	WNUT	ENES
CoNLL	92.51	40.10	11.88
WNUT	55.75	44.73	33.33
ENES	50.78	57.48	64.00

For the same experimental setup, Table 1 summarizes performance with F1-scores. Unlike the F1-score table, `CrossCheck` reveals that models trained on social media data misclassify ORG on the news data, and the news models overpredict named entities on social media data.

3.2 Reading Comprehension (RC)

Similar to NER, we trained an AllenNLP model for reading comprehension (Seo et al., 2016) that is designed to find the most relevant span for a question and paragraph input pair. The model output includes, on a question-paragraph level: the model prediction span, ground truth span, model confidence, question type and length, the number of annotators per question, and what the train and test datasets were, as shown in Figure 3b.[9] Figure 4 contrasts model correctness and confidence across question types. `CrossCheck` reveals that across all types of questions when the model is correct it has higher confidence (bottom row) and lower confidence when incorrect (top row). It also reveals that models have a higher variability in confidence when predicting "why" questions.

[9]We evaluated RC on SQuAD and TriviaQA datasets, but with space limitations only present results for SQuAD.

3.3 Clickbait Detection

Finally, we demonstrate `CrossCheck` for comparison of regression models. We use a relevant application of NLP in the domain of deception detection (clickbait detection) that was the focus of the Clickbait Challenge 2017, a shared task focused on identifying a score (from 0 to 1) of how "clickbait-y" a social media post (*i.e.,* tweet on Twitter) is, given the content of the post (text and images) and the linked article webpages. We use the validation dataset that contains 19,538 posts (4,761 identified as clickbait) and pre-trained models released on GitHub after the challenge by two teams (*blobfish* and *striped-bass*)[10].

In Figure 5 we illustrate how `CrossCheck` can be used to compare across multiple models and across multiple classes of models.[11] When filtered to show only the *striped-bass* models (shown at right), a strategy to predict coarse (0 or 1) clickbait scores versus fine-grained clickbait scores is clearly evident in the *striped-bass* model predictions. Here, there is a complete lack of predictions falling within the center three columns so even with no filters selected (shown at left), `CrossCheck` indicates that there is an inconsistency in the range of outcomes between models (an explanation for the disparity in F1-scores in Table 2). In cases

[10]Models and code were available via `github.com/clickbait-challenge/` repositories.

[11]Note, models could also be grouped by any number of shared characteristics such as the algorithms or architectures used (*e.g.,* different neural architectures used in deep learning models, or models that use deep learning versus those that do not), hyper-parameter settings, granularity of prediction outputs, ensembles versus single models, *etc.*

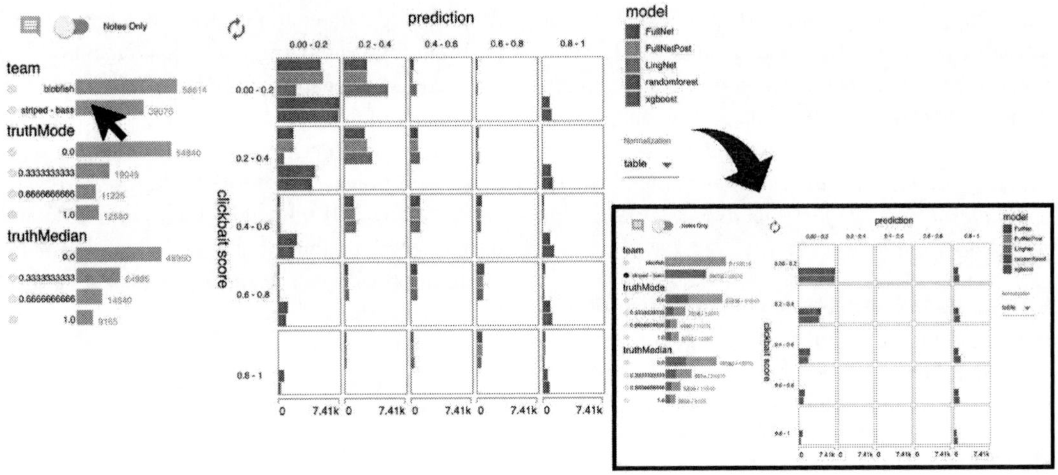

Figure 5: `CrossCheck` for cross-model comparison across two teams who competed in the Clickbait Challenge 2017 shared task, highlighting distinctions in the variety of prediction outputs with histograms normalized across the full table that become particularly clear when team filters are selected.

Table 2: Traditional evaluation summary table contrasting mean squared error (MSE) and mean absolute error (MAE) of each model's predictions.

Team	Model	MSE	MAE
	FullNetPost	0.026	0.126
blobfish	FullNet	0.027	0.130
	LingNet	0.038	0.157
striped-bass	xgboost	0.171	0.326
	randomforest	0.180	0.336

where there is a more nuanced or subtle disparity, shallow exploration with different filters within `CrossCheck` can lead to efficient, effective identification of these key differences in functional model behavior.

4 Design and Implementation

We designed `CrossCheck` following a user-centered design methodology. This is a continuous, iterative process where we identify needs and goals, implement prototypes, and solicit feedback from our users to incorporate in the tool. Our users were data scientists, specifically NLP researchers and practitioners, tasked with the aforementioned model evaluation challenge. We identified `CrossCheck`'s goals as allowing the user to: understand how instance attributes relate to model errors; provide convenient access to raw instance data; integrate into a data scientists workflow; and reveal and understand disagreement across models, and support core NLP tasks and applications.

4.1 Design Iterations

Round 1—Heatmaps (functional prototype) Our first iteration extended the confusion matrix visualization technique with a functional prototype that grouped the data by one variable, and showed a separate heatmap for each distinct value in that group. *User feedback: though heatmaps are familiar, the grouping made the visualization misleading and difficult to learn.*

Round 2—Table & Heatmap (wireframes) We wireframed a standalone tool with histogram filters, a sortable table, and a more traditional heatmap visualization with a rectangular brush to reveal raw instance data. *User feedback: the sortable table and brushing would be useful, but the heatmap has essentially the same limitations as confusion matrices.*

Round 3—Histogram Heatmap (wireframes) We wireframed a modified heatmap where each cell was replaced with a histogram showing the distribution of a third variable conditioned on the row and column variables. This modified heatmap was repeated for each variable in the dataset except for the row and column variables. *User feedback: Putting the histogram inside the heatmap seems useful, but multiple copies would be overwhelming and too small to read. We would prefer to work with just one histogram heatmap.*

Round 4—`CrossCheck` (functional prototype) We implemented a single "histogram heatmap" inside a Jupyter widget, and made raw instance data available to explore by clicking on any bar. Additionally we incorporated histogram filters from the Round 2 design and allowed the user to change the histogram normalization. *User feedback: the tool was very useful, but could use minor improvements e.g., labeled axes and filtering, as well as ability to add annotation on raw data.*

Round 5—`CrossCheck` (polished prototype) We added minor features like a legend, a matrix transpose button, axis labels, dynamic padding between rows and columns (based on normalization), and the ability to annotate instances with notes. *User feedback: the tool works very well, but screenshots aren't suitable to use in publications.*

4.2 Implementation Challenges

To overcome the rate limit between the python kernel and the web browser (see the `NotebookApp.iopub_data_rate_limit` Jupyter argument) our implementation separates raw instance data from tabular data to be visualized in `CrossCheck`'s histogram heatmap. The tool groups tabular data by each field in the table and passed as a list of each unique field/value combinations and the corresponding instances within that bin. This is computed efficiently within the python kernel (via a pandas `groupby`). This pre-grouping reduces the size of the payload passed from the python kernel to the web browser and allows for the widget to behave more responsively because visualization and filtering routines do not need to iterate over every instance in the dataset. The tool stores raw instance data as individual JSON files on disk in a path visible to the Jupyter notebook environment. When the user clicks to reveal raw instance data, this data is retrieved asynchronously using the web browser's XMLHttpRequest (XHR). This allows the web browser to only retrieve and render the few detailed instances the user is viewing at a time.

5 Discussion

`CrossCheck` is designed to quickly and easily explore many combinations of characteristics of models (*e.g.,* parameter settings, network architectures) as well as datasets used for training or evaluation. It also provides users the ability to efficiently compare and explore model behavior in specific situations and *generalizability of models* across datasets or domains. `CrossCheck` can also generalize to support model comparison, e.g. when ground truth is absent, by visualizing model agreement.

`CrossCheck` enables users to perform error analysis in an efficient, concise, and reproducible manner due to its effective integration into data scientists' workflows. The tool can be used to evaluate across models trained on image, video, tabular data, or combinations of data types with interactive exploration of specific instances on demand. A limitation of the tool is that adding new use cases might require end users to write custom JavaScript code to visualize instances in the details sidebar beyond what is currently implemented. Future work includes expanding to include additional generic components to cover more core NLP or ML tasks.

6 Conclusions

We have presented `CrossCheck`, a new interactive capability that enables rapid model evaluation and error analysis. There are several key benefits to performing evaluation and analyses using CrossCheck, especially compared to *i.e.,* adhoc or manual approaches because `CrossCheck` is generalizable across text, images, video, tabular, or combinations of multiple data types, can be integrated directly into existing workflows for rapid and highly reproducible error analysis during and after model development, users can interactively explore errors conditioning on different model/data features, and users can view specific instances of inputs that cause model errors or other interesting behavior within the tool itself.

References

Apoorv Agarwal, Ankit Agarwal, and Deepak Mittal. 2014. An error analysis tool for natural language processing and applied machine learning. In *Proceedings of COLING 2014, the 25th International Conference on Computational Linguistics: System Demonstrations*, pages 1–5.

Gustavo Aguilar, Fahad AlGhamdi, Victor Soto, Mona Diab, Julia Hirschberg, and Thamar Solorio. 2018. Named entity recognition on code-switched data: Overview of the calcs 2018 shared task. In *Proceedings of the Third Workshop on Computational Approaches to Linguistic Code-Switching*, pages 138–147.

Leon Derczynski, Eric Nichols, Marieke van Erp, and Nut Limsopatham. 2017. Results of the wnut2017 shared task on novel and emerging entity recognition. In *Proceedings of the 3rd Workshop on Noisy User-generated Text*, pages 140–147.

Finale Doshi-Velez and Been Kim. 2017. Towards a rigorous science of interpretable machine learning. *arXiv preprint arXiv:1702.08608*.

Robert Hoffman, Tim Miller, Shane T Mueller, Gary Klein, and William J Clancey. 2018. Explaining explanation, part 4: a deep dive on deep nets. *IEEE Intelligent Systems*, 33(3):87–95.

Fred Hohman, Andrew Head, Rich Caruana, Robert DeLine, and Steven M Drucker. 2019. Gamut: A design probe to understand how data scientists understand machine learning models. In *Proceedings of the 2019 CHI Conference on Human Factors in Computing Systems*, page 579. ACM.

Minsuk Kahng, Pierre Y Andrews, Aditya Kalro, and Duen Horng Polo Chau. 2017. ActiVis: Visual exploration of industry-scale deep neural network models. *IEEE Transactions on Visualization and Computer Graphics*, 24(1):88–97.

Minsuk Kahng, Dezhi Fang, and Duen Horng Polo Chau. 2016. Visual exploration of machine learning results using data cube analysis. In *Proceedings of the Workshop on Human-In-the-Loop Data Analytics*, page 1. ACM.

Todd Kulesza, Simone Stumpf, Margaret Burnett, Sherry Yang, Irwin Kwan, and Weng-Keen Wong. 2013. Too much, too little, or just right? ways explanations impact end users' mental models. In *2013 IEEE Symposium on Visual Languages and Human Centric Computing*, pages 3–10. IEEE.

Gyeongbok Lee, Sungdong Kim, and Seung-won Hwang. 2019. Qadiver: Interactive framework for diagnosing qa models. In *Proceedings of the AAAI Conference on Artificial Intelligence*, volume 33, pages 9861–9862.

Zachary C Lipton. 2016. The mythos of model interpretability. *arXiv preprint arXiv:1606.03490*.

Matthew E Peters, Waleed Ammar, Chandra Bhagavatula, and Russell Power. 2017. Semi-supervised sequence tagging with bidirectional language models. *arXiv preprint arXiv:1705.00108*.

Martin Potthast, Tim Gollub, Kristof Komlossy, Sebastian Schuster, Matti Wiegmann, Erika Patricia Garces Fernandez, Matthias Hagen, and Benno Stein. 2018. Crowdsourcing a large corpus of clickbait on twitter. In *Proceedings of the 27th International Conference on Computational Linguistics*, pages 1498–1507.

Forough Poursabzi-Sangdeh, Daniel G Goldstein, Jake M Hofman, Jennifer Wortman Vaughan, and Hanna Wallach. 2018. Manipulating and measuring model interpretability. *arXiv preprint arXiv:1802.07810*.

Pranav Rajpurkar, Jian Zhang, Konstantin Lopyrev, and Percy Liang. 2016. Squad: 100,000+ questions for machine comprehension of text. *arXiv preprint arXiv:1606.05250*.

Marco Tulio Ribeiro, Sameer Singh, and Carlos Guestrin. 2016. Why should i trust you?: Explaining the predictions of any classifier. In *Proceedings of the 22nd ACM SIGKDD international conference on knowledge discovery and data mining*, pages 1135–1144. ACM.

Tjong Kim Sang. 2003. De meulder, 2003. tjong kim sang, ef, & de meulder, f.(2003). introduction to the conll-2003 shared task: language-independent named entity recognition. In *Proceedings of the Conference on Computational Natural Language Learning. Edmonton, Canada*, pages 142–147.

Minjoon Seo, Aniruddha Kembhavi, Ali Farhadi, and Hannaneh Hajishirzi. 2016. Bidirectional attention flow for machine comprehension. *arXiv preprint arXiv:1611.01603*.

Eric Wallace, Jens Tuyls, Junlin Wang, Sanjay Subramanian, Matt Gardner, and Sameer Singh. 2019. Allennlp interpret: A framework for explaining predictions of nlp models. *arXiv preprint arXiv:1909.09251*.

Tongshuang Wu, Marco Tulio Ribeiro, Jeffrey Heer, and Daniel S Weld. 2019. Errudite: Scalable, reproducible, and testable error analysis. In *Proceedings of the 57th Annual Meeting of the Association for Computational Linguistics*, pages 747–763.

Jiawei Zhang, Yang Wang, Piero Molino, Lezhi Li, and David S Ebert. 2018. Manifold: A model-agnostic framework for interpretation and diagnosis of machine learning models. *IEEE Transactions on Visualization and Computer Graphics*, 25(1):364–373.

TopGuNN: Fast NLP Training Data Augmentation using Large Corpora

Rebecca Iglesias-Flores[1] **Megha Mishra**[1] **Ajay Patel**[1] **Akanksha Malhotra**[2]
Reno Kriz[1] **Martha Palmer**[2] **Chris Callison-Burch**[1]

University of Pennsylvania[1] University of Colorado at Boulder[2]
{irebecca, mmishra, ajayp, rekriz, ccb}@seas.upenn.edu
{akanksha.malhotra, martha.palmer}@colorado.edu

Abstract

Acquiring training data for natural language processing systems can be expensive and time-consuming. Given a few training examples crafted by experts, large corpora can be mined for thousands of semantically similar examples that provide useful variability to improve model generalization. We present TopGuNN, a fast contextualized k-NN retrieval system that can efficiently index and search over contextual embeddings generated from large corpora to easily retrieve new diverse training examples. TopGuNN is demonstrated for a semantic role labeling training data augmentation use case over the Gigaword corpus. Using approximate k-NN and an efficient architecture, TopGuNN performs queries over an embedding space of 4.63TB (approximately 1.5B embeddings) in less than a day.

1 Introduction

To collect training data for natural language processing (NLP) models, researchers have to rely on manual labor-intensive methods like crowdsourcing or hiring domain experts. Rather than relying on such techniques, we present TopGuNN, a system to make it quick and easy for researchers to create a larger training set, starting with just a few examples. Large-scale language models can be effectively used to search for similar words or sentences; however, attempting to extract the most similar words from a large corpus can become intractable and time consuming. Our system TopGuNN utilizes a fast contextualized k-NN retrieval pipeline to quickly mine for a diverse set of training examples from large corpora. The system first creates a contextual word-level index from a corpus. Then, given a query word in a training example, it finds new sentences with words used in similar contexts to the query word. Figure 1 shows an example of the results of querying for the word "diagnosis" used in different contexts.

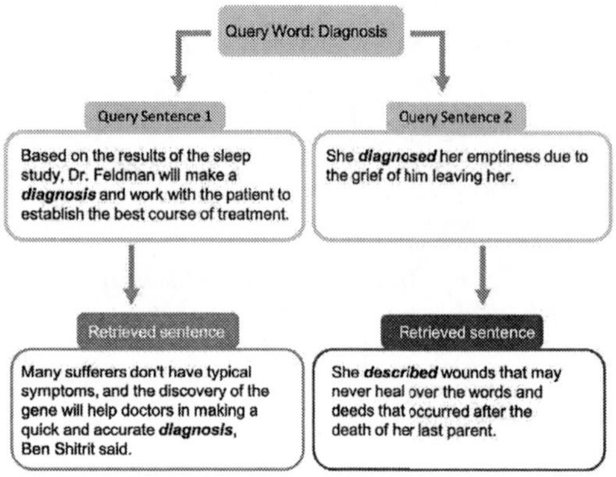

Figure 1: Retrieved results for two queries with different senses of a polysemous word searching over 183 million sentences (or 1.5B embeddings) in the Gigaword corpus with TopGuNN.

TopGuNN pre-computes BERT contextualized word embeddings over the entire corpus, and then efficiently searches through them when queried using approximate k-NN indexing algorithms. Our system has been designed with efficiency and scalability in mind. We demonstrate its use by indexing the Gigaword corpus, a large corpus for which we pre-computed 1.5B contextualized word embeddings (totaling 4.63TB), and using TopGuNN to run search queries over it. A detailed description of the system's architecture is given in Section 3.

1.1 Human-in-the-Loop with TopGuNN

Our primary use case for TopGuNN was to retrieve more training data for an event extraction and semantic role labeling task. We start with a few example sentences of each event type, identify query words within each example sentence (often the event verb), and then query TopGuNN to find new instances of similar sentences. These candidates are quickly voted on by non-expert human annotators who check the correctness of the semantic type (described in Section 2). Using active learning strategies, these filtered candidates can

Proceedings of the 2nd Workshop on Data Science with Human in the Loop: Language Advances, pages 86–101
June 11, 2021. ©2021 Association for Computational Linguistics

then be used to better tune TopGuNN's retrieval in the future. We demonstrate how our system can be used to mine for new diverse training data from large corpora with an efficient human-in-the-loop process given just a few samples to start with.

2 Use Case: KAIROS Event Primitives

Our primary use case stems from our work on the DARPA KAIROS program.[1] The DARPA KAIROS program seeks to develop a schema-based AI system that can identify complex events in unstructured text and bring them to the attention of users like intelligence analysts. KAIROS systems are based on an ontology of abstracted event schemas which are complex event templates. Complex event schemas are made up of a series of simpler events, and specify information about participant roles, temporal order, and causal relations between the simpler events. The simplest level event representations used in KAIROS are "event primitives". For each event primitive, a definition of the primitive is given along with the event's semantic roles. An example of a KAIROS event primitive is *Attack*:

Label	**Conflict.Attack**
Description	a violent physical act causing harm or damage
Slot Role	**Slot Argument Constraints**
Attacker	per, org, gpe, sid
Target	loc, gpe, fac, per, com, veh, wea, sid
Instr./Means	com, veh, wea
Place	fac, loc, gpe
Temporal	
Start and End	(times specific to event)
Duration	1 second to multiple years

Each event primitive contained 2-5 example sentences. Prior to TopGuNN, example sentences were selected by linguists who manually retrieved them from a corpus by keyword search. With TopGuNN, we can find thousands of candidate sentences automatically and then annotators can make a quick pass to filter down to the final set.

Some work attempts to create event extraction systems without extensive training data. For instance, Chen et al. (2020) discusses how training could be performed using a single "bleached statement," or a definition of an event, without needing a large set of labeled training examples. Rather than relying on such techniques, we design a system to make it quick and easy for annotators to create a larger training set .

2.1 Corpus

TopGuNN was used to index the Linguistic Data Consortium's English Gigaword Fifth Edition Corpus (Parker et al., 2011). Gigaword consists of approximately 12 gigabytes of news articles from 7 distinct international news agencies, spanning 16 years from 1994-2010, and contains a total of 183 million sentences and 4.3 billion tokens.[2]

2.2 Embedding Model

TopGuNN creates contextualized word embeddings for each content word in the corpus and for each query word in the query sentences. We use BERT (Devlin et al., 2019a) to create the embeddings because BERT produces contextually-aware embeddings unlike word2vec and GloVe (Mikolov et al., 2013; Pennington et al., 2014).[3] FastBERT or DistilBERT would also be appropriate choices, but come with an accuracy trade-off for speed (Liu et al., 2020; Sanh et al., 2019). We also investigated running TopGuNN at the sentence-level using sentence embeddings from SBERT and computing averaged sentence embeddings using BERT (Reimers and Gurevych, 2019). Qualitatively, the results from using BERT at the word-level gave us diversity in the results that we desired (see Appendix B).

2.3 Retrieving Event Primitives

A total of 60 event primitives were annotated using TopGuNN. On average, we were given 2 seed sentences per event and 1-2 viable query words per sentence with which to run through TopGuNN. The query word was typically a verb-form of the event. Approximately 120 query sentences were used to retrieve over 10,000 candidate sentences that were later sent through 2 phases of annotation: 1) sentence classification and 2) span annotation.

After annotators confirm "yes/no" on the candidate sentences meeting the event primitive definition, the sentences classified as "yes" are sent to semantic role labeling for span annotation using a semantic role labeling tool called Datasaur (lee, 2019).[4]

[1] https://www.darpa.mil/program/knowledge-directed-artificial-intelligence-reasoning-over-schemas

[2] https://catalog.ldc.upenn.edu/LDC2011T07

[3] We use the "bert-base-uncased" model from the Transformers Python package. (Wolf et al., 2020)

[4] https://datasaur.ai/

2.4 Examples of Retrieved Sentences

Our system works well in retrieving new, diverse variations of a query word used in contextually similar ways. Below, we display notable retrieved results we found to best showcase the utility of TopGuNN running over the entire Gigaword corpus for gathering both positive and abstract examples for training data.

Positive Example

- Event: Disable
- Definition: Impeding the expected functioning of an ORG, a mechanical device, or software, Ex., remove fuse from explosive

Query Word
The U.S. Army and Marine Corps also both fielded K-9 units with explosive-sniffing dogs to locate IEDs on the battlefield. Engineer Ordnance Disposal (EOD) experts ***disable*** or destroy IEDs through a variety of means, including the use of robotic ground vehicles and explosives.
Retrieved Sentence
Friday's guidelines called for deploying more Patriot interceptor missiles to ***shoot*** down ballistic missiles from North Korea, which has been developing missiles and nuclear weapons.
Cosine sim. of ***disable*** and ***shoot***: 0.641

Table 1: *Shooting down* an explosive as a positive example of *Disable*.

Abstract Example

- Event: Contaminate
- Definition: An animal (incl. people) is infected with a pathogen.

Query Word
"We detected SARS-CoV-2 RNA on eight (36%) of 22 surfaces, as well as on the pillow cover, sheet, and duvet cover," demonstrating that presymptomatic patients can easily ***contaminate*** environments, the authors said. "Our data also reaffirm the potential role of surface contamination in the transmission of SARS-CoV-2 and the importance of strict surface hygiene practices, including regarding linens of SARS-CoV-2 patients," they said.
Retrieved Sentence
Also keep in mind that ***infestations*** of adware/spyware are the leading cause of a slow computer.
Cosine sim. of ***contaminate*** and ***infestations***: 0.637

Table 2: *Infestations* of computer spyware as an abstract example of *Contaminate*.

More notable results can be seen in Appendix C.

2.4.1 Influence of Corpora Size

To validate our system retrieves more relevant results as the size of the corpus it has access to grows we ran a test comparing the results of TopGuNN retrieval on a subset of Gigaword against full Gigaword (see Appendix D). The cosine similarities of retrieved results on the full Gigaword corpus were significantly higher than those retrieved from the subset. Qualitatively, the results appear to contain more apt variations of the retrieved word used in a similar contexts as the query word.

3 System Design

A diagram of TopGuNN is given in Figure 2. TopGuNN is engineered to run in multiple stages: 1) Pre-processing, 2) Generating Embeddings, 3) Indexing, and 4) Running Queries.

3.1 Pre-Processing

During pre-processing we ingest a corpus and perform NLP analysis on each sentence. We use spaCy[5] to generate universal dependency labels and part-of-speech (POS) tags. We use the spaCy annotations to filter down the embeddings to a smaller subset that will be stored and indexed (resulting in a major reduction in the index size).

During pre-processing we also construct several tables in a database to keep track of which sentence and document each word occurs in and what its POS and dependency labels are. This information is stored in 6 lookup dictionaries in a SQLiteDict[6] database seen in Appendix E.

For our use case, we parallelized our pre-processing over each file in Gigaword. In a final step, we amalgamate the 6 lookup dictionaries per file into 6 lookup tables for the whole corpus. By doing so, we were able to use multiple CPUs for pre-processing.

3.2 Generating Embeddings

We partition the 183 million sentences in the Gigaword corpus into 960 sets of approximately 200,000 sentences each. For each partition, we pass batches of 175 sentences through BERT. Each partition is run in parallel using 16 NVIDIA GK210 GPUs on a p2.16xlarge machine with 732GB RAM on AWS, taking approximately 2 days to compute the BERT embeddings for all sentences in Gigaword.

BERT tokenizes its input using the WordPiece tokenization scheme (Devlin et al., 2019b). In TopGuNN, we operate on word-level tokenization

[5]https://spacy.io/

[6]https://pypi.org/project/sqlitedict/

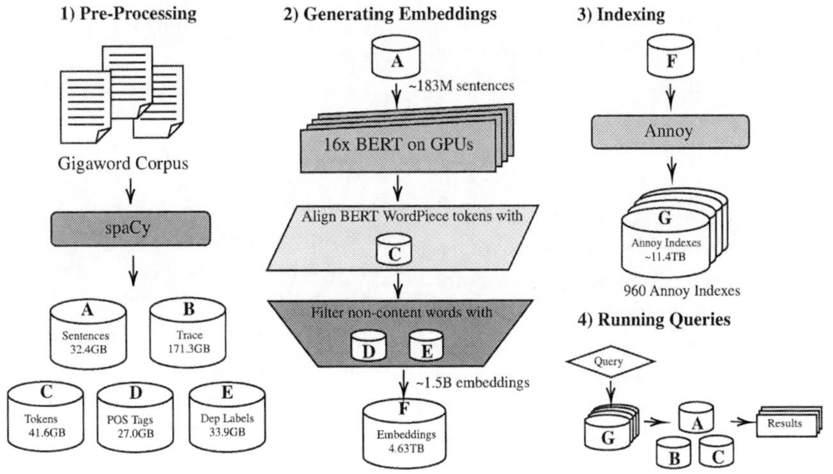

Figure 2: TopGuNN runs in four stages: Pre-Processing, Generating Embeddings, Indexing, and Querying

for indexing and queries, not on word pieces, so we align BERT's WordPiece tokenization scheme to our word-level tokenization scheme. We aligned the BERT-style model's tokenization with spaCy's tokenization using the method described in a blog post by Sterbak (ste, 2018).[7] We then took the mean of the WordPiece embeddings in a word to represent the embedding for the full word.

In order to reduce the number of embeddings we need to store on disk, only content words are kept from each sentence. *Content words* consist of non-proper nouns, verbs, adverbs, and adjectives only. We use POS tags to identify content words and use dependency labels in conjunction with POS tags to further filter out auxiliary verbs. We store the final filtered embeddings using NumPy's memory mapped format as our underlying data store. [8] We discuss the savings in disk space in Section 4.1.

3.3 Indexing

All of the embeddings saved in the previous step for each of the 960 partitions are added to an Annoy index, to create 960 Annoy indexes that span our entire corpus. We use Spotify's Annoy indexing system created by Bernhardsson (2018) for approximate k-NN search, which has been shown to be significantly faster than exact k-NN (Patel et al., 2018). While, there are various competing implementations for approximate k-NN, we ultimately used Annoy to power our similarity search for its ability to build and query on-disk indexes and reduce the amount of RAM required for search.[9]

3.4 Running Queries

TopGuNN allows you to query either a single query word or multiple query words batched together in a search query for performance. The input is a query matrix, which is a matrix of BERT embeddings for all query words in the batch.

Each query word is queried against the 960 Annoy indexes. In order to retrieve the overall top-N results, we query each Annoy index for its top-N results, and we then combine and sort the results from all the Annoy indexes to return the final compiled top-N results. We use our look-up dictionaries to return the document, the sentence, and the word of each result. Search results from each of the query words over the Annoy indexes are combined at the end and exported to a `.tsv` for human annotation and active learning.

3.4.1 Enhancing Query Performance

Sequentially searching each query word against the 960 Annoy indexes before moving on to the next query word is slow. To perform searches more efficiently, we sequentially query each of the 960 Annoy indexes with all query words. This leverages the operating system page cache in such a way that allows for the system to scale better to larger batches of queries. By querying in this manner, we only need to load each of the 960 Annoy index files (each index is ~6GB) into memory once, instead

[7]https://www.depends-on-the-definition.com/named-entity-recognition-with-bert/

[8]https://numpy.org/doc/stable/reference/generated/numpy.memmap.html

[9]https://github.com/spotify/annoy

of once per query word. This is a constant time fixed cost that we must pay for a single query, but subsequent queries will benefit from not having to load the Annoy index again. This fixed cost of loading the Annoy indexes can be amortized over all queries in a batch (see Table 4).[10] Using this method we get performance gains in speed, but we trade it off for higher-memory usage as now we have to hold the intermediate results in memory for all query words in the batch until all Annoy indexes are queried. This means that our memory usage grows linearly with the number of queries in each batch. In practice, we found this trade-off to be tolerable. For a batch of 189 queries, we had a peak memory usage of ~70GB.

3.4.2 Iterative Requery Method

Since this could possibly yield no results if the top-N is sufficiently small and all results are filtered out, we add a parameter that is the number of unique results desired for each query. However, setting top-N to be a very large would hinder the performance of the search queries.

To strike a balance, we employ an iterative requery method that begins with a low top-N and incrementally requeries, increasing N by k (a configurable parameter) while the number of desired unique results retrieved is not met. A current search is halted once the number of desired unique results is met or terminated if the max top-N threshold is reached without meeting the number of desired unique results. This allows us to search the minimum possible amount of nearest neighbors required to reach the best unique results for maximal performance.

4 Performance Details

4.1 Index Size

The size of the Annoy index relies heavily on two parameters set at build time during post-processing: the number of trees (`num_trees`) and the number of nodes to inspect during searching (`search_k`). We also greatly reduce the size of the Annoy index by deciding to exclude non-content words from our index during the Section 3.2 stage.

We use the following heuristic following Patel et al. (2018) to maintain similar search performance across our indexes:

```
num_trees =
max(50,int((num_vecs/3000000.0) * 50.0))
search_k = top_n * num_trees
```

Algorithm 1: Heuristic for Annoy parameters

Excluding Non-content Words We computed the number of words in the entire Gigaword corpus to be 4.3B words. We made the decision to exclude non-content words (defined in Section 3.2) which helped us save resources by a factor of 2.8X while maintaining a high search speed. Using content words only for the Gigaword corpus resulted in a total file size of 16TB (see **F** and **G** in Figure 2).

4.2 Sample Running Times

To give an idea of the TopGuNN system's performance on a corpus as large as Gigaword, we report times for building an index for Gigaword and querying it. Our system design is deconstructed into 4 different stages (as previously described in Section 3) separating out the CPU from the GPU processes in order to streamline the workflow and save on costs. For each stage, we utilized a machine with the best RAM and CPU configuration profile for each particular task and only used a machine with GPUs for Stage 2. For pre-processing, we used a total of 384 cores on a CPU cluster. For our "Generating Embeddings" stage, we utilized a machine with 732GB RAM and 16 GPUs. For post-processing, we used a 16 core machine with 128GB of RAM.

Build Times The times for running the different stages of TopGuNN on the entire Gigaword corpus can be seen in Table 3.

	Build Time
Pre-Processing	76.7 hours
Generating Embeddings	48.8 hours
Post-Processing	23.7 hours

Table 3: Build times for TopGuNN on Gigaword

Query Times The times for querying TopGuNN on the entire Gigaword corpus can be seen in Table 4. The first query word in the batch of queries takes longer as it must load each Annoy index into memory from disk. For subsequent queries in the batch, the Annoy index is already loaded into memory. (see Section 3.4.1)

[10]For example, after searching a query word "identify" on a particular Annoy index all subsequent queried words like "hired" or "launched" on that same Annoy index will leverage the operating system page cache of the Annoy index file and perform faster

	Query Time
Query Batch *(n = 189)*	21.4 hours
First Query *(1)*	19.4 hours
Subsequent Queries *(2-189)*	0.63 minutes

Table 4: Query times for TopGuNN on Gigaword

Because the Annoy indexes are partitioned, the first step could be parallelized to further reduce the 19.4 hours. Keeping cost management in mind, we ran this step serially to highlight its relevant use case even with limited budget (our budget was approximately $2,000).

5 Other NLP Applications

5.1 Sentence- and Document-Level Retrieval

For a sentence-level application, TopGuNN could be useful for training data in story generation. In Ippolito et al. (2020), the author predicts the likely embedding of the next sentence. To facilitate the diversity and speed of candidate sentences used to generate the next sentence in the story, TopGuNN could be employed with sentence embeddings to retrieve sentences from large corpora. For document-retrieval training data, Kriz et al. (2020) recasts text-simplification as a document-retrieval task. The author generates document-level embeddings from the Newsela corpus using BERT and SBERT and similarly adds them to an Annoy index to find documents with similar complexity levels as the query document.

5.2 Multilingual Information Retrieval

DAPRA KAIROS' events are similar to the events found in the IARPA BETTER multilingual information retrieval project.[11] A future application of TopGuNN could be querying in English and retrieving training examples in another language (or vice versa) by substituting BERT for GigaBERT (Lan et al., 2020) in TopGuNN. With this modification, TopGuNN could help facilitate multilingual retrieval of training examples.

6 Related Work

Previous work that parallels our work to search and index large corpora includes projects like Lin et al. (2010), which created an index of n-gram counts over a web-scale sized corpus. Similarly, as an extension to work completed by Lin et al. (1997) and Gao et al. (2002), Moore and Lewis (2010) propose a method for gathering domain-specific training data for languages models for use in tasks such as Machine Translation. By utilizing contextual word embeddings from a modern language model like BERT instead of techniques like n-grams or perplexity analysis as seen in previous approaches, TopGuNN aims to achieve higher quality results.

Our work directly builds upon prior research on approximate k-NN algorithms for cosine similarity search. We chose to use the Annoy package for indexing our embeddings in TopGuNN for its particular ability to build on-disk indexes, however, another package could be used instead. Aumüller et al. (2018) discusses various approximate k-NN algorithms that could alternatively be utilized for TopGuNN with alternate trade-offs in speed, memory, and other hardware requirements. By utilizing on-disk indexes on SSDs, which have fast random-access reads and high-throughput, we are able to use significantly cheaper machines than would be required to hold terabytes of indexes in RAM.

7 Getting started with TopGuNN

You can get started with TopGuNN on GitHub: https://github.com/Penn-TopGuNN/TopGuNN

8 Conclusion

We have presented a system for fast training data augmentation from a large corpus. To the best of our knowledge, existing search approaches do not make use of contextual word embeddings to produce the high quality diverse results needed in training examples for tasks like our event extraction use case. We have open sourced our efficient, scalable system that makes the most efficient use of human-in-the-loop annotation. We also highlight several other NLP tasks where our system could facilitate training data augmentation in Section 5.

Future work may include enabling TopGuNN to query for multi-word expressions (i.e. *"put a name to"*), hyphenated expressions (i.e. *"pre-existing conditions"*), or in the form of natural language questions as seen in (Yu et al., 2019). Finally, identifying antonymy as studied in (Rajana et al., 2017) would be a valuable extension for more fine-grained search results as synonyms and antonyms often occupy the same embedding space.

[11] https://www.iarpa.gov/index.php/research-programs/better

Acknowledgements

We would like to thank Erik Bernhardsson for the useful feedback on integrating Annoy indexing.

Special thanks to Ashley Nobi for spearheading the annotation effort and Katie Conger at University of Colorado at Boulder for the training sessions on semantic role labeling she gave for the span annotation effort.

We would like to thank the Fall 2020 semester students of *CIS 421/521 - Artificial Intelligence* and Leila Pearlman at the University of Pennsylvania, and the University of Colorado at Boulder's Team of Linguists for annotating TopGuNN results.

We would like to thank Ivan Lee, CEO of Datasaur Inc., Hartono Sulaiman and Nadya Nurhafidzah of Datasaur, for providing a seamless annotation tool for us to use and with around-the-clock customer service in navigating the system.

I would like to thank my post-doc Dr. Mohammad Sadegh Rasooli and my PhD labmate Aditya Kashyap for their invaluable input and constant availability to us throughout the project.

Special thanks to my senior PhD labmate Reno Kriz for his mentorship during this project.

The first author was funded by NSF for the University of Pennsylvania under grant number DGE-1845298 (the Graduate Research Fellowships Program). This research is also supported in part by the DARPA KAIROS Program (contract FA8750-19-2-1004), the DARPA LwLL Program (contract FA8750-19-2-0201), and the IARPA BETTER Program (contract 2019-19051600004). Approved for Public Release, Distribution Unlimited. The views and conclusions contained herein are those of the authors and should not be interpreted as necessarily representing the official policies, either expressed or implied, of DARPA, IARPA, or the U.S. Government.

The U.S. Government is authorized to reproduce and distribute reprints for Governmental purposes. The views and conclusions contained in this publication are those of the authors and should not be interpreted as representing official policies or endorsements of NSF, DARPA, and the U.S. Government.

And to the timeless 1986 American cult-classic "Top Gun," thanks for the inspiration on naming our retrieval system... ***I feel the need for speed!***

References

2018. *Named entity recognition with Bert*. Tobias Sterbak Consulting, Akazienstraße 3A, 10823 Berlin, Germany.

2019. *Ivan Lee, CEO., Datasaur*. Datasaur, Inc., Sunnyvale, California, United States.

Martin Aumüller, Erik Bernhardsson, and Alexander Faithfull. 2018. Ann-benchmarks: A benchmarking tool for approximate nearest neighbor algorithms.

Erik Bernhardsson. 2018. *Annoy: Approximate Nearest Neighbors in C++/Python*. Python package version 1.13.0.

Yunmo Chen, Tongfei Chen, Seth Ebner, Aaron Steven White, and Benjamin Van Durme. 2020. Reading the manual: Event extraction as definition comprehension.

Jacob Devlin, Ming-Wei Chang, Kenton Lee, and Kristina Toutanova. 2019a. BERT: Pre-training of deep bidirectional transformers for language understanding. In *Proceedings of the 2019 Conference of the North American Chapter of the Association for Computational Linguistics: Human Language Technologies, Volume 1 (Long and Short Papers)*, pages 4171–4186, Minneapolis, Minnesota. Association for Computational Linguistics.

Jacob Devlin, Ming-Wei Chang, Kenton Lee, and Kristina Toutanova. 2019b. BERT: Pre-training of deep bidirectional transformers for language understanding. In *Proceedings of the 2019 Conference of the North American Chapter of the Association for Computational Linguistics: Human Language Technologies, Volume 1 (Long and Short Papers)*, pages 4171–4186, Minneapolis, Minnesota. Association for Computational Linguistics.

Jianfeng Gao, Joshua Goodman, Mingjing Li, and Kai-Fu Lee. 2002. Toward a unified approach to statistical language modeling for chinese. *ACM Transactions on Asian Language Information Processing*, 1(1):3–33.

Daphne Ippolito, David Grangier, Douglas Eck, and Chris Callison-Burch. 2020. Toward better storylines with sentence-level language models.

Reno Kriz, Eleni Miltsakaki, Jaime Rojas, Rebecca Iglesias-Flores, Megha Mishra, Marianna Apidianaki, and Chris Callison-Burch. 2020. Recasting text simplification as a document retrieval task. *In Submission*.

Keita Kurita, Nidhi Vyas, Ayush Pareek, Alan W Black, and Yulia Tsvetkov. 2019. Measuring bias in contextualized word representations.

Wuwei Lan, Yang Chen, Wei Xu, and Alan Ritter. 2020. An empirical study of pre-trained transformers for arabic information extraction.

Dekang Lin, Kenneth Ward Church, Heng Ji, Satoshi Sekine, David Yarowsky, Shane Bergsma, Kailash Patil, Emily Pitler, Rachel Lathbury, Vikram Rao, et al. 2010. New tools for web-scale n-grams. In *LREC*.

Sung-Chien Lin, Chi-Lung Tsai, Lee-Feng Chien, Keh-Jiann Chen, and Lin-Shan Lee. 1997. Chinese language model adaptation based on document classification and multiple domain-specific language models. In *EUROSPEECH*. ISCA.

Weijie Liu, Peng Zhou, Zhe Zhao, Zhiruo Wang, Haotang Deng, and Qi Ju. 2020. Fastbert: a self-distilling bert with adaptive inference time.

Tomas Mikolov, Kai Chen, G. S. Corrado, and J. Dean. 2013. Efficient estimation of word representations in vector space. In *ICLR*.

Robert C. Moore and William Lewis. 2010. Intelligent selection of language model training data. In *Proceedings of the ACL 2010 Conference Short Papers*, pages 220–224, Uppsala, Sweden. Association for Computational Linguistics.

Robert Parker, David Graff, Junbo Kong, Ke Chen, and Kazuaki Maeda. 2011. *English Gigaword Fifth Edition LDC2011T07*. Web Download.

Ajay Patel, Alexander Sands, Chris Callison-Burch, and Marianna Apidianaki. 2018. Magnitude: A fast, efficient universal vector embedding utility package. In *Proceedings of the 2018 Conference on Empirical Methods in Natural Language Processing: System Demonstrations*, pages 120–126, Brussels, Belgium. Association for Computational Linguistics.

Jeffrey Pennington, Richard Socher, and Christopher Manning. 2014. Glove: Global vectors for word representation. In *Proceedings of the 2014 Conference on Empirical Methods in Natural Language Processing (EMNLP)*, pages 1532–1543, Doha, Qatar. Association for Computational Linguistics.

Yusu Qian, Urwa Muaz, Ben Zhang, and Jae Won Hyun. 2019. Reducing gender bias in word-level language models with a gender-equalizing loss function. In *Proceedings of the 57th Annual Meeting of the Association for Computational Linguistics: Student Research Workshop*, pages 223–228, Florence, Italy. Association for Computational Linguistics.

Sneha Rajana, Chris Callison-Burch, Marianna Apidianaki, and Vered Shwartz. 2017. Learning antonyms with paraphrases and a morphology-aware neural network. In *Proceedings of the 6th Joint Conference on Lexical and Computational Semantics (*SEM 2017)*, pages 12–21, Vancouver, Canada. Association for Computational Linguistics.

Nils Reimers and Iryna Gurevych. 2019. Sentence-BERT: Sentence embeddings using Siamese BERT-networks. In *Proceedings of the 2019 Conference on Empirical Methods in Natural Language Processing and the 9th International Joint Conference on Natural Language Processing (EMNLP-IJCNLP)*, pages 3982–3992, Hong Kong, China. Association for Computational Linguistics.

Victor Sanh, Lysandre Debut, Julien Chaumond, and Thomas Wolf. 2019. Distilbert, a distilled version of BERT: smaller, faster, cheaper and lighter. *CoRR*, abs/1910.01108.

Thomas Wolf, Lysandre Debut, Victor Sanh, Julien Chaumond, Clement Delangue, Anthony Moi, Pierric Cistac, Tim Rault, Rémi Louf, Morgan Funtowicz, Joe Davison, Sam Shleifer, Patrick von Platen, Clara Ma, Yacine Jernite, Julien Plu, Canwen Xu, Teven Le Scao, Sylvain Gugger, Mariama Drame, Quentin Lhoest, and Alexander M. Rush. 2020. Huggingface's transformers: State-of-the-art natural language processing.

Tao Yu, Rui Zhang, Kai Yang, Michihiro Yasunaga, Dongxu Wang, Zifan Li, James Ma, Irene Li, Qingning Yao, Shanelle Roman, Zilin Zhang, and Dragomir Radev. 2019. Spider: A large-scale human-labeled dataset for complex and cross-domain semantic parsing and text-to-sql task.

A Ethical Considerations/Discussion

Our work utilizes BERT and therefore it contains the inherent biases that exist in language models trained on large amounts of unsupervised data collected from the internet. Kurita et al. (2019) analyzes the various biases that exist specifically in BERT.

In our own tests, we directly observed some of these biases when querying for the DARPA KAIROS DETONATE:EXPLODE event over a subset of Gigaword. Querying the word **bombing** in the sentence *"Rabee'a owned a drill rig, and his friend had heard stories from elsewhere in Yemen about jets **bombing** well sites."* yielded the word **Muslim** as the top result from the sentence *"Amid the tension, **Muslim** leaders say their communities are doing more than ever to help in investigations – a point they say is overlooked by many Americans."* with a cosine similarity of 0.602. Moreover, 9 out of the 20 top results were the words "muslim" or "mosque".

When using TopGuNN to help bootstrap training data for event extraction models or running search queries, care must be taken to ensure these biases do not leak into a downstream applications by a thorough manual review to prevent unintentional harm. Debiasing language models is an active area of research and techniques like Qian et al. (2019) could be utilized to attempt to debias language models at train time that could then replace BERT in TopGuNN.

B Testing Various Embedding Models with TopGuNN

We explored 3 different embedding models for the TopGuNN system:

1. SBERT automatically has its own sentence representation to retrieve sentences.
2. AVG-BERT uses the mean of the word embeddings as the sentence representation to retrieve sentences.
3. BERT returns results for a single query word and retrieves sentences with words that were used in a similar context as the query word in the query sentence.
   Note: To show diversity of results for BERT, the Top-10 unique nearest neighbors are shown and not necessarily the first Top-10 as seen in SBERT and AVG-BERT.

Table 5: Results comparing SBERT, AVG-BERT, and BERT

Method	Cosine Sim	Retrieved Result
Query Sentence: "President Barack Obama's hopes of winning Senate approval for a new arms control treaty with Russia by the end of the year were encouraged Tuesday by two Republican senators, including John McCain."		
	0.908	WASHINGTON -The US Senate, in a key test vote, moved Tuesday toward final passage of a nuclear arms pact with Russia, setting up a likely foreign policy victory for President Obama and a hard-won achievement for Senator John F. Kerry of Massachusetts, who shepherded the treaty through fierce GOP opposition.
	0.888	Fresh from winning Senate approval for a new strategic arms treaty, President Barack Obama plans to return to the negotiating table with Russia next year in hopes of securing the first legal limits imposed on the smaller, battlefield nuclear weapons viewed as most vulnerable to theft or diversion.

Continued on next page

Table 5 – continued from previous page

Method	Cosine Sim	Retrieved Result
SBERT	0.882	McCain, one of his party's leading voices on national security, said he thought that Republican concerns over missile defense and nuclear modernization could be resolved in time to vote on the so-called New Start treaty during the lame-duck session of Congress this month, as Obama has sought.
	0.878	To press their point, Republicans pushed through a side resolution calling on Obama to open talks with Russia on such weapons within a year.
	0.872	The Senate moved closer Monday to approving a new arms control treaty with Russia over the opposition of Republican leaders as lawmakers worked on a side deal to assure skeptics that the arms pact would not inhibit U.S. plans to build missile defense systems.
	0.872	Beyond his behind-the-scenes role in negotiating the tax deal with Republicans – a path that Biden and Obama decided on in a recent conversation at the White House, aides say – the vice president has also been trying to win Republican votes in the Senate for ratification of the START nuclear arms treaty with Russia.
	0.856	On Tuesday, Sen. John McCain – who is inexplicably playing second fiddle to Kyl – told ABC: "I believe that we could move forward with the START treaty and satisfy Senator Kyl's concerns and mine about missile defense and others, and I hope that we can do that."
	0.848	White House officials, meanwhile, expressed hope of sealing a deal swiftly, perhaps by midweek, and clearing the congressional calendar for a long list of other priorities they aim to accomplish by the end of the year, including ratification of the New START arms treaty with Russia and the repeal of the "don't ask, don't tell" policy for gay service members as part of a wider Pentagon policy bill.
	0.832	While President Barack Obama presses the Senate to embrace a new arms control treaty with Russia, another nuclear pact with Moscow secured final approval after more than four years on Thursday with virtually no notice but potentially significant impact.
	0.828	In the interview, Putin also warned that Russia would develop and deploy new nuclear weapons if the United States did not accept its proposals on integrating Russian and European missile defense forces – amplifying a comment made by Medvedev in his annual state of the nation address Tuesday.
	0.920	WASHINGTON - Senator John F. Kerry and other top Democrats said Tuesday they have secured enough bipartisan backing to ratify the START nuclear arms treaty with Russia, a vote that would be a substantial foreign policy victory for President Obama.
	0.911	Immediately after the tax vote Wednesday, Senate Democrats began angling for passage of a new U.S.-Russian nuclear arms treaty, a priority of President Barack Obama that has been on the agenda for months.
	0.904	McCain, one of his party's leading voices on national security, said he thought that Republican concerns over missile defense and nuclear modernization could be resolved in time to vote on the so-called New Start treaty during the lame-duck session of Congress this month, as Obama has sought.

Continued on next page

Table 5 – continued from previous page

Method	Cosine Sim	Retrieved Result
AVG-BERT	0.896	Sen. John McCain of Arizona had previously said he hoped to vote for the treaty as long as concerns over missile defense were addressed, and it was not clear whether he was signaling a shift or using the opportunity to vent his longstanding frustration with Russian behavior.
	0.894	A Republican senator announced that he would vote for the treaty and two others said they were leaning toward it, and at the same time, Sen. John McCain, R-Ariz., produced separate legislation that could reassure fellow Republicans worried about the treaty's impact on missile defense.
	0.893	Obama brought up the treaty Tuesday during a White House meeting with congressional leaders, pressing them to vote this month to strengthen the relationship with Russia.
	0.892	President Barack Obama on Tuesday strongly defended his tax cut deal with congressional Republicans against intense criticism from his own party, insisting it was "a good deal for the American people."
	0.887	Sen. Harry Reid of Nevada, the majority leader and crucial proponent of the repeal, noted that some Republicans had indicated they may try to block Senate approval of a nuclear arms treaty with Russia due to their pique over the Senate action on the ban on gays in the military.
	0.887	Obama has insisted that the Senate approve it before the end of the month rather than wait until a new Senate with more Republicans takes office, and a number of Republican senators have signaled tentative support.
	0.885	Obama, in his brief remarks Wednesday during a meeting with the president of Poland, suggested that Republicans for the next two years will still be defending the Bush tax rates while he is looking forward to a new, better code.
Query Word: "President Barack Obama's hopes of ***winning*** Senate approval for a new arms control treaty with Russia by the end of the year were encouraged Tuesday by two Republican senators, including John McCain."		
BERT	0.953	TWO REPUBLICANS HINT AT HOPE FOR ARMS PACT WITH RUSSIA President Barack Obama's hopes of ***winning*** Senate approval for a new arms control treaty with Russia by the end of the year were encouraged Tuesday by two Republican senators, including John McCain.
	0.825	Obama's failure to ***win*** passage of comprehensive immigration reform was a disappointment to many Latinos, he conceded.
	0.802	Aides to Reid said they had mapped out a path to ***securing*** votes on all of the legislation, which would mean staying in session until next Thursday, two days before Christmas, and potentially returning the week before New Year's Day.
	0.793	While he has a fair chance of ***securing*** the votes of the two other Democrats, he faces a potential fight with one of those commissioners, Michael J. Copps, who has been public in his support for stricter regulation of broadband Internet service.
	0.756	With a week before Election Day, Perry, who is thought to have the best chance of ***gaining*** a seat for Republicans in the state, is struggling to fend off accusations that he witnessed and covered up the illegal strip search of a teenage girl in 1991, when he was a police sergeant in Wareham, Mass.

Continued on next page

Table 5 – continued from previous page

Method	Cosine Sim	Retrieved Result
	0.755	The White House is negotiating with Sen. Jon Kyl, R-Ariz., whose support is crucial to ***getting*** other Republican votes, to meet his price: more money to modernize the nuclear arsenal.
	0.744	Republican confidence about ***capturing*** control of the House remained high, though even Republicans considered the Senate more of a question mark, given the number of excruciatingly close races across the country.
	0.731	Obama bested the chamber in the first two years of his term, ***passing*** health care legislation and an overhaul of financial regulations over the group's heated opposition.
	0.731	Like most of her 18 opponents nearing the Nov. 28 election, Manigat's campaign trail stretches northward from Port-au-Prince to Miami, New York, Boston and Montreal in hopes of ***garnering*** money and influence from the large Haitian diaspora.
	0.730	Still, with Republicans ***challenging*** every element of the new law, the Obama administration is likely to be handcuffed in its efforts to expand the revamping of the health care system.

C Notable Results

Positive Example

- Event: Defeat
- Definition: Defeat in a conflict or an election (but not a game-style competition)

Query Word
Most democratic activists and lawmakers ***rejected*** the deal as a sham and it was eventually defeated in the city's legislatures after a botched walkout by pro-government legislatures.
Retrieved Sentence
The White House and Senate Democrats ***considered*** the amendment a treaty killer because any change to the text would require both countries to go back to the negotiating table.
Cosine sim. of ***rejected*** and ***considered***: 0.745

Table 6: *Treaty killer* as a positive example of *Defeat*.

Positive Example

- Event: Disable
- Definition: Impeding the expected functioning of an ORG, a mechanical device, or software, Ex., remove fuse from explosive

Query Word
Soldiers and personnel have to be trained to be aware of the enemy's behaviors, to look for indicators of IEDs in their patrol areas and to use technology to dispose or ***disable*** them.
Retrieved Sentence
And he assured his audience that he had made clear to senior Pakistani military officials my strong desire to see more action taken against these places and to ***root*** out the terrorists.
Cosine sim. of ***disable*** and ***root***: 0.616

Table 7: *Rooting out terrorist* organizations as a positive example of *Disable*.

Positive Example

- Event: Block Passage
- Definition: Preventing entry or exit from a location

Query Word
...archipelagic defense would have the holders of islands adjoining straits and other narrow seas fortify those islands with mobile anti-ship and anti-air missiles while deploying surface, subsurface, and aerial assets to ***block*** passage through these seaways. In effect these forces string a barricade between geographic features—interdicting shipping and overflight while bringing economic and military pressure on adversaries.
Retrieved Sentence
Assad Ismail, a local council president in Sadiya, a village along the disputed territories northeast of Baghdad, said that only the Americans were able to settle a recent dispute that flared when Iraqi soldiers trying to ***restrict*** the movement of insurgents closed off local farmers' access to their date palms, tomatoes and peanuts.
Cosine sim. of ***block*** and ***restrict***: 0.637

Table 8: *Restricting movement* as a positive example of *Block Passage*.

Positive Example

- Event: Destroy
- Definition: Damage property, organization or natural resource

Query Word
"These actions challenge national sovereignty, threaten one country, two systems, and will ***destroy*** the city's prosperity and stability," she said, referring to slogans of "Liberate Hong Kong, revolution of our times" and the act of throwing a Chinese flag in the sea.
Retrieved Sentence
"Letting it expire would threaten jobs, harm the environment, ***weaken*** our renewable fuel industries, and increase our dependence on foreign oil," they wrote.
Cosine sim. of ***destroy*** and ***weaken***: 0.732

Table 9: *Weaken renewable fuel* as a positive example of *Destroy*.

Abstract Example

- Event: Destroy
- Definition: Damage property, organization or natural resource

Query Word
"These actions challenge national sovereignty, threaten one country, two systems, and will ***destroy*** the city's prosperity and stability," she said, referring to slogans of "Liberate Hong Kong, revolution of our times" and the act of throwing a Chinese flag in the sea.
Retrieved Sentence
Adopting an orthodox view, he said in 1976 that a projected budget deficit estimated at 60 billion was "very scary" and would "***wreck***" the economy.
Cosine sim. of ***destroy*** and ***wreck***: 0.752

Table 10: *Wrecked the economy* as an abstract example of *Destroy*.

Abstract Example

- Event: Block Passage
- Definition: (Physically) preventing entry or exit from a location

Query Word
...archipelagic defense would have the holders of islands adjoining straits and other narrow seas fortify those islands with mobile anti-ship and anti-air missiles while deploying surface, subsurface, and aerial assets to ***block*** passage through these seaways. In effect these forces string a barricade between geographic features—interdicting shipping and overflight while bringing economic and military pressure on adversaries.
Retrieved Sentence
Even as Pakistan's army vows to take on militants spreading chaos and mayhem inside Pakistan, the intelligence service still sees the Afghan Taliban as a way to ensure influence on the other side of the border and ***keep*** India's influence at bay.
Cosine sim. of ***block*** and ***keep***: 0.649

Table 11: *Keeping influence at bay* as an abstract example of *Block Passage*.

D TopGuNN Results Using Different Sized Corpora

We compared the top 10 unique results from a small subset of the Gigaword corpus (400,000 sentences) compared to results ran on the full Gigaword corpus (183 million sentences) for the event primitive **Sentence** (as in the judicial meaning).

Current findings have shown us some interesting, but unexpected results. The cosine similarities of retrieved results for full Gigaword are significantly higher, but TopGuNN still works extremely well on a small subset in terms of quality and diversity of results. Other researchers who need to prioritize high-speed in retrieving positive or abstract examples for their training data could retrieve similar sentences even faster on a smaller subset of a uniform corpus like Gigaword without having to sacrifice much in terms of quality.

Table 12: Top-10 unique results querying the event primitive 'Sentence' (as in the judicial meaning) over a subset of Gigaword (400K sentences) vs. full Gigaword (183M sentences).

Method	**Cosine Sim**	**Retrieved Result**
Query Sentence: "The judge ***sentenced*** him to death."		
Gigaword Subset *(400K sentences)*	0.742	When she explained to the court that she could not afford to pay, Nowlin was ***sent*** to prison.
	0.701	"It matters little if they ***condemn*** me, even to the heaviest sentence.
	0.695	True, the court could have gone further and actually ***jailed*** the two defendants.
	0.693	He ***received*** a life sentence.
	0.680	A federal judge ***spared*** him prison time but ordered him to leave the country within 90 days or be deported.
	0.676	The jury came within two votes of ***convicting*** Megahed.
	0.670	Bush ***commuted*** the sentences, and the men are now free.
	0.666	At 6:28 p.m., she found him ***hanged***.
	0.664	He eventually pleaded guilty to manslaughter and ***spent*** 15 years in prison.

Continued on next page

Table 12 – continued from previous page

Method	Cosine Sim	Retrieved Result
	0.659	That convinced a jury to find him guilty of aggravated sexual assault and ***send*** him to prison for 75 years.
Full Gigaword *(183M sentences)*	0.881	A jury didn't believe him, and a ***judge*** sentenced him to eight years in prison.
	0.863	Seven years later, a Paris court ***condemned*** him in absentia to life in jail for the murders.
	0.847	The jury decided unanimously to ***sentence*** him to death.
	0.845	The jury ***convicted*** him to life in prison, where he will spend the rest of his life.
	0.841	"There are some things you just can't run from, this being one of those," Rolling told Circuit Judge Stan R. Morris, who accepted the pleas and found him guilty and ***later*** sentenced him to death.
	0.833	The presiding judge agreed, ***sentencing*** the two young men to life imprisonment.
	0.830	The judge ***sent*** them to prison.
	0.828	It wasn't until last October – a decade later – that ***courts*** sentenced 34 men to 26 years each for the killings.
	0.814	They unanimously ***acquitted*** him on all counts.
	0.812	But the U.N. court decided he was not directly involved and ***punished*** him with a light two years in prison.

E Lookup Dictionaries

1. Sentences (32.4GB):
   `sent_id → (sentence)`
2. Document Traceability (15.0GB):
   `sent_id → (doc_id)`
3. Tokens (41.6GB):
   `sent_id → (sentence tokens)`
4. Parts-of-Speech Tags (27.0GB):
   `sent_id → (sentence pos_tags)`
5. Dependency Labels (33.9GB):
   `sent_id → (sentence dep_labels)`
6. Words Trace (156.3 GB):
   `word_id → (word_id, word, (doc_id, sent_id))`

F Querying Polysemous Words

We demonstrate TopGuNN's ability to perform contextual similarity search of a query word in its corresponding sentence using polysemous words, which have two distinct sentences. Figure 3 and Figure 4 are further examples of querying two distinct sentences with different senses of the same word to retrieve sentences that capture both polysemies.

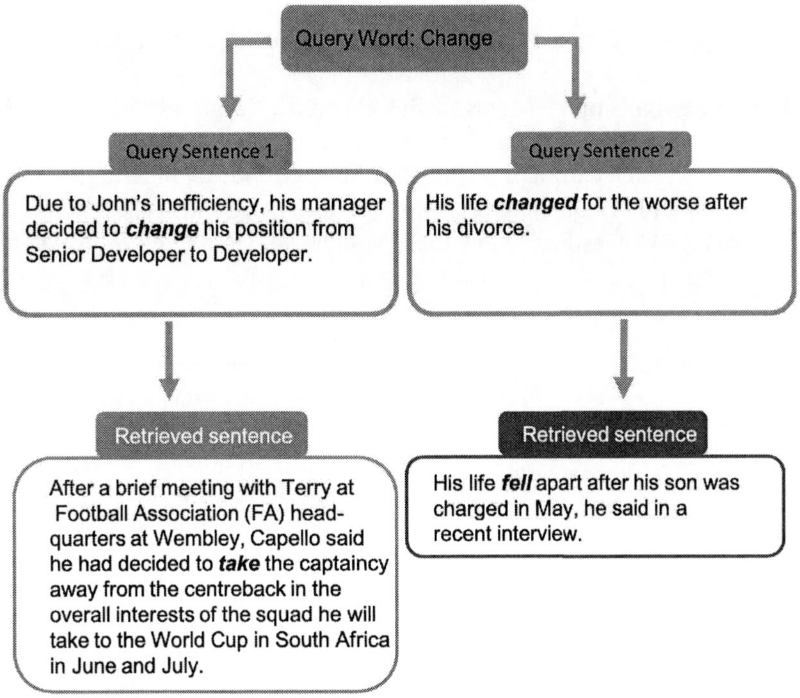

Figure 3: TopGuNN results on the the polysemous word *change*.

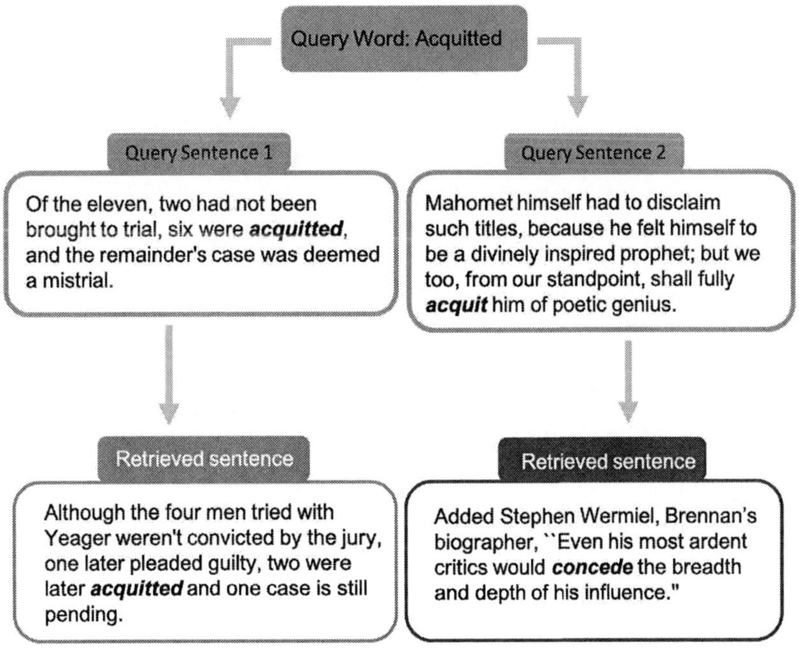

Figure 4: TopGuNN results on the the polysemous word *acquit*.

Everyday Living Artificial Intelligence Hub

Raymond Finzel[1], Esha Singh[2], Martin Michalowski[3], Serguei Pakhomov[1], Maria Gini[2]
[1]Department of Pharmaceutical Care and Health Systems, College of Pharmacy,
[2]CSE Department, College of Science and Engineering,
[3]Population Health and Systems Cooperative, School of Nursing,
University of Minnesota, Twin Cities, Minnesota, United States of America.
{finze006,sing0640,martinm,pakh0002,gini}@umn.edu

Abstract

We present the Everyday Living Artificial Intelligence (AI) Hub, a novel proof-of-concept framework for enhancing human health and wellbeing via a combination of tailored wearable and Conversational Agent (CA) solutions for non-invasive monitoring of physiological signals, assessment of behaviors through unobtrusive wearable devices, and the provision of personalized interventions to reduce stress and anxiety. We utilize recent advancements and industry standards in Internet of Things (IoT) and AI technologies to develop this proof-of-concept framework.

1 Introduction

The significance of stress in disease development and progression has been established for multiple therapeutic areas including cardiovascular disease (Kivimäki and Steptoe, 2018), type 2 diabetes (Hackett and Steptoe, 2017), obesity (Sinha and Jastreboff, 2013), sleep disorders (Han et al., 2012) , depression (Madsen et al., 2017), stroke (O'Donnell et al., 2016) drug addiction (including opioid, tobacco, cannabis, and cocaine use) (Airagnes et al., 2018; Preston et al., 2017) , and Alzheimer's disease (Justice, 2018). As demonstrated for cardiovascular disease, stressors associated with increased risk of events include those commonly encountered in life such as work stressors, anger episodes and even the viewing of stressful sporting events (Smyth et al., 2016). Exposure to stressful events is therefore a major risk factor for morbidity and mortality rates especially for conditions that have a great impact on public health.

As the commercial IoT sector continues to grow, our homes and bodies are increasingly instrumented. We now have digital personal assistants that listen and respond to voice commands and wearable devices equipped with multiple sensors. The availability and maturity of this technology affords an unprecedented opportunity to develop holistic systems to advance the health and wellbeing of many groups including one of the most vulnerable sectors of our population: elders aging in-place. To provide personalized and effective interventions, such a system must be capable of sensing, integrating, responding to physical, emotional, and cognitive status in an accessible way.

Towards this vision, we have developed a proof-of-concept framework for individually tailored detection and management of mental stress and anxiety in everyday life. We target the development and deployment of a novel personalized technology that integrates conversational voice assistants with wearable sensors and smart-textile clothing technology to provide real-time, in-home, unobtrusive sensing and on-body stimulation solutions (e.g., pressure, heat, etc.). The proposed proof-of-concept framework integrates three major components: 1) natural language interaction with the user via a conversational voice assistant; 2) physiological signal sensing of activity, heart rate, body temperature, and electrical conductivity of skin; and 3) garment-based delivery of heat and compression interventions to reduce stress and anxiety detected via voice and wearable sensors.

2 Methodology

The Everyday Living AI Hub is a holistic framework that orchestrates the 3 components discussed in section 1, coordinating multiple streams of biometric data and physical interventions (Figure 1). The Hub framework allows for the analysis of self-supplied information (such as information about a user's schedule, habits, and preferences) alongside biometric data collected from OTC wearable devices with the goal of providing interventions into the user's life to help them self-regulate. These interventions are in the form of notifications (reminders to breathe, reminders that a meeting or other scheduled time is coming up), or bindings with devices that operate "In Real Life (IRL)" such

Proceedings of the 2nd Workshop on Data Science with Human in the Loop: Language Advances, pages 102–104
June 11, 2021.

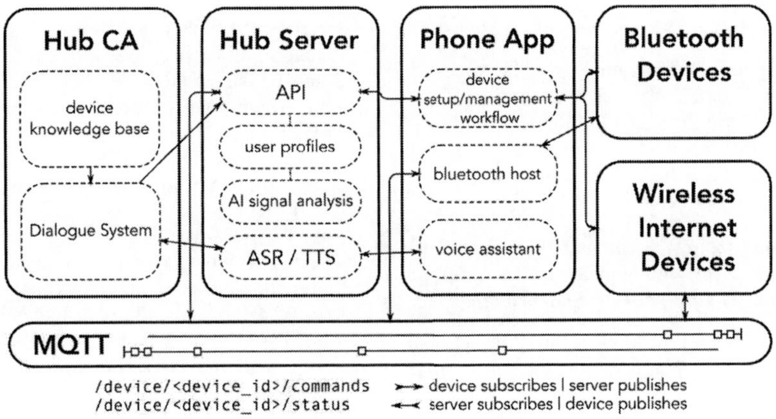

Figure 1: Architecture for Everyday Living AI Hub and end-point user interaction flow.

as the SmartHugs Garment (Pettys-Baker et al., 2018), a wearable shirt designed to perform compression on dysregulated individuals. Detected stress events are confirmed with the user via the Hub Conversational Agent (Hub CA), which can ask questions about the severity and timing of the stressful event, and confirm whether an intervention is necessary or desirable.

Earlier stress measures were mainly questionnaires such as Demand–Control–Support model (Johnson and Hall, 1988, Pozo-Antúnez et al., 2018, Karasek and Theorell, 1990). Lu et al. proposed a framework for real-time stress measurement, monitoring and intervention. Like our proposed system, they used physiological indicators to detect stress level using a wearable smart bracelet. Our contribution adds human-in-the-loop voice control and the ability to incorporate interventions via IoT devices to the milieu of this prior work.

2.1 Architecture

By utilizing many industry-standard IoT protocols, the framework is designed to be flexible. User accounts and profiles are maintained via a web service based on Responder (Reitz, 2018), a free Python framework for microservice development. Monitoring devices collect data and send it through Bluetooth to a cell-phone companion app, or send it directly to the Hub Server's AI collection point via a lightweight publish/subscribe protocol called MQTT (Figure 1). Everyday interactions with the framework are performed either by interacting with a web-service Application Programming Interface (API) via mobile application, website, or by using natural language to converse with the voice assistant, which passes speech data through an Automatic Speech Recognition (ASR) service to the Hub CA which is based on MindMeld (Raghuvanshi et al., 2018), a framework for conversational agent development. The Hub CA then performs actions on behalf of the user by interacting with the API, and speaks to the user using the integrated Text-To-Speech (TTS) service.

2.2 Project Status

Completed modules include system architecture components such as MQTT services, web APIs for data collection and intervention applications, a phone app for the management of Bluetooth connected devices, ASR and TTS modules, and a prototype stress management garment. Active development is underway for AI signal analysis, in-the-loop conversational device setup, and intervention management in the Hub CA.

3 Challenges

The Everyday Living AI Hub requires many practical and theoretical advances. While preliminary studies have shown that commercial IoT wearables can detect changes in heart-rate that correspond to stress in a naturalistic environment (Pakhomov et al., 2020), existing machine-learning models are not equipped to reliably predict stressful events in real-time. Collection of data and the creation of an adequate model are ongoing work. The Hub CA is based on established chatbot paradigms, but models and dialog flows are still under development for the new domain of stress management.

Acknowledgements

UMN Grand Challenges Research Initiative.

References

Guillaume Airagnes, Cédric Lemogne, Marcel Goldberg, Nicolas Hoertel, Yves Roquelaure, Frédéric Limosin, and Marie Zins. 2018. Job exposure to the public in relation with alcohol, tobacco and cannabis use: Findings from the constances cohort study. *PLOS ONE*, 13:e0196330.

Ruth Hackett and Andrew Steptoe. 2017. Type 2 diabetes mellitus and psychological stress - a modifiable risk factor. *Nature reviews. Endocrinology*, 13.

Kuem Han, Lin Kim, and Insop Shim. 2012. Stress and sleep disorder. *Experimental neurobiology*, 21:141–50.

Jeffrey Johnson and E.M. Hall. 1988. Job strain, work place social support, and cardiovascular disease: A cross-sectional study of a random sample of the swedish working population. *American journal of public health*, 78:1336–42.

Nicholas J. Justice. 2018. The relationship between stress and alzheimer's disease. *Neurobiology of Stress*, 8:127–133.

Robert Karasek and Töres Theorell. 1990. *Healthy Work: Stress, Productivity, and The Reconstruction Of Working Life*.

M. Kivimäki and A. Steptoe. 2018. Effects of stress on the development and progression of cardiovascular disease. *Nature Reviews Cardiology*, 15:215–229.

Peixian Lu, Wei Zhang, Liang Ma, and Qichao Zhao. 2020. *A Framework of Real-Time Stress Monitoring and Intervention System*, pages 166–175.

Ida E. H. Madsen, S. Nyberg, Linda Magnusson Hanson, Jane Ferrie, Kirsi Ahola, Lars Alfredsson, G. Batty, Jakob Bjorner, Marianne Borritz, Hermann Burr, J.-F Chastang, Ron Graaf, Nico Dragano, Mark Hamer, M. Jokela, Anders Knutsson, M. Koskenvuo, Aki Koskinen, Constanze Leineweber, and Minna Kivimäki. 2017. Job strain as a risk factor for clinical depression: systematic review and meta-analysis with additional individual participant data. *Psychological Medicine*, 47:1–15.

Martin O'Donnell, Siu Chin, Sumathy Rangarajan, Denis Xavier, Lixin Liu, Hongye Zhang, Purnima Rao-Melacini, Xiaohe Zhang, Prem Pais, Steven Agapay, Patricio Lopez-Jaramillo, Albertino Damasceno, Peter Langhorne, Matthew McQueen, Annika Rosengren, Mahshid Dehghan, Graeme Hankey, Antonio Dans, Ahmed Elsayed, and Yan Duarte. 2016. Global and regional effects of potentially modifiable risk factors associated with acute stroke in 32 countries (interstroke): A case-control study. *The Lancet*, 388.

Serguei Pakhomov, Paul Thuras, Raymond Finzel, Jerika Eppel, and Michael Kotlyar. 2020. Using consumer-wearable technology for remote assessment of physiological response to stress in the naturalistic environment. *PLOS ONE*, 15:e0229942.

Robert Pettys-Baker, Nicholas Schleif, J. Walter Lee, Sophia Utset-Ward, Mary Ellen Berglund, Lucy E. Dunne, Brad Holschuh, Christopher Johnson, Kevin Kelly, Bruce Johnson, and Michael Joyner. 2018. Tension-Controlled Active Compression Garment for Treatment of Orthostatic Intolerance. 2018 Design of Medical Devices Conference. V001T10A005.

José Pozo-Antúnez, Antonio Ariza-Montes, Francisco Fernández-Navarro, and Horacio Molina. 2018. Effect of a job demand-control-social support model on accounting professionals' health perception. *International Journal of Environmental Research and Public Health*, 15.

Jonathan Preston, Megan Leece, Kerry McNamara, and Edwin Maas. 2017. Variable practice to enhance speech learning in ultrasound biofeedback treatment for childhood apraxia of speech: A single case experimental study. *American Journal of Speech-Language Pathology*, 26:1.

Arushi Raghuvanshi, Lucien Carroll, and Karthik Raghunathan. 2018. Developing production-level conversational interfaces with shallow semantic parsing. In *Proceedings of the 2018 Conference on Empirical Methods in Natural Language Processing: System Demonstrations*, pages 157–162.

Kenneth Reitz. 2018. A familiar http service framework.

R. Sinha and A. Jastreboff. 2013. Stress as a common risk factor for obesity and addiction. *Biological Psychiatry*, 73:827–835.

Elizabeth Smyth, Matteo Fassan, David Cunningham, William Allum, Alicia Okines, Andrea Lampis, Jens Hahne, Massimo Rugge, Clare Peckitt, Matthew Nankivell, Ruth Langley, Michele Ghidini, Chiara Braconi, Andrew Wotherspoon, Heike Grabsch, and Nicola Valeri. 2016. Effect of pathologic tumor response and nodal status on survival in the medical research council adjuvant gastric infusional chemotherapy trial. *Journal of Clinical Oncology*, 34.

A Computational Model for Interactive Transcription

William Lane, Mat Bettinson, Steven Bird
Northern Institute, Charles Darwin University

Abstract

Transcribing low resource languages can be challenging in the absence of a comprehensive lexicon and proficient transcribers. Accordingly, we seek a way to enable interactive transcription, whereby the machine amplifies human efforts. This paper presents a computational model for interactive transcription, supporting multiple modes of interactivity and increasing the likelihood of finding tasks that stimulate local participation. The approach also supports other applications which are useful in low resource contexts, including spoken document retrieval and language learning.

1 Introduction

Understanding the "transcription challenge" is a prerequisite to designing effective solutions, minimizing bottlenecks (Himmelmann, 2018). We must face realities such as the lack of a good lexicon, the short supply of transcribers, and the difficulty of engaging people in arduous work. *Sparse transcription* is an approach to transcribing speech in these low-resource situations, an approach which is well suited to places where there is limited capacity for transcription. Sparse transcription admits multi-user workflows built around shared data, for human-in-the-loop transcriptional practices, or "interactive transcription" (Bird, 2020b; Le Ferrand et al., 2020).

Sparse transcription is 'sparse' because we do not produce contiguous transcriptions up front. Instead, we transcribe what we can, and lean on computational support to amplify those efforts across the corpus. This is not suggested as an alternative to contiguous transcription, but as a more efficient way to produce it, especially in those situations where linguists and speakers are "learning to transcribe" (Bird, 2020b, page 716). Sparse transcription relies on word spotting. Wordforms that occur frequently in the transcribed portion of a corpus are used to spot forms in the untranscribed portion. These are presented for manual verification, speeding up the contiguous transcription work while indexing the entire corpus.

Sparse transcription accepts the realities of early transcription: we lack a good lexicon; we need to grow the lexicon as we go; and we do not have a ready workforce of transcribers. Moreover, in the context of language documentation, transcription is iterative and interactive. Linguists and speakers leverage complementary skills to accomplish the task (Crowley, 2007; Austin, 2007; Rice, 2009).

Sparse transcription leverages the kind of work speakers are motivated to do. For example, when it comes to recordings, speakers tend to engage with the content more than the particular form of expression (Maddieson, 2001, page 215). Identifying key words and clarifying their meanings is often more engaging than puzzling over the transcription of unclear passages (Bird, 2020b). An indexed corpus can be searched to identify additional high-value recordings for transcription.

We report on a computational model for interactive transcription in low-resource situations. We discuss the kinds of interactivity which the sparse transcription model enables, and propose an extension which provides real-time word discovery in a sparse transcription system. For concreteness we also present a user interface which provides real-time suggestions as the user enters words.

We work with speakers of Kunwinjku (ISO gup), a polysynthetic Indigenous language of northern Australia. Members of this community have expressed interest using technology to support their own language goals. Through this work we hope to support language learning and corpus indexing, and produce locally meaningful results that help to decolonize the practice of language technology (Bird, 2020a).

This paper is organized as follows. Section 2 gives an overview of the sparse transcription model. Section 3 describes a particular use case of sparse

Proceedings of the 2nd Workshop on Data Science with Human in the Loop: Language Advances, pages 105–111
June 11, 2021.

transcription: interactive transcription. In Section 4 we describe the system architecture and the design decisions which enable an interactive human-computer workflow. Section 5 describes the user interface and shows screenshots of the implementation. We conclude with a summary in Section 6.

2 The Sparse Transcription Model

Following Bird (2020b), we understand transcription to be the task of identifying meaningful units in connected speech. These units belong to a growing inventory (the glossary, or lexicon); their orthographic representation is generally not settled. We add each new meaningful unit to the glossary as it is encountered, initializing the entry with a form and a gloss. Thus, a transcriptional token is a pairing of a locus in the speech stream with a glossary entry. We are agnostic about the size of this unit; it could be a morpheme, word, or multi-word expression.

Transcription begins with a lexicon. There is always a word list, since this is what is used for establishing the distinct identity of a language. There may also be some historical transcriptions, and these words can be included in the initial lexicon. From this point on, transcription involves growing the lexicon.

The speech stream is broken up into 'breath groups' which we use as manageable chunks for transcription. In the course of transcription, it is a natural thing for a non-speaker linguist to attempt to repeat any new word and have a speaker say it correctly and give a meaning. Thus, the process is interactive in the interpersonal sense. We hear and confirm the word in context, and record it in the lexicon with a lexical identifier and a pointer to where it occurs in the media. In the background, a sparse transcription system uses this confirmed glossary entry to spot more instances.

Word spotting is an automatic task which discovers putative tokens of glossary entries. Glossary entries are already stored with pointers to occurrences in particular breath groups. Discovering new instances through word spotting then becomes a retrieval task, where each breath group is seen as a mini-document. Breath groups which are determined to contain the exemplar lexical entry are queued for speaker confirmation. Confirmed spottings are updated with pointers to their respective breath groups.

Word spotting proceeds iteratively and interactively, continually expanding the lexicon while transcribing more speech. As we focus on completing the contiguous transcription of a particular text, we grow the lexicon and the system attempts to discover other instances across the wider corpus. As the system calls our attention to untranscribed regions, which may be difficult to complete for a variety of reasons, we effectively marshall the whole corpus to help us.

A sparse transcription system is a form of computer supported collaborative work, in that it alleviates productivity bottlenecks via automation and asynchronous workflows (Greif, 1988; Hanke, 2017). The sparse transcription model—organized around a growing glossary of entries with pointers to instances in speech—can underlie a variety of special-purpose apps which support various tasks in the transcription workflow. For example, Le Ferrand et al. (2020) demonstrate the use of a word confirmation app based on word-spotted data for the purpose of confirming automatically-generated hypotheses.

We have prototyped a system which implements the core functionalities described in this section, and which includes a user interface which supports interactive transcription. Figure 2 gives a schematic view of the sparse transcription model.[1]

3 Learning to Transcribe

A linguist, learning to transcribe, is capable of listening to audio and quickly transcribing the lexemes they recognize. As lexemes are recorded, they are added to the transcriber's personal glossary. Entries in this glossary may be morphs, words, or other longer units such as multi-word expressions. The record-keeping of the glossary helps manage the linguist's uncertainty in an accountable way, as they give the task their best first-pass. As is the standard behavior in sparse transcription, a glossary is updated with links from glossary entries to the segment of audio in which they were found.

Speakers of the language can access a view of the linguist's glossary entries, and confirm entry tokens for admission to the global glossary. The design decision to maintain personal glossaries for individual users and postpone adjudication with a shared, canonical glossary is an extension of the concept defined in the sparse transcription model.

[1]The system prototype and a reference implementation of the sparse transcription model can both be found at `https://cdu-tell.gitlab.io/tech-resources/`.

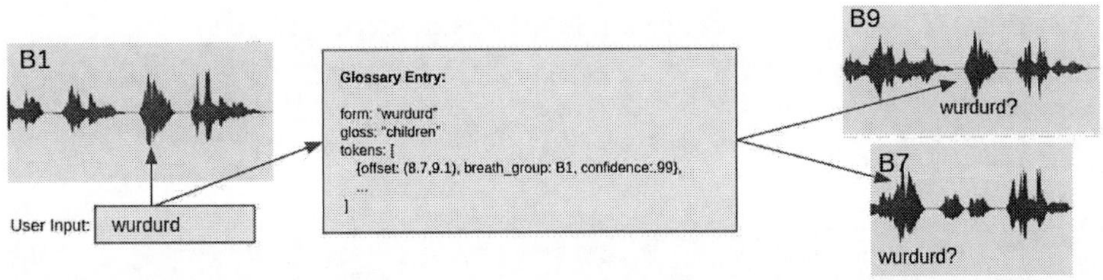

Figure 1: Word spotting in the sparse transcription model begins when the user confirms the existence of a glossary entry in the audio. A token is created for that instance of the glossary entry, and can be used to spot similar instances in other breath groups across the corpus.

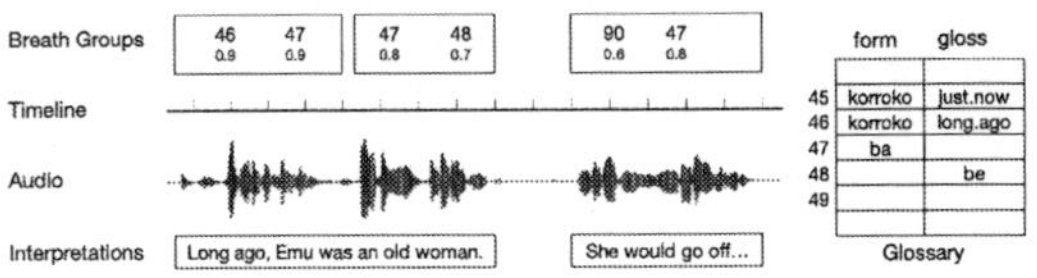

Figure 2: The Sparse Transcription Model: Audio is segmented into breath groups, each one a mini spoken document where words may be spotted (with given probability); interpretations span one or more breath groups (Bird, 2020b).

Multiple transcribers can contribute to the shared glossary, initializing their own project with the current state of the global lexicon.

Confirmed glossary entries can be used to spot similar entries across the whole corpus, maximizing the efforts of the learner, and providing more pointers from a glossary entry to breath groups where it occurs. Over time, this process leads to more contiguous transcriptions as the transcriber revisits and revises their lexicon in the course of their transcription work.

However, there is an opportunity here to get more immediate feedback from the system. A sparsely transcribed breath group (whether system or human transcribed) provides signal about the breath group as a whole. Combined with the fact that the human is currently engaged in entering their hypotheses, we can provide system suggestions conditioned on sparsely transcribed data which are updated interactively as the user types. Anchored at the locus of a known lexeme, and conditioned on additional available signal i.e., a predicted phone sequence, the system posits suggestions for untranscribed regions. We can refer to this as 'local word discovery' (Fig. 3).

Working together with the system, a linguist's hypotheses can be queued for confirmation in the same way that word spotting queues hypotheses for speaker confirmation. Simultaneously, the transcriber leverages a model to get immediate feedback on the connections between what they hear and what a model encodes about the language, potentially aiding language learning (Hermes and Engman, 2017).

Up to this point, we have established the interactive nature of transcription on three levels. First, it is interpersonally interactive, as a linguist works with speakers to associate forms with meanings. Second, sparse transcription is interactive in the sense that it attempts to amplify the effort of transcribers by propagating lexical entries across the whole corpus via word spotting.

Finally, the implementation of local word discovery is interactive in the context of the "learning to transcribe" use case. It occupies a distinct niche with a smaller feedback loop than word spotting: transcription hints are polled from the model and filtered with every keystroke (Figs. 6-8). It is improved by word spotting because contiguous transcriptions reduce uncertainty in the input to the local word discovery model. It allows a linguist to prepare and prioritize work for the interpersonally interactive task of confirming entries with a speaker.

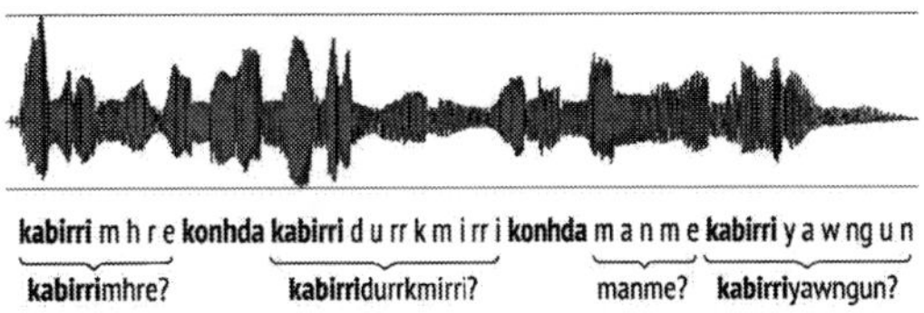

Figure 3: Sparsely transcribed input can be leveraged for local word discovery methods which are complementary to word spotting.

4 System Architecture

The interactive transcription use case calls for a variety of computational agents. Some agents ser-

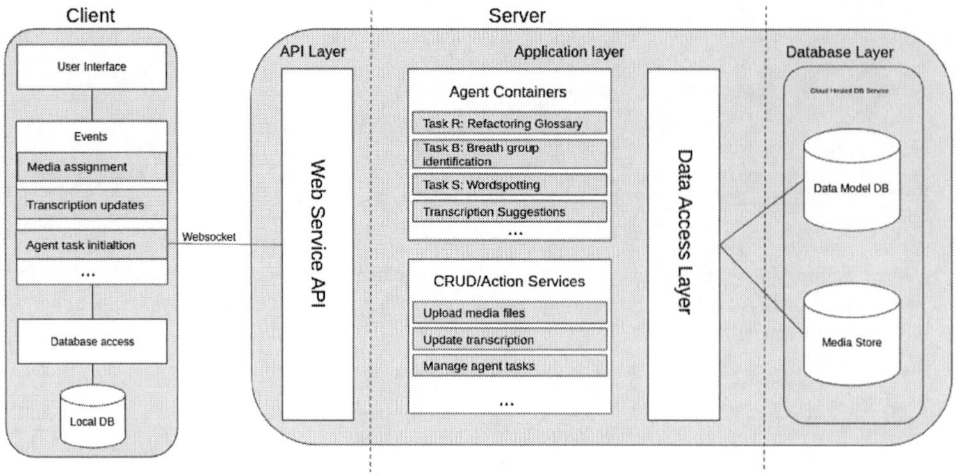

Figure 4: The system architecture

vice computationally-expensive batch tasks, while others are coupled with user events down to the level of keystrokes.

Agents are implemented as containerized services, some corresponding to long-running tasks, e.g. media processing, while others are integral to the user interface, e.g. phone alignment. The implementation supports RESTful endpoints, and a real-time websocket-based API.

The API layer responds to events in the client, and endpoints support the methods in the data model. There are three main kinds of operation; simple CRUD operations like uploading media, data model operations such as adding a token to a glossary, and real-time queries such as word discovery. Data validation is distributed across the client and the server, for performance reasons and to mitigate the effects of network dropouts. The client replicates a subset of the server data model, storing this in the browser's database and synchronizing it with the server opportunistically.

We utilise a continuous web socket session to relay user input to the server, fetching and displaying results in real time. Commonly seen in web search, this is a form of distributed user interface where computational resources are distributed across platforms and architectures (Elmqvist, 2011). This is achieved via asynchronous programming with observable streams, via implementations of the Reactive X pattern for JavaScript (rxjs) on the client and Python (rxpy) on the server. Input events from the browser are filtered, debounced and piped through a websocket transport to a session handler on the back end. Similarly, components of the client subscribe to session event streams coming from the back end, such as aligning user input to a phone stream, and presenting a series of word completions.

The system makes use of several agents whose implementation may vary across contexts or evolve over time. We have implemented the following agents:

Audio pre-processing. When a user adds an audio file to a transcription project, the audio is preprocessed and we store metadata and alternative representations which are useful for downstream tasks. For example, the pipeline includes voice activity detection (VAD), which identifies breath groups. Next, we calculate peaks–acoustic amplitude values–which we use to visualize speech activity over time. Finally, the audio is resampled and sent to the phone recognition agent, and the results are displayed beneath the waveform as extra information to support transcription.

Phone recognition. Allosaurus is a universal phone recognizer trained on over 2,000 languages (Li et al., 2020). The model can be used as-is to provide phones from a universal set, or it can be fine-tuned with language specific phonemic transcriptions. The model currently we currently deploy is fine-tuned on 68 minutes of Kunwinjku speech across 5 speakers. We calculated a 25.6% phone error rate on 10 minutes of speech from a hold-out speaker.

Word spotting. Word spotting traditionally is audio exemplar matching against spans of raw audio

(Myers et al., 1980). It has been shown to be feasible in low resource scenarios using neural approaches (Menon et al., 2018b,a). Le Ferrand et al. (2020) describes several plausible speech representations suited for low-resource word spotting.

Local word discovery. This is distinct from word spotting, which locates more tokens of existing glossary entries. Local word discovery attempts to fill in untranscribed regions between existing tokens. This agent provides transcription hints via a smaller feedback loop, the third kind of interactivity discussed in Section 3. The system retrieves the potentially large set of suggested words, and filters it down interactively as the transcriber types. The model is free to favor recall, because the raw suggestions do not need to be immediately revealed.

We implement local word discovery using a finite state analyzer for Kunwinjku (Lane and Bird, 2019), modified to recognize possible word-forms given a stream of phones and the offsets of known lexemes. We use PanPhon to estimate articulatory distances between lexemes and phone subsequences to obtain rough alignments (Mortensen et al., 2016).

5 User Interface

The user interface (Fig. 5) is inspired by minimalist design, motivated by the need for an inclusive agenda in language work (cf. Hatton, 2013). In the left column is a waveform which has been automatically segmented into breath groups. Below the waveform is a map of waveform peaks, to facilitate navigation across long audio files. Useful context is also displayed, including the transcript of the preceding breath group, followed by the sequence of phones produced from the audio, with user transcriptions aligned roughly to the phone sequence. Below this is the input box, scoped to the current breath group, where users enter lexemes, with occasional suggestions offered by the local word discovery module, and which filter interactively per keystroke (Figs. 6-8).

In the right column, there is a running transcript of the audio file, with the text of the transcript for the current breath group shown in bold.

The user interface is designed to be navigable entirely through the keyboard, to support ergonomic transcription (cf. Luz et al., 2008).

6 Conclusion

Transcription is especially challenging when we lack a good lexicon and trained transcribers. Consequently, we seek to bring all available resources to bear, including the knowledge of speakers, linguists, and a system, all of whom are "learning to transcribe."

We presented a use case for interactive transcription and showed how this can be supported within the sparse transcription model. In designing and implementing a sparse transcription system for a specific use case, we elaborated on some concepts presented in (Bird, 2020b). We examined various kinds of interactivity in low-resource language transcription, and we proposed local word discovery as a grammatically-informed approach to word spotting. This allows individual users to manage their local lexicon independently of the task of curating a canonical lexicon, enabling multi-user workflows.

Finally, we reported on the architecture and implementation of an interactive transcription system. It enables a transcriber to take care of much of the arduous transcription task up front, and to allocate more meaningful work for speakers. The product of interaction with the system is an expanded lexicon, which can be used to index the corpus for information retrieval, thus supporting the community goal of access to knowledge locked up in many hours of recorded audio. Additionally, we anticipate that support for growing personal lexicons will be a valuable resource for the language learning that takes place alongside transcription. In short, the system is designed to produce the content that language communities care about, in a way that leverages the kind of language work that people are willing to do.

Operationalizing the sparse transcription model makes it possible to streamline field-based transcriptional practices, and is expected to lead to further implementations of special purpose interfaces that support transcription of low-resource languages.

Acknowledgments

We are grateful for the support of the Warddeken Rangers of West Arnhem. This work was covered by a research permit from the Northern Land Council, and was sponsored by the Australian government through a PhD scholarship, and grants from the Australian Research Council and the Indigenous Language and Arts Program.

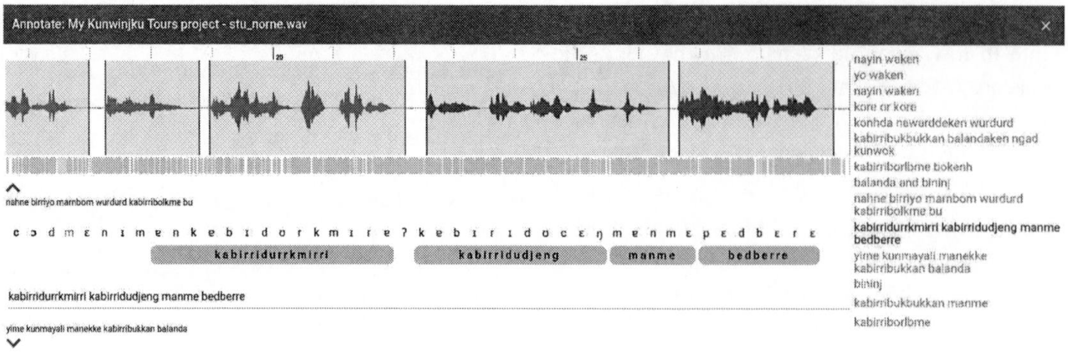

Figure 5: The transcription user interface connects to the data model, which facilitates word spotting and local word discovery agents.

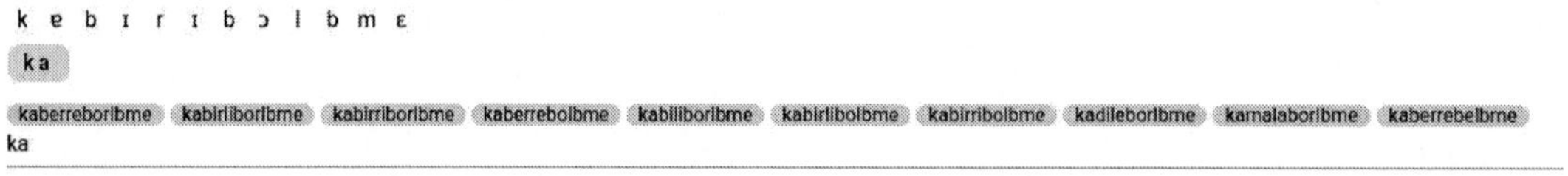

Figure 6: Local word discovery predicts possible words in the audio, conditioned on known lexemes and a flexible interpretation of the surrounding sounds.

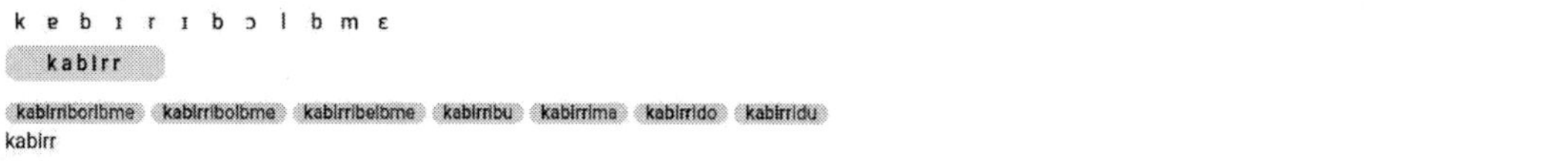

Figure 7: As the user continues typing, the list of suggestions is filtered down to those which remain compatible.

Figure 8: Thus, the user is guided to grammatically valid transcriptions which can be added to their lexicon.

References

Peter Austin. 2007. Training for language documentation: Experiences at the School of Oriental and African Studies. In Victoria Rau and Margaret Florey, editors, *Documenting and Revitalizing Austronesian Languages*, number 1 in Language Documentation and Conservation Special Issue, pages 25–41. University of Hawai'i Press.

Steven Bird. 2020a. Decolonising speech and language technology. In *Proceedings of the 28th International Conference on Computational Linguistics*, page 3504–19, Barcelona, Spain.

Steven Bird. 2020b. Sparse transcription. *Computational Linguistics*, 46:713–744.

Terry Crowley. 2007. *Field Linguistics: A Beginner's Guide*. Oxford University Press.

Niklas Elmqvist. 2011. Distributed user interfaces: State of the art. In *Distributed User Interfaces*, pages 1–12. Springer.

Irene Greif. 1988. *Computer-Supported Cooperative Work: A Book of Readings*. Morgan Kaufmann.

Florian Hanke. 2017. *Computer-Supported Cooperative Language Documentation*. Ph.D. thesis, University of Melbourne.

John Hatton. 2013. SayMore: Language documentation productivity. Presentation at International Conference Language Documentation and Conservation.

Mary Hermes and Mel Engman. 2017. Resounding the clarion call: Indigenous language learners and documentation. *Language Documentation and Description*, 14:59–87.

Nikolaus P Himmelmann. 2018. Meeting the transcription challenge. In *Reflections on Language Documentation 20 Years after Himmelmann 1998*, volume 15 of *Language Documentation and Conservation Special Publication*, pages 33–40. University of Hawai'i Press.

William Lane and Steven Bird. 2019. Towards a robust morphological analyzer for Kunwinjku. In *Proceedings of the 17th Annual Workshop of the Australasian Language Technology Association*, pages 1–9.

Éric Le Ferrand, Steven Bird, and Laurent Besacier. 2020. Enabling interactive transcription in an Indigenous community. In *Proceedings of the 28th International Conference on Computational Linguistics*, pages 3422–28. International Committee on Computational Linguistics.

Xinjian Li, Siddharth Dalmia, Juncheng Li, Matthew Lee, Patrick Littell, Jiali Yao, Antonios Anastasopoulos, David R Mortensen, Graham Neubig, Alan Black, and Florian Metze. 2020. Universal phone recognition with a multilingual allophone system. In *Proceedings of the International Conference on Acoustics, Speech and Signal Processing*, pages 8249–53. IEEE.

Saturnino Luz, Masood Masoodian, Bill Rogers, and Chris Deering. 2008. Interface design strategies for computer-assisted speech transcription. In *Proceedings of the 20th Australasian Conference on Computer-Human Interaction: Designing for Habitus and Habitat*, pages 203–10.

Ian Maddieson. 2001. Phonetic fieldwork. In Paul Newman and Martha Ratcliff, editors, *Linguistic Fieldwork*, pages 211–229. Cambridge University Press.

Raghav Menon, Herman Kamper, John Quinn, and Thomas Niesler. 2018a. Fast ASR-free and almost zero-resource keyword spotting using DTW and CNNs for humanitarian monitoring. In *Interspeech*, pages 3475–79.

Raghav Menon, Herman Kamper, Emre Yilmaz, John Quinn, and Thomas Niesler. 2018b. ASR-free CNN-DTW keyword spotting using multilingual bottleneck features for almost zero-resource languages. In *Proceedings of the 6th International Workshop on Spoken Language Technologies for Under-Resourced Languages*, pages 182–186.

David R. Mortensen, Patrick Littell, Akash Bharadwaj, Kartik Goyal, Chris Dyer, and Lori Levin. 2016. Panphon: A resource for mapping IPA segments to articulatory feature vectors. In *Proceedings of the 26th International Conference on Computational Linguistics*, pages 3475–84. Association for Computational Linguistics.

Cory Myers, Lawrence Rabiner, and Andrew Rosenberg. 1980. An investigation of the use of dynamic time warping for word spotting and connected speech recognition. In *Proceedings of the International Conference on Acoustics, Speech, and Signal Processing*, volume 5, pages 173–177. IEEE.

Keren Rice. 2009. Must there be two solitudes? Language activists and linguists working together. In Jon Reyhner and Louise Lockhard, editors, *Indigenous language revitalization: Encouragement, guidance, and lessons learned*, pages 37–59. Northern Arizona University.

Author Index

Association for Computational Linguistics
209 N. Eighth Street
Stroudsburg, Pennsylvania 18360

CURRAN ASSOCIATES INC.
proceedings.com

ISBN 978-1-7138-3021-4

9 781713 830214